The Writers' Castle

The Writers' Castle

Reporting History at Nuremberg

Uwe Neumahr

Translated from the German
by Jefferson Chase

Pushkin Press

Pushkin Press
Somerset House, Strand
London WC2R 1LA

The right of Uwe Neumahr to be identified as the author of this Work has been
asserted by him in accordance with the Copyright, Designs & Patents Act 1988

Original text © Uwe Neumahr 2023
English translation © 2024 Jefferson Chase

The Writers' Castle was first published as *Das Schloss der
Schriftsteller* by Verlag C.H. Beck oHG, München 2023

First published by Pushkin Press in 2024

The translation of this book was supported by a grant from the Goethe-Institut

1 3 5 7 9 8 6 4 2

ISBN 13: 978-1-80533-069-1

Designed and typeset by Tetragon, London
Printed and bound in the United Kingdom by Clays Ltd, Elcograf S.p.A.

www.pushkinpress.com

CONTENTS

FOREWORD

Xiao Qian was amazed. Walking for the first time through the ruins of Nuremberg in October 1945, it was the only European city that reminded him of Beijing, not just because of its walls around the old town, the river that snaked through its midst or its many weeping willows, but also because of the calm it emanated. Xiao (1910–99) had crossed the river with British Armed Forces earlier that year as a Chinese correspondent during the Second World War. After a stop in defeated Berlin, he reached Nuremberg in the autumn. Xiao knew that the former home of the Nazis' annual party rallies had once been a tourist destination. "But right now, the tourists aren't here for the cultural and historical attractions, which are buried beneath rubble anyway, or Nuremberg's famous gingerbread," he told his readers on 9th October 1945. "Today, Nuremberg is the focus of the world's attention because twenty-three of the biggest criminals of the Nazi regime are being put on trial... It is a great event."[1]

The "great event" was the international response to an unimaginable horror, the moment when Germany's war criminals would be held accountable for what they had done. People around the world longed for the Nazi dictatorship to be unmasked to reveal the true faces of the men behind it. Some observers saw the Nuremberg Major War Criminals Trial* as the foundation for the enforcement of modern standards for crimes against humanity. The presence of famous Nazis in the courtroom dock, the judicial novelty of a tribunal carried out by the four victors in the war, and public curiosity about a country many people regarded as a mystery in fact made the trial a spectacular event. Large numbers of journalists were dispatched to Nuremberg, including the lone reporter from China, Xiao Qian, who later become the chairman of the Chinese Writers' Association. These journalists were to serve as a window into a sealed enclave, so that the outside world would know what transpired there.

Taking the lead, US occupation authorities set about identifying a facility capable of handling the flood of reporters, but locating a building suitable for accommodating several hundred press representatives was no mean task in a city that had been so heavily bombed. In the end, they found what they were looking for in the nearby town of Stein, to the south-west of Nuremberg proper. It was there, in a latter-day mock castle seized from the pen and pencil manufacturing dynasty Faber-Castell, that the international "press camp" was set up. The castle was a place to both live and work.[2] Correspondents slept there in rooms with up to ten beds and dutifully recorded events from the trial a few kilometres away, as men like Göring, Ribbentrop,

---

* The Nuremberg Major War Criminals Trial is the trial of Nazi leaders including Hermann Göring in 1945–46. For brevity's sake, it will subsequently be referred to as simply the Nuremberg Trial. The other trials of war criminals, which went on in Nuremberg until 1949, will be referred to as the subsequent trials or individually by the groups concerned, i.e. The Doctors Trial.

Streicher and Hess waited in their cells to learn the verdicts of
the International Military Tribunal.

Some of the world's most important journalists and best-
known writers were deployed to Nuremberg to report for
newspapers, news agencies and radio broadcasters. The list
of names reads like the crème de la crème of the journalistic
and literary scene of the day—Erika Mann, Erich Kästner,
John Dos Passos, Ilya Ehrenburg, Elsa Triolet, Rebecca West
and Martha Gellhorn, to name a few—but it also included
men and women who would only later go on to achieve literary, media or political fame. Their ranks encompassed the
German novelist Wolfgang Hildesheimer, who served at the
trial as a translator; Augusto Roa Bastos, widely considered
Paraguay's leading author; Austrian writer and peace cam-
paigner Robert Jungk; legendary US television news anchor-
man Walter Cronkite; and Walter Lippmann, regarded as the
most influential political writer in the United States. Also on
hand were later German Chancellor Willy Brandt; the head of
state surveillance in Communist East Germany, Markus Wolf;
and a bevy of other somewhat lesser-known authors, including
Joseph Kessel, Peter de Mendelssohn and Gregor von Rezzori.
Never before and never since had so many famous writers from
all over the world come together as during this "zero hour". In
Schloss Faber-Castell, world literature encountered world history. It was a meeting point for returnees from exile or "inner
emigration" and battle-hardened officers, for Resistance fighters and Holocaust survivors, Communists and Western media
conglomerates, war correspondents from the trenches and star
reporters with extravagant lifestyles. All were eager to find out
how such a human catastrophe could have happened, what sort

of people the accused were and how they would seek to defend themselves.

Within the press corps, the body in which history was literally being written, opposites collided. Erika Mann, who was officially employed by the US Armed Forces, cohabitated with her female partner, an American journalist, even though homosexuality was prohibited by the US military. Brandt, then a correspondent for a working-class Scandinavian newspaper, came together with Wolf, the very man who would later, as the head of the Communist East German Foreign Intelligence Agency, bring him down as West German Chancellor. The legendary American military photographer Ray D'Addario, who was to remain in Nuremberg until 1949, would celebrate his wedding in the castle and have it catered by Hitler's former head of household, Arthur Kannenberg.

Having officially undergone de-Nazification, Kannenberg ran the kitchen at Schloss Faber-Castell, but before the Second World War he had entertained the Führer with his singing and accordion-playing. He was envied for his proximity to Germany's leader. "What is granted to only a very few mortals but is the wish of millions is your great fortune, you who are in His presence every day," a friend once wrote to him in a mawkish letter.[3] But Hitler's "court fool on the squeeze box", as Wolfgang Wagner once mockingly dubbed him, now served the representatives of the international press instead of the Führer and his entourage.[4]

The press camp, which remained open until the last of the subsequent trials in Nuremberg had concluded in 1949, was a hive not only of journalistic activity but of artistic creativity, the birthplace of drawings, cartoons, novels and short stories, along with countless articles, features and radio reports on the legal proceedings. Boris Polevoy's novel *The Story of a Real Man*, upon which Prokofiev's opera of the same name would be based, was written in the press camp—the composer called it the "most intense literary experience of recent times" and insisted on setting it to music. Wolfgang Hildesheimer, whose first love was the visual arts, also painted a number of abstract works in the castle.

The Schloss was essentially a multinational hostel with a variety of idiosyncratic mores and habits, as a correspondent for *Pravda* noted in his journal. Coexisting in such confined space generated tensions. Competition was fierce, particularly among American journalists. Reporters who had conversed pleasantly enough over breakfast could turn into fierce rivals by the afternoon. Everyone was after a scoop. Hermann Göring's wife, Emmy, was inundated with interview requests, and aggressive press photographers also hounded the spouses of the other defendants. One famous Associated Press image showed journalist Wes Gallagher sprinting out of the court building to be the first reporter to pass on the news of the verdict via overseas telephone. Competition led some correspondents to exaggerate what they reported. False news—intended to boost circulations or serve propaganda purposes—was repeatedly reported. Even a respected author like the novelist Alfred Döblin, who covered the trial under a pseudonym for the French occupation authorities, pretended to be present in the courtroom although he wasn't even in Nuremberg.

The international event attracted no shortage of would-be profiteers, and publishers working for large American conglomerates sensed the chance to earn small fortunes. Sometimes they met up for dinner in the press camp immediately after negotiating with the lawyers of the war criminals on trial for the rights to their memoirs.

The growing mistrust between the victorious powers amid the incipient Cold War meant that Soviet and Western correspondents weren't supposed to get too close to one another. Moscow kept its journalists on an especially short leash. They were given strict instructions on how to behave and risked being informed on if they disobeyed. The tiniest deviation or one false word might see them immediately recalled and their careers ended, with their families punished as well.

During the day, those present in the courtroom were confronted with the incomprehensible crimes of the defendants, documented by photos of the death camps and mass executions and testimonies from eyewitnesses and victims. In the evening, many of these people numbed themselves with alcohol. Inhibitions disappeared. There was lots of dancing and drinking. "The Americans drink as though they get paid for it, and it's not uncommon for one of them to be recalled home because he (or she) is suffering from delirium tremens," noted Hildesheimer. "Otherwise, they're prudish, friendly and naive."[5]

As a place where so many cultures converged, the press camp was a very progressive social experiment for its time. The Western media aimed to show the occupied Germans what the ideal of freedom of the press looked like in practice. In terms of women's liberation, the microcosm of Schloss Faber-Castell was far ahead of mainstream German society, still informed by National Socialist ideology. One of the accused at the Nuremberg Trial, the Nazi ideologue and author of *Der Mythus des zwanzigsten Jahrhunderts* (*The Myth of the Twentieth Century*), Alfred Rosenberg, had called for German women to be "emancipated

from women's emancipation", and the Nazi dictatorship had
encouraged a patriarchal social order in which women were
mothers first and working people second. Rosenberg and his
fellow defendants must have been bewildered to see so many
female correspondents in the courtroom. Only 13 per cent of the
members of the Reich Association of the German Press in 1944
had been women, most of them employed by magazines and
only a handful in political journalism,[6] whereas the proportion
of women within the international press corps was far higher.
Although it would be too much to claim that there was gender
equality, the international press corps did approximate that
ideal. Female journalists were housed in a separate building,
the Villa im Schlosspark. *The New York Times* alone sent two
women to report on the proceedings: Kathleen McLaughlin and
the Pulitzer Prize winner Anne O'Hare McCormick. Tullia Zevi,
later the President of the Union of Italian Jewish Communities,
wrote for the *Religious News Service*. Among the many other
respected female writers in Nuremberg were West, Nora Waln,
Gellhorn, Dominique Desanti, Janet Flanner and Erika Mann.

Their interests went beyond politics. Some of the female
reporters addressed feminist issues and criticized the main trial
as an exclusively male affair. "There were no women among
the defendants—was this perhaps the reason that there was
no woman to be found among the judges?" asked Argentinian
writer Victoria Ocampo. "Shouldn't they have been represented,
precisely here? If the results of the Nuremberg trials are to play
a significant role in determining the future of Europe, wouldn't
it have been just to let women have a say, too?"[7]

Nuremberg was also the place where the future of Germany
was decided, and most of the men and women who chronicled

the trials there resided in the press camp in Stein. The reports they produced included not only legal details and current affairs, political issues and individual life stories, but also their fair share of rumours and gossip. As a microcosm within what was already the microcosm of Nuremberg, the press camp provides a perfect setting to examine both political and cultural history and individual biographies. This book is the first attempt at a comprehensive narrative of this unique place and its temporary residents. In 2015, to mark the seventieth anniversary of the start of the trials, the culture editor of the *Nürnberger Nachrichten* newspaper, Steffen Radlmaier, published a fifty-page catalogue full of illustrations, titled "The Pencil Castle as Press Camp", for an exhibition held at Schloss Faber-Castell. This book owes much to Radlmaier's pioneering work, especially the collection he edited of reports on the trials by international correspondents.[8]

We will begin with a general introduction of the press camp, followed by examinations of some of the prominent personalities who lived and worked there. Each chapter will focus on one such extraordinary individual. Who were these people before they came to Nuremberg? How did their time there influence them? What impression did the trials make? No one was left untouched by the terrible deeds being adjudicated in the courtroom or by the ruins of the surrounding city. Some correspondents asked to be recalled because they could no longer take the horror. If we believe one of his peers, Wolfgang Hildesheimer's increasingly apocalyptic view of the world as he got older could be traced back directly to his experiences in Nuremberg. Erika Mann's lover stayed on in the city after the Nuremberg Trial and became an opponent of the death penalty and "victors' justice".

The Nuremberg trials did not just change the lives of those who witnessed them; they also altered the way they wrote. Janet Flanner, known for her "Flanner touch" of satirical punchlines and denouements, expressed herself very differently in the Franconian city. Her wit and sarcasm were no match for the horrific dimensions of the crimes in question. Erich Kästner, otherwise never at a loss for words, stated that, after viewing documentary film footage of the death camps, he was unable to write "a single coherent article about this unimaginable, infernal insanity". The present volume is thus also a book about speechlessness and literary approaches to the unspeakable.

The central protagonist of this study is the main Nuremberg Trial itself. The dramaturgy of the chapters will conform to the chronology of the legal proceedings: from the start of the trial of the main defendants in November 1945 (Dos Passos) to the cross-examination of Göring (Flanner) and the rendering of the verdict in the autumn of 1946 (Gellhorn) to the subsequent trials (Hildesheimer.) We will take a detour to look at the aristocratic owners of the castle, and the book will conclude with how historian Golo Mann came to advocate for Rudolf Hess to be released from his military prison in Spandau. Together, these stories will form a literary chronicle of the Nuremberg trials and a collective biography of the reporters lodged in Schloss Faber-Castell.

A Castle Made of Pencils

"But such is the Press Camp—either very exciting
or very dull, seldom mid-way between."

ERNEST CECIL DEANE, LETTER TO HIS WIFE
LOIS ON 9TH OCTOBER 1945

I n November 1945, the eyes of the world were upon
Nuremberg. For the first time in the history of humanity,
a criminal regime's wielders of political and military power
were to be held to account before a court of law. The express
will of the US occupation forces in charge of organizing the
Nuremberg Trial was that they be an act of justice, not vengeance. The International Military Tribunal, which convened from
20th November 1945 to 1st October 1946, was formed with the
purpose of rendering legal judgment upon leading representatives of the Nazi apparatus. Twenty-one men were to answer
for themselves in the courtroom, while Martin Bormann would
be tried in absentia—although Gustav Krupp von Bohlen und
Halbach was deemed unable to stand trial, and Robert Ley, the
director of the German Labour Front, hanged himself in his
cell before the hearings could begin. Thus what took place was
a trial of "Göring and associates", as the files drily noted. The

most major of Nazi war criminals, Adolf Hitler, had of course avoided responsibility by committing suicide, as had two of his main henchmen, Joseph Goebbels and Heinrich Himmler.

The trial officially opened in Berlin on 18th October 1945, but it was moved to Nuremberg because the Americans insisted that it be held in the US occupation zone. The city was chosen for both practical and symbolic reasons. The huge complex of the Palace of Justice on Fürther Strasse, inaugurated in 1916, had suffered only minor war damage and had a directly adjacent prison. But most importantly, Nuremberg was where Hitler had held his Nazi Party rallies. This was where the regime's cruellest and most notorious laws had been proclaimed, including the "Law for the Protection of German Blood and German Honour". Thus there was a special symbolism in making prominent Nazis face a tribunal in Nuremberg. The Nuremberg Trial was neither a court martial, as Winston Churchill had called for, nor a Soviet-style bit of legal theatre. The justice to be done in the Franconian capital was supposed to be worthy of the name, and the proceedings were intended to exemplify an ethical antipode to the brutal capriciousness of the Nazi regime. The trial was a historic chance to debunk the idea of the legal immunity of governments and establish a multilateral global system based on the rule of law and democracy.

The Americans, in particular, wanted the world to see the proceedings as just, which required measuring the culpability of each defendant individually. Nonetheless, along with individuals, prosecutors sought to prove that central Nazi organizations were fundamentally criminal in nature: the Reich government, the corps of Nazi Party political directors, the Gestapo, the SS and the Security Service (SD), and the Wehrmacht Supreme

Command and general staff. Everyone involved knew that the trial would be a huge experiment. There were no laws on the books specifying what a marshal or minister of the Third Reich was and wasn't allowed to do. In such uncharted judicial waters, improvisation would be crucial. Still, as US chief counsel Justice Robert H. Jackson put it in his opening statement, "The wrongs which we seek to condemn and punish have been so calculated, so malignant, and so devastating, that civilization cannot tolerate their being ignored, because it cannot survive their being repeated." The trial aimed at not only atonement and catharsis, but also deterrence.

Even before the end of the Second World War, amid constant reports of Nazi atrocities, the Allies had agreed that the leaders of the Third Reich had to be punished. The Charter of the International Military Tribunal, signed in London in August 1945, laid out the legal basis for trying the primary German war criminals, determining the procedure and defining what sort of offences could be adjudicated. A list of accused was drawn up. The committee of judges in the tribunal consisted of one representative from each of the four main Allies along with deputies. Each of the four powers also had a legal team with a chief prosecutor and assistants. The defendants were charged on four counts: crimes against peace, war crimes, crimes against humanity and conspiracy to commit those three categories of crimes. Since France and the Soviet Union had suffered so greatly under German occupation, it was logical for those two nations to lead the prosecution on the charges of war crimes and crimes against humanity. The British and Americans were responsible for the charges of having conspired to destroy peace and planned a war of aggression.

The Nuremberg Trial got under way in Nuremberg on 20th
November 1945. For the first time in judicial history, proceedings were conducted in four languages. The American company
IBM provided the court, free of charge, with special equipment
for simultaneous translations. By flicking switches mounted on
the courtroom seats, the prosecution could listen in via headphones in English, Russian, German or French. The tribunal
was thus a truly international event. Reporters, too, could choose
the language in which they wanted to follow the proceedings.
Unfortunately, the new technology was prone to occasional
untimely malfunctions, most prominently when the death sentence for Hermann Göring was announced on 1st October 1946.

The media presence in Nuremberg, encompassing journalists from all over the world, reflected the event's enormous
significance. This was a news spectacle of the first order. The
publicly declared aim of the authorities who organized the trial
was to leave not just a written but also a visual and aural record
of the proceedings for posterity. Organizers saw it as both a
history lesson and, in the words of Alfred Döblin, a "learning
process" for generations to come. The courtroom was equipped
with technologically sophisticated "radio boxes" attached to
the ceiling like swallows' nests. They allowed commentators to
broadcast live from trial for the first time ever. For instance, one
eyewitness reported for Radio Stuttgart: "250 journalists and
radio reporters, as well as eleven photographers and cameramen
from all over the world, follow the proceedings constantly. The
American contingent is the largest, with 100 representatives,
while the British Empire has 50, France 40 to 50 and Russia
25 to 30."[1] Journalist Madeleine Jacob later recalled the entire
French press landscape being present, and in fact just about

every well-known French publication—from the conservative *Le Figaro* and the Christian Democratic *L'Aube* to the Communist *L'Humanité* and the voice of the Resistance, *Libération*, to regional newspapers like *L'Est républicain*—covered at least parts of the trial.[2] The press corps was a disconcerting sight for the defendants. "In the courtroom... we encountered only hostile faces," Albert Speer wrote in his memoirs. "I was taken aback when the journalists began laying bets on the extent of our penalties, and their list of those slated for hanging sometimes included us too."[3]

Flanked by US soldiers in white helmets and gloves, the defendants recognized some familiar faces among the correspondents, including William Shirer, Howard Smith, Louis Lochner and Frederick Oechsner, who had reported from Germany for various US media up until the early 1940s. Oechsner had been the Central European manager for the United Press in Berlin, where his underlings included later CIA Director Richard Helms. After the USA entered the Second World War, Oechsner and other journalists had been interned for five months in Bad Nauheim before being released as part of a prisoner exchange. Now they were back in Germany under completely altered circumstances.

German reporters had a special task in Nuremberg. German journalism was starting over. After the war, the occupying powers had immediately banned all organs of the Nazi-controlled press, but during the summer of 1945, having discarded the practice of pre-censorship and initially publishing only news written by the military government, the occupiers issued the first licences for German newspapers. A new German press, it was felt, was needed to service the populace's hunger for information and

The press section in the Nuremberg courtroom, with future German Chancellor Willy Brandt in the middle of the third row.

encourage a climate of reconciliation between the occupiers and the occupied. The first officially licensed, post-war newspaper, the *Aachener Nachrichten*, appeared on 20th June 1945, with the first issue of the *Frankfurter Rundschau* following on 1st August. By the time the Nuremberg Trial began, US authorities had licensed twenty newspapers, which, because of paper shortages, appeared only two to three times a week and had few pages. Ultimately, four super-regional papers established themselves as leaders in the four occupation zones: *Die Welt* in the British zone, *Nouvelles de France* in the French zone, *Die Neue Zeitung* in the American zone and the *Tägliche Rundschau* in the Soviet zone.

As part of their three-pronged strategy of demilitarization, de-Nazification and democratization, occupation authorities were particularly keen on keeping journalists with Nazi pasts out of the Nuremberg press corps. The correspondents reporting from the court building for the licensed German newspapers initially came almost exclusively from the victorious nations of the Second World War. Their articles were explicitly intended to re-educate the German people. But eventually authorities warmed to the notion of "Germans reporting to Germans", and German journalists were also admitted to the Palace of Justice. They took turns occupying the seven seats they were allocated among 250 press spots. The Soviets also gave five seats from their contingent to German reporters—among the beneficiaries was Markus Wolf.[4]

For their part, German journalists insisted they had a right to report independently and form their own opinions. Theodor Heuss, the editor-in-chief of the *Rhein-Neckar Zeitung* and later President of West Germany, wrote in a remarkably self-confident editorial on 5th September 1945: "There is now a chance that German men, having freely accepted their responsibility towards the military government and the German people, begin to interpret Germany's destiny themselves and serve as well as they know how the difficult and long process of convalescence. We have seized this chance in full knowledge of the psychological and objective difficulties. We welcome supportive engagement while remaining completely indifferent to derisive mockery."[5]

American authorities didn't always make the right calls when handing out accreditations, as the story of the fraudster Walter Ullmann shows. When US troops set the Vienna-born Ullmann free from a prison in Moosburg near Munich shortly before the end of the war, he claimed to have been persecuted by the Nazi regime. In the 1920s, under the pseudonym Dr Jo Lherman, Ullmann had run an experimental theatre in Berlin that had attracted the attention of no less than Erich Kästner. Now, having served jail time for a series of frauds, he changed his alias to Dr Gaston Oulmán and claimed to be the head of the Cuban press service. In reality, Ullmann had reported on the Spanish Civil War for various Austrian newspapers, but, using his new identity, he succeeded in gaining the trust of the American officials responsible for Radio Munich. Oulmán, kitted out in a self-designed uniform with a Cuban flag on his left shoulder, was made the official Bavarian radio correspondent in Nuremberg, in part because he spoke such excellent German.

Every day except Sundays, in the prime-time slot starting at 8.15 p.m., Oulmán commented on the proceedings. All told, until the conclusion of the trial, he delivered some 300 commentaries, composed in a controversially pompous, biting tone. Oulmán continually mocked witnesses, dismissing the

Resistance fighter General Erwin Lahousen, for instance, on account of his appearance as being like a "postmaster". Millions of listeners heard his critical opinions on the verdicts with their transparent sympathy for the defendants. When Göring was found guilty, Oulmán commented: "This verdict could be seen as exaggerated in its declaration that the trial had not uncovered one characteristic that spoke in his favour or could have served as moderating circumstance, and that his crimes had been almost without precedent."[6]

Statements like that got him in hot water with the American authorities, and his contract with Radio Munich wasn't extended. Ullmann's deception was revealed when the American consulate in Munich wrote to Cuba requesting proof-of-identity documents, which he claimed to have lost, so that he could be issued new papers in Germany. No one in Havana had ever heard of the man. "We regret to inform you that we cannot issue you the requested papers since there is no proof of your Cuban citizenship," the consulate wrote to Oulmán.[7] But American authorities, wanting to avoid a scandal, kept the deception under wraps until the end of the trial. At most, Oulmán's fellow correspondents in Nuremberg may have suspected that there was something fishy about their fluent-German-speaking Cuban colleague.

Another journalist accredited by American authorities was Ernst Michel, a Jewish-German born in Mannheim, who wrote for the *Rhein-Neckar-Zeitung*. With the backing of Theodor Heuss, in the spring of 1946 Michel was the only Holocaust survivor to report on the Nuremberg Trial. Several of the supplemental personal articles he wrote were attributed to "Special Correspondent Ernst Michel, Auschwitz Inmate Number

104995". It was a miracle he had survived, having raised a finger
at the right time in the barracks for ill prisoners when his captors
asked if any of the prisoners had particularly neat handwriting.
As a result he was made a scribe, responsible for drawing up
the lists of sick captives. Both his parents were murdered in
Auschwitz. Michel was able to escape from a death march in
Saxony. After the war, he returned to Mannheim and began
looking for surviving relatives. A recommendation secured him
a meeting with Heuss, who hired him to work for the newspaper.

It is impossible to imagine what Michel must have felt in the
Nuremberg court in March 1946 when he first shared a room
with former Nazi grandees like Julius Streicher, the publisher of
the anti-Semitic hate-rag *Der Stürmer*, "Deputy Führer" Rudolf
Hess or the head of the Security Police and Security Service,
Ernst Kaltenbrunner. When Göring learned that a survivor of
Auschwitz was covering the trial, he wanted to meet the man
and had his attorney invite Michel to his cell. "The meeting was
arranged under the condition it remain off the record," Michel
would write in his autobiography. "I was nervous. What should
I say? Should I shake hands? Ask questions? Since I couldn't
write about it, why did I want to go through such a painful experience? Goering [*sic*] stood up when Dr Stahmer and I entered
his cell, which was constantly under guard. 'This is the young
reporter you asked me about,' Dr Stahmer said, motioning to
me. Goering looked at me, started to reach out to shake hands
and, sensing my reaction, turned away for a moment. I stood
frozen. What the hell am I doing here? How can I possibly be
in the same room with this monster and carry on a conversation?
How could I talk logically, unemotionally? Mr Goering, how
does it feel to be here? What do you think of the proceedings?

Are they treating you well? Should I shout at him, tell him that he was responsible for my six years in the camps? Should I blame him for my lost childhood? For the death of my parents? I did nothing of the sort. I stood there and stared while Dr Stahmer discussed the next day's proceedings. Then, on an impulse, I bolted for the door and asked the MP to let me out. I couldn't take it. I couldn't remain. I had to get away. There was no discussion, not a word was exchanged, no comments or statements were made. I was there, and then I was gone. Period."[8]

While Michel wrote for a German newspaper, Jewish correspondents reported on the trial for the Hebrew press in Palestine. One of them was Robert Weltsch, a journalist for Tel Aviv's *Haaretz*. Weltsch shared a room in the press camp with Robert Jungk, who covered the proceedings for the Zurich newspaper *Weltwoche*. Meanwhile, Shabse Klugman wrote in Yiddish for the publication of the Central Committee of Liberated Jews in Bavaria, *Undzer veg*. At the start of the trial, many Jewish correspondents praised the Allies and were confident that the liberators would act on behalf of Jews everywhere in prosecuting the murderers. The summary of the charges presented at the beginning of the trial in *Undzer veg* indeed gave the impression that the genocide against European Jews would be the main issue. But this optimism would quickly be disappointed. Nine days later Klugman wrote: "The oceans of our blood have been squeezed into a small framework called 'Crimes Against Humanity.' Within it, there is a special section titled 'Crimes against the Jews.'" Increasingly frustrated, he asked a short time later: "Where is our case, our enormous tragedy, at this tribunal?" And in fact, of the 139 witnesses invited to testify at the trial only three were Jewish. One of them, the Lithuanian poet Avrom Sutzkever, who testified on 27th February 1946, was introduced by the Russian prosecutor L.M. Smirnov as a Soviet citizen. When Sutzkever started speaking Yiddish, he was told that there was no interpreter for that tongue and that he would have to use Russian.

Since the French were responsible for "crimes against humanity" during the proceedings, they were the ones who should have focused on the Holocaust, but French prosecutors tried to marginalize the topic in favour of crimes against Gentile French people and Resistance fighters. The calling of a Gentile Auschwitz survivor, Marie-Claude Vaillant-Couturier, as a witness was symptomatic of their insensitivity.[9] On the other hand, psychological repression may also have been at play. The sheer unimaginability of the Holocaust probably hindered people from acknowledging the extent of the crimes. British judge Normal Birkett found the testimony of Soviet witnesses exaggerated, while US chief counsel Jackson worried that Jewish witnesses could be more vengeful and less reliable than others, potentially damaging the prosecution's case.[10]

German journalists frequently complained about second-class treatment in the courtroom and felt disadvantaged vis-à-vis correspondents from other countries. Articles in German were carefully scrutinized and censored, and in the Soviet occupation zone articles could not be published at all without pre-clearance. While the Allies explicitly promoted the idea of extensive journalistic coverage, critical analyses were unwelcome. The authorities responsible for the press in occupied Germany also required the newspapers covering the trial to feature reports from it prominently, and roughly a third of texts appeared on the front page and a further fifth in special supplements.[11] The arrangement was intended to make it more difficult for readers to ignore the story. In the US occupation zone, the American-established German General News Agency (DANA) pre-edited reports and monitored trial coverage.[12]

Early on, German journalists were also physically marginalized. Because of strictures against fraternizing with the former enemy, reporters of other nationalities avoided them. Germans were only admitted to the courtroom with a yellow press pass via a separate entrance. Others had a blue pass that also granted them admission to the American PX (commissary). German reporters had to arrange their own accommodation in Nuremberg and were barred from the press camp. In a letter dated 9th April 1946 to General Robert A. McClure, the head of American Information Control Division, eight German journalists complained that "the physical and psychological conditions for the accredited German press representatives do not measure up to what we would wish for and expect in order to do the job".[13] After McClure intervened, the situation for German correspondents improved in the spring of 1946. They were given adequate workspaces and were allowed to communicate with reporters from Allied countries and eat in the court canteen, which had previously been prohibited. But accommodation and supplies remained problematic.

Press representatives of other nationalities were better off. Not only were they housed and fed in the international press camp in the well-protected confines of Schloss Faber-Castell, they also enjoyed a free shuttle to the court building in Nuremberg. The castle itself consisted of two sections, built in the nineteenth and twentieth centuries, and the grounds encompassed a park, a villa and other buildings; seven were used for the press camp, with the castle proper serving as the main building with dining rooms and a bar. A sign hanging by the entrance read: "Off limits to Germans".

Journalist Hans Rudolf Berndorff found out the hard way how strictly this prohibition was meant. Berndorff, formerly a leading reporter for the Ullstein publishing conglomerate, had come to Nuremberg with a certain Mr Forrest, a correspondent for the English German News Service. The likeable Englishman, who spoke only broken German, stood up for his colleague. "I got thrown out of the castle as quickly as I entered it," Berndorff wrote; referring to himself in the third person, he continued: "But Forrest was an imaginative fellow. He said to me, 'Herr Berndorff out on the street? Nonsense! I won't go to bed until Herr Berndorff does as well.' He drove to the local mayor and asked: 'Who was a Nazi here?' The mayor thought this over and answered: 'As far as I know, everyone.' Forrest pointed to a small house and asked if the man who lived there was a Nazi. 'Yes.' In the end, Forrest succeeded using gifts of butter and chocolate to convince the family who lived there [to take me in]. That was how Berndorff remained in Stein, if outside the press camp."[14]

Trial authorities took care to divide up the court building by sex and profession—and also according to the political realities of the day. In a reflection of the polarization of East and West, Soviet correspondents were separately accommodated in the so-called Red House. Women and married couples were given the run of the villa in the castle park. Radio technicians stayed in the so-called Green House.[15]

The interior of the castle was impressive, but also stained and damaged from military use during the war, when flak artillery had been deployed in the tower. Jackson refused to have the prosecutorial staffs quartered there, but it was deemed adequate for the international press community. Several correspondents, including William Shirer, disagreed with that assessment. They were used to the greater comfort of places like the luxurious Hôtel Scribe in central Paris, which had served as the press camp when the French capital was liberated in 1944,[16] and complained about the overcrowded, substandard and chaotic living conditions in Stein, where some reporters had to sleep ten to a room on army cots. Residents also often quarrelled over the intermittently functional telephone connections. There weren't enough sanitary facilities, and long queues formed every morning in front of the few lavatories. Pyjama-clad journalists walked across the interior courtyard in icy temperatures, reported Peter de Mendelssohn, to use the bathrooms in the adjacent building.

It was virtually impossible for reporters to concentrate on their work in the castle. "Life here is so darned complicated and uncomfortable that I find it very difficult to do anything properly," Mendelssohn wrote. "This place, the castle in which we are billeted, is so enormous and at the same time so overcrowded that it is almost impossible to find a quiet place to sit and write or think. We have a large 'work room,' for all the correspondents, and there are always up to 30 or 40 typewriters clattering away, in addition to a loudspeaker blaring announcements and a pianist outside the door playing for all his worth for the entertainment of those lounging round the bar which is just outside the workroom. It is a difficult atmosphere."[17]

Willy Brandt, who though German was allowed to stay in the castle because he held a Norwegian passport, was more pragmatically accepting of his quarters. "When you think of castle life, you imagine something different than sleeping bags and

field cots," he wrote. "But they do suit the title war correspondent."[18] That was in fact how the correspondents were officially
classified even many months after the war had ended.

Not all the inhabitants were fans of the massive castle's
architecture, which was described as an eyesore, an example of
"German hideousness", "a monumental example of bad taste"
and a "complete nightmare". Some blamed the Faber-Castells.
"How many pencils and pens did it take for the Fabers to be
able to build such a thoroughly ugly castle?" asked Elsa Triolet.
Rebecca West also saw the exterior architecture and interior
design of the building as reflecting negative German traits.
Admittedly, many foreign correspondents rarely had anything
good to say about anything German after the war, especially
not in Nuremberg, as the full extent of crimes committed by
Germany were being revealed for the first time. There was
an imposing number of so-called Vansittartists—named after
the hardcore anti-German Permanent Under-Secretary at
the Foreign Office, Baron Vansittart—among the ranks of the
American and British correspondents. Some, including Janet
Flanner and Martha Gellhorn, admitted in their private correspondence that they loathed Germans on principle. We should
also recall that the journalists also saw the castle—considered
today a "remarkable example" of Franconian historicism and art
nouveau—in a state of urgently needed repair.[19]

Working conditions varied according to the technological
infrastructure and the capacities of the nations they represented.
Brandt, for instance, was unable to phone Oslo because there
were no connections between Nuremberg and the Norwegian
capital, so he was forced to send telegrams to his office via
London or Copenhagen. Because it took so long to pass on news

he had to take care, when writing his reports, that they wouldn't become obsolete before they were published.[20]

Living and working conditions improved for the journalists who covered the subsequent trials between December 1946 and April 1949. Services and organization got better, and fewer reporters needed to be accommodated. The interpreters working for the occupation powers also lived in the castle and, as Wolfgang Hildesheimer, who was one of them, enthused, had "access at all times to huge en-suite rooms, fantastic food, drink, social spaces, and cars".[21] But even during the main trial, the reporters inhabiting the castle generally felt at home, as evidenced by surviving photos of representatives of the global press clearly enjoying intoxicated dinners in the ballroom or playing chess while seated in the building's sumptuous armchairs.[22]

A Better Class of Accommodation

Some reporters' dissatisfaction with Schloss Faber-Castell was fuelled by comparisons with the more comfortable accommodation reserved for VIPs: the Grand Hotel near Nuremberg's central train station, which had served during the Second World War as an outpost of the Reich Chancellery. The US military administration had set it aside for reasons of prestige, and it was repeatedly the site of high-profile receptions. Located in the centre of the city, the hotel hosted short-term official visitors, including top members of the victorious powers' delegations sent to the trial and renowned media guests. Children and those maimed in the war used to hurl themselves on the ground to claim the cigarette butts tossed away by the privileged guests.

Russian authors Ilya Ehrenburg and Konstantin Fedin and French Prix Goncourt winner Elsa Triolet stayed in the Grand Hotel, as did Marlene Dietrich, who served for a short time as a trial observer and who would later play one of the leads in the film *Judgment at Nuremberg*. In contrast to the field cots at the castle, hotel guests at least slept in repurposed hospital beds made no less comfortable by sometimes still having medical charts attached to them. More off-putting was the dining-room cutlery, which still bore Reich eagles and swastikas. Soviet journalists nicknamed the hotel the "luminarium" because so many luminaries resided there, while the latter mockingly referred to the press camp as the "Chaldeum" after the well-known press photographer Yevgeny Khaldei, who was housed in the castle.

Despite the serious damage the hotel had suffered in the war—power cables hung down from the ceilings of the hallways, and replacement toilets, bathtubs and sinks lay around waiting to be installed—it remained the centre of downtown Nuremberg social life. The city was subjected to a night-time curfew, but the main figures at the trial could still meet in the Grand Hotel after work to unwind. "The marble hall… is full to the rafters," wrote Triolet. "Women and men in uniform and civilian dress. There you can see lawyers, secretaries, interpreters, the press and prosecutors dancing. Even the judges cut a rug there— that's no myth."[23] Nor were the two residences for reporters by any means isolated from one another. Residents of one visited the other to amuse themselves or exchange information. Hotel guests regularly travelled out to the castle because of the atmosphere there, which, to the particular delight of the star Soviet correspondents, was far more relaxed and rustic. The castle's expansive grounds were a welcome change of scenery for those depressed by the sight of the devastated city centre.

Graphic Artists

The press camp was also home to court illustrators and cartoonists who made drawings of the defendants for newspapers and magazines. These graphic artists played a major role in documenting the trials since photographers weren't allowed in the courtroom. The spectrum of the illustrators' work ranged from more or less lifelike pencil and ink portraits to spontaneous sketches to cartoons. One of the more realistic artists was Edward Vebell, who worked for the American Armed Forces newspaper *Stars and Stripes*. The cartoonists included David Low of the London *Evening Standard*, with his excellent eye for Göring's physical demeanour, and the Soviet caricaturist Boris Yefimov, who often depicted the defendants with bird-of-prey beaks and surreally long, clutching fingers.

One exceptional figure was the British Impressionist painter Laura Knight, who, in keeping with her status as a well-known fine artist, lodged as of January 1946 in a suite in the Grand Hotel. During the war she had painted scenes of the conflict for the War Artists' Advisory Committee. Now she was sent to Nuremberg to capture the trial for posterity in an oil painting to be shown at the Summer Exhibition in London's Royal Academy. Her work *The Nuremberg Trial* departed from the realism of her war scenes. Although it depicted the defendants sitting in the dock naturalistically, she wholly omitted the rear and side walls of the courtroom so that viewers looked out on the devastated

Laura Knight, *The Nuremberg Trial* (1946), oil on canvas.

city of Nuremberg, parts of which stood in flames. This horrid panoramic backdrop of destruction was a greater indictment than Knight's depiction of the court itself. In a letter to the War Artists' Advisory Committee, she explained: "In that ruined city death and destruction are ever present. They had to come into the picture, without them, it would not be the Nuremberg as it now is during the trial, when the death of millions and utter devastation are the sole topics of conversation wherever one goes—whatever one is doing." But the painting received a rather cool reception at the Academy.[24]

Like Knight, caricaturist Günter Peis didn't stay in Schloss Faber-Castell, although in his case that was due to nationality and not status. Born in Austria, Peis had been forced to join the Volkssturm militia at the age of seventeen as part of Nazi Germany's last-ditch efforts to defend itself. After the war, he had attended an American re-education programme at a journalism school in Munich. From there he was sent to Nuremberg, where at nineteen he was the youngest correspondent and personally witnessed the execution of the convicted war criminals from an attic window. Peis, today considered a pioneer of investigative journalism, was a man of many talents, writing several articles about the proceedings but also reaching for his sketchbook to document the trial and capture the characteristics of the defendants. His caricatures, also made of the judges, prosecutors and witnesses, were a bit of light relief in the otherwise emotionally charged atmosphere. The Jewish-Austrian journalist William Stricker wrote of Peis's illustrations in the *Nürnberger Extra Blatt*, a humorous, self-mocking brochure published by the correspondents themselves, saying they were "the expression of the right of a free press for people to make fun of themselves after their work was done".[25]

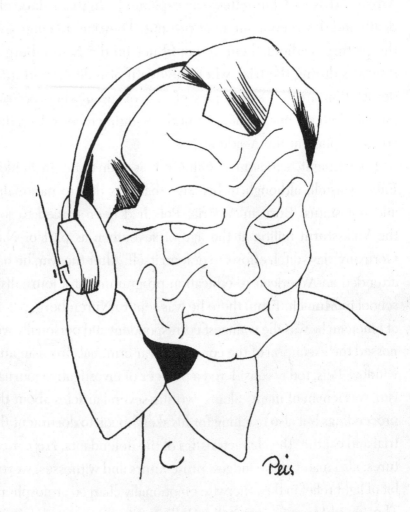

Günter Peis, caricature of Hermann Göring in the courtroom, October 1946.

The Problem Solver: Ernest Cecil Deane

In October 1945 the press camp came under the command of General Lucian Truscott, Patton's successor as military governor of Bavaria. Truscott delegated responsibility on the ground in the camp to US press officer Charles Madary, who started preparing the castle for the journalists' arrival in August 1945 by rearranging and repurposing rooms, among other things. The imposing Gobelin hall became an open workspace in which correspondents typed away at their articles. Field cots were lined in rows in the once-luxurious private chambers. There was a salon, a game room and a library, and a cinema was set up in the stables. Residents took meals together with those housed in the other buildings in the former ballroom and the main dining room.

We have Madary's assistant, Ernest Cecil Deane, to thank for some vivid descriptions of everyday life in the press camp. "Ernie Deane", whose letters are preserved in the Stanford University archive, wrote home to his wife, Lois, several times a week. Because Madary was often absent from Germany for long periods Deane actually ran the camp, serving as a point of contact for the correspondents until June 1946. The thirty-four-year-old, who had studied journalism at the University of Arkansas, joined the US Army as a press officer in 1942 and arrived in Bavaria with advancing American troops in 1945. That October, he wrote to his wife from a spa town called Bad Wiessee about his new task: "The press will be housed and fed on the former Faber estate, a fabulous place with a small palace, and all of the works. Faber was the pencil magnate of Germany—you may know Eberhardt-Faber pencils, I used to

use a lot of them. Anyhow, old man Faber built himself a beautiful place, marble stairways, mother-of-pearl decorative work
along the walls, etc... My job is entitled 'liaison officer' between
the press camp and the courthouse, which means I'll probably
be a trouble shooter trying to calm down irate correspondents
who get griped over all sorts of things—transportation, food,
communications, news, etc. It should be a lively assignment."[26]

Deane's job was indeed a challenging and varied one, since
he not only had to serve as a troubleshooter and a liaison but
as a *maître de plaisir* as well. Along with being a place to reside
and eat, the camp was where journalists amused themselves.
Guests were constantly showing up in search of a good time,
not just from the Grand Hotel but also from Zirndorf, where
the French delegation stayed, or Dambach, where the American
chief counsel and his staff were housed in seven separate villas.
Conversations were lively, and visitors interested in news beyond
what they could get in *Stars and Stripes* eagerly snapped up
information. Frequently, generals, ranking officers and US
newspaper publishers enjoyed multi-course dinners in the castle's imposing main dining room and other social spaces. Deane
even put together a small women's chorus consisting of German
waitresses who regaled the international guests with native
folk songs and, for comic relief, heavily accented versions of
American popular ditties. On one occasion, he asked his wife to
send him sheet music of Americans songs for the German piano
player at the bar.

The game room was particularly popular. Markus Wolf,
who was allowed in the castle as a Soviet passport holder, later
recalled learning to play poker there. Visitors' horizons were
expanded not only by unfamiliar card games, previously unheard

forms of music and a Babylonian variety of languages, but also by national cultural peculiarities. Wolf was dumbfounded the first time he saw a troupe of kilted bagpipe players booked for Burns Supper. Meanwhile, the canteen in the Nuremberg court building introduced the Russian-French Elsa Triolet to the idea of a cafeteria, inspiring her to write of a place "where you find a selection of food atop a long counter you approach in a synchronised march". In addition, the press camp offered correspondents the opportunity to engage in sporting pursuits. Walter Cronkite, later the "most trusted man in America", was very accomplished at table tennis.[27] And representatives of East and West constantly faced off over the chessboards.

On 9th December 1945 there was a large ball attended even by Robert H. Jackson, but according to Deane, who organized it, the event was a flop: "All sorts of things went wrong—the justice and the general and their party arrived an hour and a half after they were supposed to show up, correspondents had occupied all of the tables we set up for the visitors and we had to set up more, and just as the justice seated himself to enjoy the evening the negro orchestra played one long blast and started packing its instruments. I dashed over to find out what the hell was going on, and the sergeant in charge told me that they were supposed to stop playing at 11 p.m." Deane was able to convince the members of the orchestra to keep playing by offering them an extra ration of gin.[28]

According to various accounts, despite the obvious risks it entailed, alcohol was an essential component of the smooth running of the camp. Whisky, vodka and cognac helped to surmount language barriers and bring the various nationalities together. An amused Deane described a completely legless

Soviet correspondent slurring "I luff you" to his American colleagues and new-found drinking buddies. After the defendants
in the main trial were executed as war criminals, the international press corps threw a huge party in the castle to celebrate the conclusion of the proceedings. Great quantities of
the national drinks of the correspondents' home countries were
flown in for the occasion. They did not go to waste.

Deane was also invested with wide-ranging authority to maintain order. His duties included such unpleasantries as handing
over to the military police an American kitchen hand who had
secretly been selling food to Germans. In the courtroom, several correspondents were found stealing headphone covers as
souvenirs. Blankets from the press camp were also popular
keepsakes. Deane had to confiscate the stolen items and even
found himself compelled to temporarily restrict the availability
of alcohol in the camp after residents consumed more than was
good for them. He was also on the receiving end of complaints,
for instance, Erika Mann's disgruntlement with the postal service, which had mistakenly forwarded two months' worth of her
mail to Paris.[29]

For Germans in the region, the press camp was an employer.
Some 150 locals, including several POWs, were hired to work
at the castle, for instance in the kitchen. Deane had to monitor
the quality of the food, answer to his superiors after inspections
and ensure that the beds were made. People were constantly
coming and going. Correspondents had to be tough to stick it
out in Nuremberg and keep reporting on the trial. The more
spectacular the proceedings became, the more correspondents resided in the press camp, whose population was directly
proportional to the level of sensation on offer. Three hundred

journalists were crammed into the castle at the beginning of the trial, but by January 1946 that number was down to 175. It rose back to 200 during Göring's cross-examination. "Hermann the German", as Deane referred to the prominent Nazi and former Hitler favourite, was a big draw. After that the number of residents again declined, only to swell back to such a level shortly before the rendering of the verdicts that Walter Gong wrote in the German newspaper *Main-Post* of a "battle of reporters".[30] The importance of the Nuremberg Trial as a media event was underscored by the fact that, for the first time since the end of the war, individual broadcasters linked up in larger networks.

Deane was not uncritical of American media representatives. While remaining friendly and even somewhat subservient in his face-to-face dealings with them, he made no bones about what he thought in his private correspondence. Some of the Americans were pushy and arrogant, insisting that he organize vehicles for day trips, requesting preferential treatment and making impossible demands. Others misbehaved, got drunk, fell down and injured themselves and got into fights. Deane also distrusted the tendency of many US correspondents to exaggerate and, encouraged by their editors, to make their reports as lurid as possible.

On 10th December 1945 the US magazine *Newsweek* wrote of "The Nuremberg Show", but the proceedings were often anything but spectacular, with the testimony trying the patience of many observers and yielding nothing new to report. Under such circumstances, the detonation of an unexploded bomb from the war in Nuremberg, in which no one was hurt, was eagerly interpreted as a terrorist attack, or a commonplace act of street violence portrayed as a political assault. "Don't get too worried

over the things you read about Nuremberg in the papers,"
Deane wrote to his wife. "You see, the correspondents are here
in droves, and the trial is very full most of the time. They have
to scratch around for sensational stories in order to keep their
bosses in New York thinking they're working, and even the
smallest bit of violence around these parts gets a big play."[31]

Name-dropping was a popular pastime. George W. Herald,
who reported for the American INS News Agency, claimed
to have run into the literary crème de la crème one day in
a press-camp bathroom, after mistaking his own toothbrush
for John Steinbeck's (monogrammed) one. In Herald's telling,
John Dos Passos contentedly splashed around in the tub in the
background, while Hemingway, clad only in a terrycloth towel
around his waist, complained about the local wines.[32] As amusing as this anecdote may have been, there is no evidence that
Hemingway or Steinbeck were ever present either in the castle
or at the trial.

East–West Conflicts

Deane was often required to mediate in political and cultural
squabbles. For example, while the Western correspondents were
happy with the camp's arrangements for Christmas holidays, as
the court went into recess from 21st December until New Year's
Day, Soviet residents felt slighted when no arrangements were
made for their plans for the Russian Orthodox holiday on 7th
January. Soviet correspondents also complained that the Russian
newspapers put out every morning for general use were stolen
by colleagues trying to learn the language.[33]

Soviet journalists were housed separately on the other side of the intersection in front of the castle, in a former civil servants' canteen the Americans called the Russian or Red Palace. Initially, as photographer Eddie Worth recalled, Soviet correspondents lived with their colleagues of other nations, but the Soviet secret police intervened to end that experiment in multiculturalism. The defenders of Communist political rectitude, it seems, were nonplussed by how quickly Soviet journalists became accustomed to the relative comfort of the castle and to the opportunity to exchange ideas with their peers from the West. "The Russians would come down in the morning, take a pint glass and crack as many eggs into it as they could, and then go down the table pouring in Heinz tomato sauce and all the things that they'd never seen before—and that was just for starters!" Eddie Worth later wrote. "We were being looked after by an old German soldier from the First World War, and we came back one day and noticed that there were no Russians around, and asked him what was going on. He told us that some very nasty-looking gentlemen, with red bands round their hats, had come in. Obviously some of the Russians had been talking about the tremendous time they very having—there was a grand piano on each floor, and singsongs and booze-ups every night—and they had rounded them all up and put them in some stables down the road."[34]

The former civil servants' canteen building was hardly a livestock stable, but the physical separation within the camp was a manifestation of the East–West conflict beginning to emerge on the world stage. Instructions coming from Moscow were strict in both a social and professional sense. Soviet media representatives were forbidden from maintaining personal relationships with non-Soviets, and their articles were monitored and censored to ensure ideological conformity. Whereas British and American journalists reported with professional distance, their Soviet colleagues tended to engage in the emotional anti-Nazi tone used by the prosecution.

Representatives of the two blocs pulled no punches during the evening debates in the press camp, where alcohol flowed freely, and encounters took place despite the best efforts of the ideological wardens. If we believe *Pravda* correspondent Boris Polevoy, differences of opinion were loud but respectful, albeit with an unmistakable undercurrent of mistrust. "'You see in my newspaper I can take every senator and every congressman to task and nothing will happen to me,' opined one representative of an American newspaper group," Polevoy wrote. "'Can you say the same?' he provokingly asked a Soviet colleague. The Russian countered coolly: 'And what about your boss? Can you also take to task a senator or congressman who's a friend of your boss or agrees with him politically. Well? Will you still get into print? And if you do, what happens next?'"[35]

There was a lot of truth to questions like that. No less than William Shirer would eventually be fired from television station CBS for disagreeing with his boss. Nonetheless, journalists from East and West did operate under different conditions in Nuremberg. American correspondents critically evaluated the trial, a few to the point of even questioning its legality, something their Soviet counterparts would never have been allowed to do. Even the conservative *Chicago Tribune* and *Stars and Stripes* expressed scepticism about trying German generals who, in the eyes of many American military officers, had done nothing but their duty, and *The New York Times* comprehensively reported on the debate.[36]

Winston Churchill's famous speech of 5th March 1946, in which he described an "iron curtain" descending on Europe from Szczecin to Trieste, disrupted the fragile coexistence of the Soviet and Western correspondents. Churchill's words and his call for the Western allies to form a common front against Moscow marked the start of the Cold War. The front page in *Stars and Stripes* bore the headline: "Unite to Stop Russians, Churchill Warns at Fulton". *Pravda* immediately responded by calling the former Prime Minister an "anti-Soviet warmonger". Soviet journalists in the press camp were more relaxed. They had been on the receiving end of so many harsh capitalist words in the past that a few thousand more from Churchill made no difference.[37] And in any case, they scoffed, the main point of the British ex-leader's cantankerous speech was merely to remind people he still existed.

But when the British radical leftist journalist Ralph Parker arrived in the camp, there was no more concealing the political animosity. As a *New York Times* correspondent in the Soviet Union, Parker had reported on events on the Eastern Front during the early years of the war. In time, though, he came to disagree with British policies towards the Soviets, claiming that pre-war policies in London had sought to bolster pro-fascist regimes as a way of rallying anti-Soviet powers. For that he was suspected of being an agent of the Soviet secret police. His Russian wife, with whom he lived in Moscow from 1941, was even said to have collaborated with the NKVD. After the war, Parker began working for the British Communist Party newspaper *The Daily Worker*. Much to Deane's disgruntlement, when Parker arrived he insisted on socializing exclusively with the Soviet friends he had made during his time reporting from the

One of the castle's two dining rooms during the days of the press camp.

front. As an American, Deane felt unable to deny the requests of a reporter from such a close ally as Britain. "There weren't enough armchairs in the [castle's] Blue Salon so people sat on the windowsills and the floor," recalled Boris Polevoy. "The toasts to the Soviet Union ended with the words hurrah, *vivat*, *prosit*, cheers and even *hoch!*"[38]

The castle's social centre was the large bar between the two dining rooms, in which, as Deane remarked, there was frequently more activity than in the courtroom. The master of ceremonies was the barkeeper David, described by Polevoy as an "amusing American with gleaming teeth". He was considered a true alchemist with cocktails—another reason for outsiders as well as residents to seek out the press-camp bar. According to Polevoy, he was adept at defusing political and cultural tensions, calming down heated tempers with his easy-going manner and skills as a mixologist. His reaction to Churchill's speech in Fulton was to create a new cocktail called the "Sir Winny". No one found it particularly palatable, but as Polevoy noted in his journal, that seemed to be precisely David's intention.

In a Foreign Land

During the Christmas holidays, the judges and prosecutors left Nuremberg, and US chief counsel Jackson toured post-war Europe. Under the Christmas tree in the castle were bottles of booze, dried fruit, writing implements and cameras, and many of the correspondents took part in a charity event, raising money for fifty Latvian children who had been forcibly taken, along with their parents, from their home country to Germany. Once again, it was Deane who organized everything. His contacts also made him a much-coveted source of information for his journalistic colleagues. On Christmas Day he interviewed the prison chaplain and reported on how the Nazi inmates were celebrating the holiday. When Hitler's political testament and marriage certificate were found in nearby Tegernsee, Deane read the documents aloud to the correspondents.[39] Like many other members of the military, he also smuggled items left behind by high-ranking Nazis. For example, on 8th November 1945 he sent his mother in the USA a book that, he proudly informed her, came from Heinrich Himmler's library.

Deane's correspondence is full of the homesickness felt by many US soldiers in Germany, who saw their work as done now that the war was over. He repeatedly complained that the trial was inexplicably dragging on. It had been years since Deane had seen his parents, his wife or his young daughter. Still, instead of pressing to be sent home, he stayed on because the trial was a chance to make valuable connections. When he returned to the USA he intended to re-enter civilian life and work as a journalist, and where else could he meet so many influential people from the American media as in the press camp? "I think my experience here will pay dividends one of these days," he wrote to Lois.

Sometimes, at weekends, the correspondents went on excursions. The US Army had requisitioned hotels and spas in Garmisch-Partenkirchen and Berchtesgaden, and soldiers' letters are full of their amazement at the natural beauty of Alpine Bavaria—as well as the strangeness of local customs. Most of the reporters had never witnessed cows wearing bells or livestock being driven from mountain pastures into valleys. A popular joke ran that the Bavarians' secret weapon was actually their cows, since nothing else could disrupt traffic so effectively.[40]

The joke played upon the idea that underground Nazis might still represent a military threat. In September 1944 Himmler had founded "Operation Werewolf", a clandestine insurgent operation that was supposed to fight on using sabotage and acts of terrorism in the event that Germany was occupied. Fear of "werewolves" proved to be unfounded, but it still meant that the Nuremberg court was heavily fortified to guard against the war criminals being freed in a guerrilla action. Correspondents were subjected to tight security and required to show press cards and allow their briefcases to be searched to be admitted to the trial. Machine-gun-toting military police patrolled the corridors, and a control post of piled-up sandbags was constructed in the hallway in front of the courtroom. "There is strict control on the ground floor," wrote Erich Kästner. "There is also strict control on the second floor, and on the third floor there are two strict controls. Many people are turned away despite their uniforms and identification."[41]

In February 1946, when the US Army received a tip that an underground network of fugitive SS men were planning attacks on foreigners and a jailbreak in Nuremberg, a tank unit was brought for protection. The exasperated French journalist Sacha Simon remarked: "More than twenty times, I have walked at night the five kilometres from Fürther Strasse to Stein. I have lost my way in dark narrow alleyways and asked shadowy figures in front of walls a hundred times for directions and have always arrived back in the best of health from these nocturnal expeditions."[42]

"Deutschland, Deutschland ohne alles"

The reports from the correspondents in Nuremberg often used the metaphor of "zero hour". Many of them were acquainted with the city from the Nazi Party rallies there, and precisely because of its symbolic associations Nuremberg was frequently treated as a microcosm of Germany. Aerial bombardment had plunged city into medieval-level destitution. Survivors rummaged through debris looking for food, lived from hand to mouth, drank from rain gutters, cooked over campfires and existed in bombed-out buildings, bunkers or improvised huts. The extent of the devastation was immense, with the city's old town being nearly destroyed. Some 178,000 people still lived within the city limits, about half of its pre-war population. The stench of rotting flesh and disinfectant was everywhere. Thousands of corpses remained beneath the ruins. "Nuremberg was practically a dead city," remarked the art historian Philipp Fehl, an American interrogation officer. "You walked through the old town as you would through a painting by Dalí. Sometimes, the exterior of a building would collapse right before your eyes with a dull noise—one step, one rolling stone could cause a breathtakingly beautiful building to disintegrate into a pile of rubble."[43]

Reuters correspondent and press camp inhabitant Seaghan Maynes told of walking his German secretary home one evening. As the well-dressed and well-groomed woman told him to stop in front of a ruin, he was confused and protested: "'Well, look I'll bring you home! I can't leave you here!' And she said, 'No, this is it.' And I saw where she went: she went into a hole in the ground. Her mother and two other youngsters were there, living in this hole which had been the cellar of a house. And yet this girl appeared as though she had come out of a very nice home where the laundry had taken care of her clothes."[44]

The people of Nuremberg were too preoccupied with their precarious personal existences to take much interest in the trial. Like most Germans, they had worries enough of their own, were trying to deal with the loss of family members and didn't have coal to heat their homes or enough to eat. And after twelve years of Nazi propaganda, many no longer trusted the press. Others, recalcitrant and defiant, dismissed the trial as a political show rather than an attempt to serve the cause of justice. Germany's collapse had encouraged a mentality of self-sufficiency and obstinance. Many Germans also wallowed in narcissistic self-pity, leading to what psychoanalyst Alexander Mitscherlich would call twenty years later an "inability to mourn".

Billy Wilder, who as a member of the US Army attended a test showing of the re-education film *KZ* (Concentration Camp) in Nuremberg's twin city of Erlangen in June 1945, was astonished that, after being forced to watch horrific scenes of piled-up corpses, the audience remained in their seats for a Western that was shown afterwards. Novelist Alfred Döblin, a trained psychiatrist, showed understanding for German obstreperousness, drawing a connection between the food crisis, political apathy, occupation and disenchantment: "You see lots of emaciated and pale faces among older people, and the youths on the street are also emaciated. Hunger in this country is a terrible force. In particular, it makes people sinister and rebellious. As is well known, it's difficult to negotiate with a person whose guts are grumbling, and if he normally gets no joy from politics, how can it be different now that he especially hates those people whom he believes are stealing his daily bread."[45]

Another well-known novelist took an active role in combatting hunger in Germany: George Orwell. His attitudes towards Germany were characterized by, to quote English literature scholar Werner von Koppenfels, "paradoxical fairness", and they reflected his keen eye for the infectiousness of totalitarian thinking. Orwell didn't see the predilection for Nazism as a purely German phenomenon. He was a democratic socialist who had regularly warned against totalitarianism since witnessing the Spanish Civil War first-hand. But the basis for his famous dystopian novel *1984* came not only from that conflict, where he had almost fallen victim to Stalinesque "purges". *The Observer* had also sent him in April and May 1945 to Germany, where he reported from Nuremberg and a completely bombed-out Cologne. In his writings from the two cities, he expressed his horror at the destruction of their neoclassical and Romantic architecture. Unlike many of his compatriots at the time, he didn't hate Germans. Indeed, he respected them as a nation of culture, a sentiment few British people shared.[46]

Even before the war ended, in January 1945, Orwell had mocked crass British anti-German hostility in two columns for the socialist magazine *Tribune*. When he read an old edition of the *Quarterly Review* from the Napoleonic Wars, he was impressed at how respectfully French books had been reviewed, even as Britain was fighting for survival in a bloody war. It would be impossible for similar reviews of German literature to appear in the British press, he complained, although in his eyes the situations were similar. After the war ended, Orwell's unusual sympathy for Germans reached its peak. By early 1946, he supported a public campaign to improve food provision on the European continent and particularly in the British occupation zone in Germany. The "Save Europe Now" initiative was the brainchild of Jewish-British publisher and peace activist Victor Gollancz. It collected clothing, food, medicine and other urgently needed emergency aid for struggling places in Germany and elsewhere. By 1948, some 30,000 care packages had arrived in the British occupation zone. Orwell's main act of support was his essay "The Politics of Starvation", published in *Tribune* on 18th January 1946, in which he argued that even if the British were comparatively well-off, another catastrophe would be inevitable if large parts of continental Europe were going hungry.

Criticism of the Trial

The correspondents in the press camp fiercely debated the issue of whether the Nuremberg Trial lived up to its elevated sense of purpose and served the cause of justice. And the tribunal did in fact deserve critical questioning. For starters, it suspended the classic legal principle that no one should be tried for violating laws instituted after the deeds in question (*nulla poena sine lege*). The Allies' primary goal was a final reckoning with Nazi ideology. As one German constitutional law expert would later write, this led to an "overemphasis of political events, while war crimes and crimes against humanity took a back seat and sometimes completely receded into the background".[47] This didn't exactly encourage political nuance in reporting on the trial. Military, political and criminal events were conflated to such an extent that neutral observers had difficulty untangling them.

Willy Brandt criticized the lack of any representatives of the "other Germany" on the judges' bench. "From the very beginning, many others and I have questioned why no way was found to allow German anti-Nazis a place on the court," Brandt wrote. "Did persecuted Germans not have a right to a reckoning with their tormentors?"[48] Many Germans asked themselves that very question. They saw the absence of a German judge as evidence of Allied hypocrisy. After all, US chief counsel Jackson had said in his opening remarks that the Germans had become the victims of a criminal regime. Why, then, weren't they allowed to have a say in the judgments rendered upon the most important living representatives of that regime?

Moreover, many correspondents knew only too well that the Soviet Union hadn't acknowledged the international convention upon which the court justified itself. The main defendants were accused of crimes the Soviet Union had itself committed: starting a war (Stalin had attacked Poland and Finland), massacring prisoners (for instance in Katyn) and inhuman brutality. Operating under direct instructions from Moscow, Soviet prosecutors tried to publicize German crimes against humanity while concealing those of their own nation. Their credibility wasn't bolstered by the fact that the lead Soviet judge in Nuremberg was Iona Nikitchenko, who had presided over some of Stalin's show trials in the 1930s. "We felt like foreign elements in the tribunal, which treated everything that had become normality for us under Stalin as a crime," wrote Soviet translator Michael Voslensky.[49] His colleague Tatiana Stupnikova, an interpreter, was horrified at the parallels between the cruelty of the Nazi regime and Stalin's dictatorship. Her own parents had been arrested as "enemies of the state" of the Soviet Union when she was just a child, and even decades later she was still terrified that she could be next every time there was a knock on the door.

Hans Habe, who resigned as editor-in-chief of the *Neue Zeitung* because of his critical stance towards the occupation policies, objected to the selective interrogation of the witnesses. With few exceptions, the requests of the prosecution were granted and those of the defence dismissed. There was reason to suspect, Habe complained, that the court had no interest in hearing from some potential witnesses, including former Allied foreign ministers: "A cross-examination of Lord Halifax, as Göring's lawyer requested, would have brought to light the glaringly catastrophic policies of the Munich Agreement. A cross-examination of Molotov would have shown how the Non-Aggression Pact between Germany and the USSR had come about."[50] Deane, too, surmised that the cross-examination of high-ranking British witnesses, as also requested by Ribbentrop's attorney, would have made public the content of confidential pre-war German–British discussions. The discrimination against the defence also manifested itself in the fact that defence lawyers, unlike the prosecutors, weren't allowed to have any assistants.

Australian correspondent Osmar White was so critical of the trial and the Allied occupation policies that no publisher would touch the book he wrote in 1946, *Conquerors' Road*. The manuscript would remain in his desk drawer for fifty years until HarperCollins and Cambridge University Press brought it out. As a war reporter for the *Herald* and *Weekly Times* group, White had crossed the German border with Patton's Third Army in the winter of 1944–45, staying with the troops until they reached Berlin's Brandenburg Gate. He had witnessed the liberation of the Buchenwald concentration camp and reported on the capitulation of the Wehrmacht. A keen and unbiased observer, he focused particularly on the mental states of the victors and vanquished. But White was also a nonconformist, determined to be objective and speak his mind. As much as he despised the craven Germans protesting their innocence whom he encountered everywhere in the country, he was also capable of respecting his adversaries. In this vein, he told the story of a protective mother who saved the lives of her sons, both battle-willing Hitler Youth members, by dragging them away from a planned ambush of American tanks. Conversely, he also wrote unflattering accounts of General Patton's brutal obsessiveness and GIs who engaged in plunder and rape.

White had little good to say about the Nuremberg Trial. After relaxing on vacation in England, he arrived in the city shortly before the start of proceedings to report on the preparations. But he quickly became disillusioned. He considered the distinctions between the four main charges legalistic hair-splitting and the trial itself an "unpleasant caricature of the processes of civilised justice". And he didn't stop there. "From the outset," White wrote, "it was clear that the 'trials' could have no more moral or judicial status than any trial by a kangaroo court in the backwoods of Tennessee. The men in the dock were already condemned. They were self-confessed members of, or executive agents for, an evil regime which had been destroyed only at the cost of millions of lives. There could be no reasonable doubt about their guilt." The tribunal was thus an unnecessary act of "carnival retribution", a collection of "rites so inherently hypocritical that they must surely be adjudged contemptible showmanship in years to come". White also dismissed the idea that "this public vivisection of Nazi felons… would deter criminal politicians and bureaucrats from evil-doing in the future any more than hanging, drawing or quartering on the public gallows had deterred psychopaths from committing atrocious acts in the past".

White may have overshot the mark by denigrating the entire trial as a theatrical ritual of vengeance, but his pessimism about its effects as a deterrent for the future would prove sadly accurate. "My return to Nuremberg was a professional mistake," he wrote. "I found that I had no heart to describe the spectacle of the fat man, Goering, deprived of the wherewithal to hold up his trousers in case he should try to hang himself with belt or braces."[51] He asked his employers in London to give him a different assignment and spent most of his time waiting for new instructions in a displaced persons camp for former Soviet slave labourers near the town of Ansbach. To his mind, there was less hypocrisy there, outside Nuremberg.

The Limits of Journalistic Representation

The correspondents knew they bore great responsibility and did not simply transmit the events of the trial. They also chose which topics to address and how to put them in context. It was up to their skill with language and storytelling to illustrate the dimensions of Nazi atrocities. The material coming from the proceedings—court documents and transcripts of testimony—alone wasn't enough to fire the public imagination. As Mitscherlich wrote in his book *Bemerkungen zum Nürnberger Prozess* (*Remarks on the Nuremberg Trial*), "The Thirty Years' War lives on people's memories not because of the copious evil deeds and rampant arson, but because Grimmelshausen described them."[52] But whereas Hans Jakob Christoffel von Grimmelshausen wrote a number of marvellously imaginative, artistic novels that cathartically depicted the trauma caused by that seventeenth-century, pan-European conflict, correspondents in Nuremberg had only a few pages at their disposal. They had to find words for both the legal proceedings and the unspeakable horrors that had been committed. No one had ever tried to do anything like that before.

By Mitscherlich's standards, most of the journalistic descriptions of the trial were disappointing, sober accounts written with no great empathy—and little artistry at all. "Over the course

of the session, the focus turned to the burning of synagogues,"
wrote Robert Jungk. "In response to a question by Göring back
then about how many Jewish temples were really destroyed,
Reinhard Heydrich had proudly issued an 'official military communiqué' from what he called the Jewish theatre of war: 101
synagogues razed by fire, 75 otherwise destroyed and 7500 busi-
nesses were smashed within the Reich!" The reference to a military communiqué, as if the issue were casualties from a war, was
clearly sarcastic, and the concluding exclamation point can be
taken as an expression of horrified amazement. But otherwise,
Jungk's text was largely an empiric protocol of the testimony.

Such dry approaches were probably also a reflex by which the
observers shielded themselves from the full brunt of the benumb-
ing horror of hearing of crimes of such unimaginable dimensions.
Author Gregor von Rezzori, who worked in Nuremberg for the
Nordwestdeutscher Rundfunk radio broadcaster, remarked that
while one murder was terrible, ten monstrous, and one hundred
almost beyond comprehension, the murder of several million
people was an abstraction that made it impossible to establish any
rational proportion between the murderer and his crime. Justice
ceased to exist within such a situation. The causal connection
between crime and punishment was suspended.[53]

Correspondents weren't the only ones who had trouble
finding words for the unspeakable. Witnesses, too, faced an
unbridgeable gap between their experiences and those of their
audience. There were no comparisons with everyday post-war
reality that could illustrate what it was like to have survived the
Holocaust. It was impossible either to imagine or communicate
what Auschwitz had been, stated witness Marie-Claude Vaillant-
Couturier. How were they supposed to make the stench of

burning human flesh comprehensible? Prosecutors were well aware of this dilemma, which Hannah Arendt, among others, identified,[54] and correspondingly put their faith in the medium of film and the emotional power of images.

Along with reports and commentaries, what Germans call *Reportage* was another common genre of coverage of the Nuremberg Trial. Journalistic features—as distinct from hard-news reports—had been accepted as a reputable, vivid and often socially critical genre since the 1920s. Depicting an event from various direct eyewitness perspectives was, for instance, a good way of combining empiric documents with precise observation of people's behaviour and thinking, allowing for further insights into what had happened at a particular moment in time.[55] But the Nuremberg Trial revealed the limitations of this style of reporting as a way of getting at the truth about the past. Dry descriptions of events in the court, based largely on documents, made it more difficult to capture and locate the historical moment. The material presented to the court was too abstract. As a result, correspondents tended to focus on activity within the courtroom and to explain what they had seen rather than to explore what had happened before.

Descriptions of the destruction in Nuremberg and the defendants in the dock became recurring motifs in their writings. Reporters were fascinated by the visual spectacle of the courtroom. Many knew the Nazi leadership, with their extravagant uniforms and aggressive gestures, from Leni Riefenstahl's depiction of them in her film about the Nuremberg party rallies, *Triumph des Willens* (*Triumph of the Will*). The contrast between pre- and post-war Nuremberg couldn't have been starker. "The defendants acted like excited school children seeing their pictures flashed across the screen," wrote *New York Times* correspondent Tania Long on 12th December 1945, after the documentary film *The Nazi Plan*, compiled from extensive footage of captured Nazi propaganda and newsreel images and sound recordings, had been shown in court. "They nodded and nudged one another." Correspondents recorded the facial expressions, gestures and comportment of these dethroned deities with something bordering on obsession. Some had even equipped themselves with opera glasses and binoculars to get a closer look at the defendants seated some fifteen metres distant. Their repertoire of comparisons seemed inexhaustible. Whereas Long wrote of excited schoolchildren, Peter de Mendelssohn compared the admirals Dönitz and Rader to unemployed street-car conductors and Göring to a movie-theatre usher. Philipp Fehls more charitably described the former Reich Marshal as a "Renaissance *condottiero* [mercenary troop leader]", while Rebecca West called him the "madam of a brothel", Janet Flanner a "fleshy contralto" and Ilja Ehrenburg an "old woman".

Streicher constantly chewed gum, Hess dozed off hunched over himself, Papen was conspicuously well groomed and Keitel sat motionless in his seat, his face like a stone. The correspondents repeatedly varied their descriptions, obviously struggling to understand the "banality of evil", as Arendt would call it, and explain it to their readers. "The ordinary everydayness of the defendants hit me hardest," remarked Polevoy, while Rezzori conceded to his dismay that it was impossible to put them into a sufficient context.[56]

The result of this banality and ordinariness was that some correspondents, above all those from the tabloid press, intentionally sensationalized their reports, even if there was nothing sensational to write about. The fragmentary, superficial and intentionally exaggerated tenor of many accounts was obvious even at the time. Playing on Göring's suicide by poison after the trial's conclusion, American journalist Max Lerner complained: "All we got were bits and pieces of the Nazi story. Millions of words were, of course, cabled from Nuremberg by correspondents to the twelve corners of the world… But mainly they were color stuff, portraying the trial as a spectacle… It is some kind of commentary on our press and our ways of thought that the most important trial of our era should have ended on the cheap note of a mystery thriller entitled *The Case of the Hidden Poison*. Nuremberg is still the Trial Nobody Knows."[57]

Nonetheless, a handful of extraordinary authors did find original and profound ways in which to write about the trial. The most important reports conspicuously transgressed the boundaries of the genre of the journalistic feature, using literary techniques. Kästner, for example, broke a major taboo by including fictional elements in his piece from Nuremberg, imagining a scene from a trial of the future. West used the seemingly marginal figure of the Schloss Faber-Castell's gardener to explore the German mentality. Triolet composed collage articles with a touch of surrealism. And Dos Passos, who was already a literary legend when he arrived at the press camp, also made a special contribution to the depiction of the trial not only with his formal approach and method, but also with his attitudes towards the vanquished Germans. By the nature of the crimes they were adjudicating, the Nuremberg Trial was already rather larger than life. The fact that some of the greatest writers of a generation wrote accounts of what they observed made it all the more so.

II

American Defeats, or The Melancholy of John Dos Passos

"Never felt so much sadder and wiser in
my life as after this trip to Europe."

JOHN DOS PASSOS TO UPTON SINCLAIR, 30TH DECEMBER 1945

American novelist John Dos Passos (1896–1970) began writing war reports for *Life* magazine in 1944. Eventually collected in the volume *Tour of Duty*, they described the theatres of battle in the Pacific and the US attacks on Japan and occupied Germany between October and December 1945. In Frankfurt and the surrounding countryside, "where people still wear funny peasant costumes and have faces like andirons", he witnessed his compatriots busily trying to administer the chaos of their defeated German enemy. Overwhelmed captains and lieutenants told him of their frustration and doubts.[1] After the Allies' victory many GIs wanted to return home as soon as possible, but instead they were ordered to remain in Germany to govern the country, help put war criminals on trial and de-Nazify the rest of the population. American soldiers weren't prepared for tasks like finding politically acceptable foresters for Germany's woodlands and renters for its cinemas. And the language barrier added to GIs' confusion.

In general, they found the people they occupied neither helpful nor likeable. Germans were prone to complaining and showing up in American offices to request favours or inform on their neighbours. Nonetheless, Dos Passos later felt sympathy when he remembered the malnourished, hollow-eyed masses he had seen in Germany. With empathy and his realistic "camera-eye" technique, the writer sought to depict the consequences of military defeat, the desperation and the breakdown of civilization he observed all around him. He also didn't whitewash the difficulties his compatriots were facing, calling the third section of his war reports "In the Year of *Our* Defeat".[2]

Dos Passos saw himself in much the same vein as his former friends Hemingway and Martha Gellhorn. All three maintained serious ambitions and aspired to become respected literary authors, and although they wrote journalism for money in their younger years they were never content to be mere chroniclers or reporters. All of them were adherents of "New Reportage", as this Marxist-inflected brand of journalism was called in the USA. In the mid-1930s, the editors of the American Communist Party newspaper *The New Masses* had begun theorizing about how journalistic reports could best be written. New Reportage was to reflect the emotional participation of the author: "To the writer of reportage, the fact he is describing is no corpse, it is alive, it has a place on earth."[3] Like Hemingway, who also wrote for *The New Masses*, Dos Passos followed this dictum, which was the exact opposite of the dispassionate, documentary style of New Objectivity. New Reportage was a form of journalism that related news narratively and communicated a personal perspective yet was both uncompromising and empathetic. It represented a middle ground between literature and journalism, art and stylistic functionalism.

Dos Passos first encountered Hemingway in a regimental mess hall in Italy during the First World War. As chance had it, both writers had been sent there as medical orderlies. Later, "Dos" and "Hem", as they were known, debated the future of the novel in Parisian cafés, partied in southern France, went skiing in Austria's Vorarlberg region, watched bullfights in Pamplona and travelled together to the Caribbean. But the comparatively mild-mannered, nearly bald Dos Passos, who suffered from rheumatic heart disease, was clearly the junior partner in this relationship.

The son of a wealthy stock-market attorney, Dos Passos enjoyed a privileged upbringing, split between Brussels and London, which he later described in an autobiographical novel as a "hotel childhood". While Hemingway attended Oak Park High School and worked for his local newspaper, the *Kansas City Star*, Dos Passos studied European literature at Harvard. After university he gradually developed into a political author, whose first novel *Three Soldiers* in 1921 was considered— along with Hemingway's *A Farewell to Arms*—to be the finest American literary treatment of the First World War. Four years later, Dos Passos published his magnum opus, the revolutionary novel *Manhattan Transfer*, which featured New York City itself as its protagonist. His narrative technique was cinematic, largely eschewing lengthy descriptions and logical connection in a favour of collage—similar to the style Alfred Döblin would use in his masterpiece *Berlin Alexanderplatz*. Dos Passos' trilogy *USA*, published in 1930, 1932 and 1936, was very critical of American society, employing biographical summaries, news-paper excerpts and interior monologues to depict figures and events in the 1920s.

Like many authors of his time, the young Dos Passos was fascinated with the Communist Party. An admirer of German Communist leader Rosa Luxemburg and an enthusiastic sup-porter of the Russian Revolution and its attendant social move-ments, he visited the Soviet Union in 1928 and supported the American Communist Party candidate over Roosevelt in the subsequent US election. It would take the show trials of the 1930s to open his eyes to the true nature of Stalinism. His friendship with Hemingway ended because of the latter's insistence on the Stalinist credo that the end always justified the means, no matter how inhumane. In 1937, Dos Passos tried to intervene on behalf of the family of a Spanish friend, José Robles, who had been killed by what Dos Passos assumed were "special sections" of the Spanish Communist Party. Hemingway tried to convince him to desist from his investigations into Robles's death, arguing that he was endangering the anti-fascist film *The Spanish Earth*, whose script they co-authored. What did one human life matter in times like these, wrote Dos Passos, sarcastically summarizing Hemingway's reasoning. Personal feelings shouldn't be allowed to get in the way of the political cause.[4]

Dos Passos never forgave either Hemingway, who had just fallen in love with Gellhorn, or the Communist Party, and much to many people's dismay he became a conservative and a supporter of McCarthyist anti-Communism. "My observa-tions in Spain brought about my complete disillusionment with Communism and the Soviet Union," Dos Passos would tell the

House Un-American Activities Committee in 1953. "The Soviet Government operated in Spain a series of 'extra legal tribunals,' more accurately described as murder gangs, who put to death without mercy all whom they could reach and who stood in the way of Communists."[5]

In Germany

When Dos Passos reached Germany in October 1945, he was already a famous writer and a staunch detractor of Communism, a stance that was strengthened by a stay in the Soviet-occupied part of Berlin. In *Tour of Duty* he described how Soviet soldiers raped a German woman and her sister, forcing her husband to stand on a chair and watch, then shot him dead when they were done. Such atrocities convinced Dos Passos that the four main Allies' agreement on the occupation of Germany, which necessarily entailed appeasing Stalin, was a dangerous mistake that would open the door to Soviet expansionism.

Dos Passos always put his views into the mouths of others in his articles, only passing judgment in the subtext, although he never completely concealed his authorial presence. It remains unclear how many of the anonymous captains, lieutenants and eyewitnesses Dos Passos cited actually existed. Some were possibly invented to support the author's own opinions—although that doesn't necessarily mean that Dos Passos failed to capture the general mood. He saw himself as a chronicler inhabiting the border between fiction and non-fiction. Just as he incorporated authentic real-life texts like news bulletins into his novels, he also smuggled fictional elements into his reporting. He was

fascinated by hybrid forms of writing, and the collision of opposites was a technique he deliberately used to capture reality.

A self-proclaimed enemy of all "imperialists, militarists and
merchants of death", Dos Passos was a moralist who condemned
what his compatriots did in Germany from the safety of their
"comfortable, well-heated houses". He made no bones about
the difference between idealistic American slogans concerning
freedom and US troops' inability to fulfil their function as a protective authority. That upset the post-war moral equilibrium and
won him little favour among his compatriots—a fact of which he
was abundantly aware. He repeatedly questioned whether *Life*
magazine would actually publish his reports. Dos Passos explicitly confronted his editors with what others only dared to express
in the safety of their private correspondence. Ernest Cecil
Deane, for instance, also summed up the general confusion felt
by GIs in a letter to his wife, Lois. As they were prohibited from
fraternizing with Germans, Deane wondered how they were "to
teach the krauts anything unless we have contact with them?".[6]

Dos Passos was an exception among the American writers in
the press camp. While Martha Gellhorn, Erika Mann (who was
a member of the US Army in Nuremberg), William Shirer and
Janet Flanner almost in unison criticized the German tendency
to wail and complain, Dos Passos sympathized with the occupied people and was never angered by those who refused to
acknowledge the sins of the past. Whereas Hemingway boasted
of having killed 122 German soldiers and having shot one prisoner "so his brains came out of his mouth or I guess it was his
nose",[7] Dos Passos sketched out for his readers the pathetic
scene of Nuremberg women trying to keep their children fed
by cooking potatoes on a sheet of tin amid the ruins of the city.

American triumphalism in all its forms was foreign to Dos Passos. In one passage, he related how an anonymous young lieutenant from Brooklyn described his deployment in the western German region of Hessen: "Well, they tell you it's like the fire department… the fire department has to do a certain amount of damage, even blow up buildings, to put the fire out. Sure, but you don't see the fire department starting new fires all over town because one block is burning? Or do you? Hatred is like a fire. You have to put it out." Sometimes, added Dos Passos' possibly fictional lieutenant, he first had to feed malnourished POWs and send them to the hospital before they were strong enough to be useful sources of information. "Brutality is more contagious than typhus and a hell of a lot more difficult to stamp out… Right here at USFET [US Forces, European Theatre] in Frankfurt, we countenance things that would have given us cold chills back at home."[8]

"Melancholy Grandeur" and National Pride: Jackson's Opening Statement

When Dos Passos first came to Nuremberg, "the old picture-book city of toymakers and meistersingers", to attend the start of the start of the Major War Criminals Trial in early November 1945, he was shocked by the devastation Allied air raids had wrought. He incorporated his impressions into his 1958 novel *The Great Days*, in which he described the historic city centre as having been flattened, while the industrial suburbs had remained "strangely undamaged". The implication was, of course, that Allied economic interests had played a role in the waging of the war, casting doubt on the rectitude of the bombing campaigns.

On the evening of 22nd November, in the "castle that Eberhard Faber's family built in stone from pencil profits and pomp", he got talking with a fellow correspondent from Eastern Europe. The man, a stranger, addressed him in French on his way to the bar, as he was looking around for a buddy with whom he could drink another Scotch. The man asked him whether he had time for a couple of questions. He did, Dos Passos replied, and the two of them went out into the castle's courtyard to have an undisturbed smoke. Did he really think that the trial served the cause of justice in Europe, the man asked. He had heard that the proceedings had made a huge impression on Dos Passos. He, too, would execute the defendants, the man assured him. But was there anything to be gained from adding "yet another hypocrisy to the mountain of hypocrisy in the world"?

Dos Passos answered that while the trial was certainly not perfect, it was still an established legal principle that a war of aggression was a crime. That, however, prompted the man to ask what atrocities the Nazis had committed that justified the American carpet-bombing of civilians. Germans had been the ones to start with air raids, Dos Passos responded. But his interlocutor insisted that the carnage in German cities had been far greater than in England. "How can one justify the massacre of helpless refugees in Dresden... What have the Nazis done that compares with your handing-over of Poland, your own ally, into the hands of the darkest totalitarian tyranny in history?" Was it not a crime against humanity, the man added, that 15 million people had been driven from their homes just because they were German? Why were the Americans so obsessed with revenge? Everything US troops were doing in Europe, the man argued, reinforced the principle of revenge and the rule of violence and would eventually come back to haunt Americans. This was certainly not "our intention", said Dos Passos, taken aback. Intentions weren't enough, countered his Eastern European colleague coolly. "I could not answer him," Dos Passos later wrote. "I said goodnight, and went into the schloss and went gloomily to bed."[9]

Dos Passos often struggled with feelings of hopeless resignation like the ones he described following the conversation in Schloss Faber-Castell. On the one hand, he was disappointed by his compatriots' political errors and inability to fill the moral vacuum in post-war Germany. The USA, he noted in his journal, had made four great historical mistakes: the failure to abolish slavery in 1776, inadequate reconstruction after the Civil War, its policies towards Mussolini and Hitler, and its policies towards Stalin. Two of those mistakes were recent. "Who sups with the devil, must need a long spoon—it is time Americans got it through their heads that Democracy & Dictatorship can't cooperate,"[10] he proclaimed. Dos Passos' criticism of the situation in Germany culminated after his return to the USA in an article titled "Americans are Losing the Victory in Europe".

On the other hand, Dos Passos was beset by a general sense of unease in a Europe he was no longer able to recognize. Even Paris, which had emerged relatively unscathed from the war, felt completely foreign to him when he visited the city in October 1945. He wanted to return home as soon as he could. Although his fellow correspondents revered him as a famous novelist, appreciated his company and lively conversation and found him friendly and down-to-earth,[11] he nonetheless wrote to his wife, Katy, on 4th November: "I don't like it over here. Not us nor the squareheads nor nobody." He found Schloss Faber-Castell and the press camp horrible, using the German word *Schrecklichkeit* to underscore his antipathy: "This press camp is in a weird 'Schloss' built by members of the Faber pencil family and is full of naked ladies in ghastly white stone, hideous stairways inlaid with various marbles, gold chairs of horrid design, chandeliers that are about to fall on your head... German schrecklichkeit at its worst. The vast rooms have had the furniture taken out and are filled with rows of cots where the swarms of correspondents about to arrive will sleep. In the main gate there's a wonderful pair of Chinese lions but they are in the minority."

Another pleasant exception in Dos Passos' eyes was the American chief counsel Robert H. Jackson, whose opening remarks on 20th November filled the author with national pride. "Robert Jackson's opening for the prosecution yesterday I thought magnificent," he wrote to Katy. "A few more speeches like that and the poor old ship of state that's been wallowing rudderless in the trough of the sea will be back on its course. He really is making an effort to make some sense out of what without him would be an act of vengeance... There was a moment when the Nazis in the prisoners dock seemed to see themselves for the first time as the world sees them. I'll never forget the look of horror and terror that came over their faces when Jackson read the orders for the massacre of the Jews. Either they had not known what documents were in our possession or something like remorse swept over them for a few minutes. Jackson represented the USA as I like to see it represented."[12]

Robert H. Jackson delivering his opening remarks on 20th November 1945.

Albeit less explicitly than in his private correspondence, Dos Passos also commented upon Jackson's speech in the twenty-page "Nuremberg Diary" he included in *Tour of Duty*. It contains a kaleidoscopic description of his encounters with people in the city, a tour of the court building, an interview with the prison commandant, Burton Andres, and a recapitulation of his conversation with the Eastern European correspondent in the press camp—a unique example within American reporting of an exchange on an equal footing with a critic of US policy. The high point of the diary, however, was his account of the start of the trial, with Jackson as the main protagonist. As though viewing the scene through a camera, Dos Passos pans across the defendants in the dock. The result is a series of snapshots influenced by cinematic editing technique. "Rosenberg draws the stiff finger of one hand down his face. Streicher develops a tic in the corners of his mouth. Schacht's countenance is drawn into deep creases of nightmare. Streicher's head leans far over on his shoulder as if were to fall off his body." But the majority of the report is devoted to Jackson. About the conclusion of Jackson's remarks, Dos Passos wrote: "I doubt if there is a man or woman in the courtroom who does not feel that great and courageous words have been spoken. As Americans we get a little proudly to our feet because it was a countryman of ours who spoke them."[13]

Jackson was aware of the significance of his remarks and considered them the most important ones he had ever uttered in his life. Calmly, he laid out the charges levelled against the accused, using their own documents against them and promising that the new ordering of the world would follow the principles of law. In Jackson's view, the court was not about revenge or the might of the victors making right. "That four great nations, flushed with victory and stung with injury, stay the hand of vengeance and voluntarily submit their captive enemies to the judgment of the law is one of the most significant tributes that Power has ever paid to Reason." Specific individuals and nations had committed the crimes in question, Jackson continued, and the defendants had to be given a fair chance to defend themselves, no matter how heinous their atrocities.

Jackson was at pains to explain the meaning of the charge of conspiracy to commit crimes, which was more nebulous than the more specific crimes being prosecuted by the other victorious nations. The US chief counsel promised to show that the accused had come together to enact a common plan that could only be achieved with a war of conquest. All of their actions—from the assumption of power in the German state to the physical destruction of dissidents and enemies to the mistreatment of POWs and parts of the populace in occupied counties—had been elements of this conspiracy.

Jackson was an exceptional speaker with a reliable sense for grand gestures. His rhetorical ideal was to create what he called a "melancholy grandeur" in the courtroom. Jackson distinguished between the criminal class of Nazis and military leaders and the German populace as a whole, and his opening statement could be interpreted as an offer to Germans to distance themselves as a nation from National Socialism. In contrast to French prosecutor François Comte de Menthon, who presumed German collective guilt and accused the populace of a "latent tendency toward barbarism",[14] Jackson spoke of a people that had been seduced by a gang of criminals, arguing: "If the German populace had willingly accepted the Nazi program, no Storm-troopers would have been needed in the early days of the Party and there would have been no need for concentration camps or the Gestapo."

Today, historians and political scientists regard the generosity Jackson showed towards Germans as "almost naive".[15] The US chief counsel made no mention of the opportunists, the cult of personality around Hitler or the death camps. Instead, Jackson extended a hand of friendship, as did his admirer Dos Passos, who can also be criticized for failing to mention the Holocaust and the blind obedience of many Germans in his reports. Both men considered Germany America's ally of tomorrow. Sooner or later, their logic ran, the USA would be glad to have a few friends around the world, particularly if Stalin continued his expansionism. Upstanding Germans had to be helped back on their feet, Dos Passos quoted his exemplary lieutenant as saying—and this at a time when Henry Morgenthau published his book *Germany is Our Problem*, in which he advocated reducing post-war Germany to a pre-industrial state. Morgenthau's ideas went far beyond the punitive terms of the 1919 Treaty of Versailles. The occupied former enemy was to be demilitarized, denied economic independence and transformed into a largely agricultural region. German industry would be dismantled and the populace required to pay reparations.

Ultimately, John Dos Passos' summary of his trip through Europe was ambivalent. By 4th December 1945, when he boarded a ship at Le Havre to return home, he had personally experienced what he perceived as America's defeat in Germany, but he had also seen Jackson, whom he considered as something akin to a saviour. The US chief counsel was a symbol of all the values he himself held close to heart. "Never felt so much sadder and wiser in my life as after this trip to Europe," he wrote to fellow author Upton Sinclair. "Maybe the Russians are right and man is vile and can only be ruled by terror—but I still refuse to believe that everything the West has stood for since the first of the Forefathers tumbled out of their leaky boats to do their washing on this beach I'm looking out at as I write must go on the ash heap. My god the tide runs strong against us."[16]

III

Countess Katharina and
Gestapo Head Rudolf Diels

"Truly, the man has courage. But we admire the courage of
the Americans more in allowing him to run around freely."

FRENCH NEWSPAPER ABOUT RUDOLF DIELS

B efore moving to discuss more literary luminaries in the press
camps, it's worth looking at an unusual personal relationship
that played itself out on the margins of the trial and Schloss
Faber-Castell. Robert Jackson's opening statement in front of
the International Military Tribunal was hailed around the world,
but there was more to the Nuremberg Trial than the publicly
analysed events in Courtroom 600 of the Palace of Justice. The
trial required an enormous organizational infrastructure in the
background. The American judicial delegation alone numbered
over 2,000 individuals—the British sent 170 people, the Soviets
twenty-four and the French roughly a dozen. Meanwhile, other
countries with the status of observers also maintained small delegations.[1] There were research analysts who checked regularly
delivered truckloads of Nazi documents, rescued from mines,
castles and archives, for relevance to the proceedings. Important

material was categorized and retained. Doctors monitored the physical and psychological health of the defendants, scholars provided political and historical background information, and interrogators questioned defendants, experts and witnesses.

Among the witnesses were not only victims but also perpetrators of Nazi terror who themselves stood to be arrested, some of whom were housed in a special wing of the prison. There were also Germans who were not suspected of war crimes but who had been closely connected to major Nazis and could provide valuable information. One of them was Hitler's favourite photographer, Heinrich Hoffmann, who was kept in Nuremberg for months and subjected to repeated questioning. Another special witness was the first head of the Gestapo, Rudolf Diels (1900–57). He was an eyewitness on a variety of scores and considered an expert on the early years of the Third Reich. Despite his involvement in the persecution of Jews and the arrest of enemies of the regime such as the writer and journalist Carl von Ossietzky, he was given something of a free pass since he had been extraordinarily close to the centre of Nazi power in the early 1930s, and Allied prosecutors needed his knowledge. British authorities brought him to Nuremberg and handed him over to American prosecutors in late October 1945.[2] He would remain there for two years.

Later dubbed the "Fouché of the Third Reich" after the French Minister of Police who served under both the First Republic and Napoleon, Diels was a political opportunist who had cleverly charted a course for his career through the Nazi dictatorship. Initially a centrist liberal, he maintained extended contact with German Communists before attaching himself to Hermann Göring in the early 1930s. In 1933 he was put in charge of the Gestapo, but he soon earned the enmity of Heinrich Himmler, who considered him a turncoat. He was ousted in the wake of the power struggles between Göring and Himmler. Diels was sacrificed to resolve the conflict: Himmler's intimate, Reinhard Heydrich, assumed his position, and Diels was given the cushy job of regional president first in Cologne, then Hanover. His subsequent work was purely administrative, though his enemies continued to keep a hostile eye upon him. He was interrogated by the Gestapo on numerous occasions and even detained in 1944. But he continued to enjoy a love-hate relationship with Göring, who protected him until the final days of the Third Reich. In 1943 Diels married the widow of Göring's deceased brother, only to divorce her one and a half years later at the Reich Marshal's insistence.

Tall, attractive, dark-haired and blue-eyed, with visible scars from his past in one of Germany's conservative duelling fraternities, Diels was very popular with women. "In his appearance he was always like a Bengali tiger," read one obituary after he died. "It was hardly possible to resist his lure."[3] One of those who fell under the spell of the first head of the Gestapo and his swashbuckling aura was the lady of the castle, Countess Katharina von Faber-Castell (1917–94). They had been acquainted for quite some time, but it was during the Nuremberg Trial that their relationship took on forms potentially embarrassing to the Faber-Castell dynasty.

The Faber-Castells

To this day, the products of the Faber-Castell company bear a logo featuring a pair of knights jousting not with lances but with

pencils. This carefully chosen image harks back to the family
and career history of the factory owner Alexander zu Castell-
Rüdenhausen (1866–1928), who married into the pencil dynasty
Faber in 1898 and was subsequently made a count. This gave
rise to the new aristocratic family Faber-Castell. The Castell-
Rüdenhausens were one of the oldest aristocratic lineages in
Germany, with roots reaching back to the eleventh century. To
distinguish himself from the competition, particularly the yellow
pencils made by the Bohemian company Hardtmuth, Count
Alexander introduced a line of products in 1905 under the name
Castell. They were coloured the same green as the uniforms
of the Bavarian Cavalry in which Alexander had served as a
career soldier and captain. The logo and name were intended
to underscore his family's centuries-old tradition, in contrast
to their arriviste Bohemian rivals. Their most successful pencil
was named after the famous Persian diamond Koh-i-Noor and
conjured up the German aristocracy and the Middle Ages. It was
a huge success and remains one of the company's most popular
products today. The logo has been slightly altered over the years.
Nowadays, it no longer depicts the winner of the duel wielding a
green Castell pencil while the vanquished jouster holds a yellow
one from the Bohemian competition.[4]

The history of the family business logo partly symbolized the
life of Count Roland von Faber-Castell, Alexander's son and the
lord of the manor at the time of the press camp. He was named
after an ancestral knight depicted by an outsized statue standing
to the east of the north wing of the New Castle.[5] Count Roland
was originally brought up to be an agricultural estate owner
taking care of his land, but soon he had to devote himself to
pencil-manufacturing full-time. Like his father, he was a cavalry

captain and a military veteran who had fought in battle. And he, too, was forced to adapt to the times and fend off outside competition. In the years prior to the press camp, he led an eventful, varied and sometimes troubled life.

As a child, Roland had much to endure after his parents' scandalous divorce, which saw him denied contact with his mother, who had initiated the split. In response, Count Alexander made his children dress in black for a year.[6] In 1928, after studying agricultural science, Roland inherited the family business. He was only twenty-three years old when Alexander died but was able to rely on a staff of highly capable company administrators. The rise of the Third Reich was the start of a difficult time for the young businessman. He declined to join the Nazi Party, so the Faber-Castell corporation was placed under the control of a Nazi-appointed director named Krüger.[7]

Roland's first wife, Countess Alix-May von Frankenberg-Ludwigsdorf, came from the Oppenheim banking family, and her background attracted enormous hostility. Her grandfather, Eduard Oppenheim, was a Jewish convert to Christianity, and the region of Franconia, where Nuremberg was located, was a hotspot of anti-Semitic hatred whipped up by Julius Streicher, the *Gauleiter* (local leader) and publisher of the SS hate-rag *Der Stürmer*. Even before the Nazis assumed power, the party press ran negative articles about the Countess, and shortly after Hitler became Chancellor she was publicly attacked. A vandal painted the words "Lady Oppenheim, the Jewish swine, must be forced from the town of Stein" on the entrance to Schloss Faber-Castell. In 1933 *Der Stürmer* ran an article excoriating Alix-May's luxurious lifestyle and the fluctuations within the household personnel, while Roland was taken to task for not encouraging the company's employees to join the SA. One passage from the article concluded: "The fact that the matron of the house in Stein belongs to the Jewish race makes many things understandable that until now were a riddle."

In 1935 Roland and Alix-May's tempestuous marriage was dissolved, and she fled Germany for Czechoslovakia. A custody battle for their children ensued and, like his father, Roland won out. The Gestapo intervened in the case. "Judged on state police principles, she appears to be unfit to raise children," the secret police told the court. "In any case, because of her overall orientation, which may also be a result of her Jewish background and upbringing, she is politically unacceptable to National Socialist principles."[8] Notwithstanding those words, a post-war court determined that Count Roland had also been politically persecuted because of his first marriage.

The tragic story of Alix-May Frankenberg-Ludwigsdorf attracted public attention in 2009 in conjunction with restitution claims for a priceless work of art. On 7th April 1938 she concluded her third marriage, to Count Jaromir Czernin, a member of the old Austrian nobility, who two years later sold Jan Vermeer's *The Art of Painting* to Hitler for 1.65 million reichsmarks. Seventy years later his heirs demanded that the work be restored to them by Vienna's Kunsthistorisches Museum, arguing that Count Jaromir had been forced to sell it far below its true value. The anti-Semitic vandalism on the entrance to Schloss Faber-Castell and the article in *Der Stürmer* were introduced as evidence during the proceedings. Ultimately, the heirs' claims were dismissed after a committee of experts deemed that Count Jaromir's lawyers had actively tried to arrange the sale and that no coercion had taken place.

In 1940, while Count Jaromir's representatives were negotiating with the Reich Chancellery, Count Roland was sta-
tioned in Poland, where he only narrowly escaped being court-
martialled after refusing an order to execute some 500 Jews.[9]
Drexel Sprecher, a member of Jackson's prosecutorial team in
Nuremberg, would later confirm that Roland was by no means
a Nazi,[10] and Rebecca West would cite a statement by a French
writer supporting that view.[11] Roland had been sent to the front
in Stalingrad, but on the way there he contracted a serious case
of typhus and was discharged from military service. With the
help of his second wife, Katharina "Nina" Sprecher von Bernegg,
whom he had married in 1938, he succeeded in transforming the
family corporation into a single-member company,[12] and after
returning to Germany in 1942 he became its sole proprietor.

The Faber-Castell family hadn't resided in the castle since
April 1940 for security reasons, as it had been commandeered
by the Wehrmacht and was being used as a control centre for
a flak searchlight division. Soldiers constantly ran in and out
of the building,[13] new troops were recruited in the courtyard,
and supplies and ammunition were stored in the basement
of the Old Castle. During this period, the family lived in the
Dürrenhembach hunting lodge twenty kilometres to the south-
east. Schloss Faber-Castell was run by an administrator who
reported regularly back to Dürrenhembach.

On 19th April 1945, the Seventh US Army advanced from
Ansbach to Stein. Shortly before the arrival of the GIs the last
members of the Wehrmacht fled south, tossing their weapons
into the lake in the castle grounds. Only a few incorrigible mili-
tiamen remained behind to defend Schloss Faber-Castell against
the invaders. That evening the Americans took the property,

which had survived the war with very little damage, confined mostly to several blown-out windows from the air pressure caused by a bombardment.

Reunion in Nuremberg

The Faber-Castells no longer made pencils in Stein. Two hundred and forty-two of the people who worked for the company before the Second World War had lost their lives.[14] But because the family factory had largely escaped damage from the air raids, it was already possible in 1945 to produce medical equipment there. The Faber-Castells themselves had lost their family home, but hoping, among other things, soon to be allowed to resume their business, they accepted the situation and quickly established good relations with occupation authorities. Aiding this cause were Countess Katharina's social skills, familial connections and acquaintances from the past.

As a young woman Katharina had attended a conservatory in Zurich, and she began training as a concert pianist in Berlin in 1943. There, in the capital of the Third Reich, she met Count Roland Faber-Castell. During this period she resided in the palace of Prince Friedrich Christian zu Schaumburg-Lippe, a high-ranking Nazi functionary and, for a time, an adjutant of Goebbels. In 1945, American intelligence surmised that her family background was the reason for her early contact with leaders of the Nazi movement. One of them was Rudolf Diels, who frequented Dürrenhembach after the First World War. His friendship with Countess Katharina soon developed into something more.

In the autumn of 1945, the Faber-Castells' hunting lodge became a ritzy place of refuge where important figures in the trial could relax. Evening social events there were very popular, attracting, among others, American prosecutors Robert Kempner and Drexel Sprecher, defence attorneys like Fritz Sauter and some of the interpreters. Invited guests spent the weekend together, riding horses, hunting and playing tennis. The centre of attention was always the glamorous hostess, who could frequently be found at the piano, singing *chansons* and entertaining her guests. It was thanks to the Nuremberg Trial that Countess Katharina "Nina" von Faber-Castell became reacquainted with Diels.

Diels was nominally under house arrest but still enjoyed considerable liberties. As a former high-ranking Nazi official, well versed in fascist history and the fascist mentality, his testimony at the trial had the power to either exonerate or incriminate. He disavowed his former patron Göring, for instance, and confirmed prosecutors' accusations against the former Reich Marshal. On 24th April 1946, after Göring denied responsibility for SA violence in his function as Prussian state premier, Diels testified that not only had the Nazi leader failed to deploy the police against the brownshirts, but he had also sought to merge the two institutions and make "murder a principle of state". Diels gave his testimony behind closed doors. Only once during his time in Nuremberg was he publicly called as a witness before the court, in the case of the chemical conglomerate IG Farben, the sixth of the twelve subsequent proceedings that followed the Major War Criminals Trial.

Diels probably owed some of his liberties to Katharina, whom he had praised in the past as a "highly talented music student" and an "adventurer between worlds" who was like a soul sister.[15] The fact that he was able to move so freely between the witness section of the prison and Dürrenhembach, even though many of the prosecutors in Nuremberg would have liked to see him behind bars, was probably also down to Robert Kempner, a member of the US general counsel's staff. He had been on cordial terms with Diels and Katharina since the early 1930s, Kempner and Diels having grown particularly close. Before the Jewish-German Kempner fled to Italy in 1935 and later the USA he had worked for the Prussian Interior Ministry. There, he once saved Diels's skin when the latter accidentally left his work identification behind after a visit to a prostitute, who then tried to file charges against him. She was sent to Kempner, who swept the affair under a rug. Diels paid Kempner back by pulling strings to get him released after he had been interned in a concentration camp in Berlin's Columbia-Haus in 1935.

Another key player in the Nuremberg trials who regularly visited the Faber-Castells' hunting lodge was Drexel Sprecher, a member of Jackson's staff who would later lead the prosecution at the IG Farben trial. In the Nuremberg Trial he was responsible for the case against Hitler Youth leader Baldur von Schirach.

In the witnesses' section of the prison, Diels lived next door to Hitler's personal photographer, Heinrich Hoffmann. He used his room there, in a building that housed both victims and perpetrators, as a love nest for himself and the Countess. The historical records contain a number of scandalous details. An enraged Count Roland, for instance, once sought to confront his rival in the prison, and on another occasion Diels had his lover's negligée smuggled back to Dürrenhembach so that the cuckolded husband wouldn't notice it was missing.[16] Nonetheless, the affair seems to have been an open secret. Diels was a notorious Casanova, and people talked behind his back to the Faber-Castell family. One of his surviving letters indicates that an American officer had accused him of being bisexual and carrying on multiple affairs simultaneously. There was even talk that he was the true father of Katharina's youngest child. Diels, for his part, complained to US prosecutor Telford Taylor about being the victim of such gossip.[17]

US intelligence officials assumed that Diels and the Countess knew one another because of a family connection. Katharina was the granddaughter of Theopil Sprecher von Bernegg, the former Chief of the General Staff in the Swiss Army. The Sprecher von Bernegg family was credited with reorganizing the Swiss military after the First World War, and US intelligence suspected its members of working together with the "Black Reichswehr", the illegal paramilitary version of the Reichswehr during the Weimar Republic that allowed Germany to get round the prohibitions contained within the Treaty of Versailles. Diels, too, was thought to have had contact with the Black Reichswehr.[18]

When journalists reporting on the trial visited Dürrenhembach, politics was a regular topic of conversation, but all discussions were off the record. In this private forum guests could speak about what happened when, questions of culpability and punishment, the issue of collective German guilt for the war and the Nazi atrocities in ways they never would have in front of a court. We can no longer quantify the influence which the sociable and well-connected Katharina had on her guests, some of whom were important prosecutors. One of her husband's relatives, Clementine zu Castell-Rüdenhausen, had been a functionary in the Nazi League of German Girls, which was headed by Hitler Youth leader Baldur von Schirach. Meanwhile, her own relative Drexel Sprecher was his American prosecutor. Katharina's son, Anton-Wolfgang, later confirmed that she sympathized with some of the Nazi bigwigs,[19] although being Swiss she was always able to claim neutrality.

The Countess kept in touch with Diels, who left Nuremberg a free man in 1947, even after their affair ended. It was she who arranged a Swiss publisher for his self-serving memoir *Lucifer ante portas* in 1949.[20] The same publishing house, Interverlag, also brought out the memoirs of journalist and Nazi propagandist Hans Fritzsche. Its director, Wilhelm Frick—not to be confused with the Nazi Interior Minister of the same name—had been a leader of the Swiss "Confederate Front" (*Eidgenössische Front*), which had maintained close ties to the Nazis.[21]

IV

Erich Kästner's Broken Promise

"At fault for all devilment taking place are not only
those doing but also those not stopping it."

ERICH KÄSTNER

"**E**rich Kästner is here," wrote Peter de Mendelssohn (1908–
82) to his wife, Hilde Spiel, from the press camp on 26th
November 1945. "I'm helping [him] along as much as I can
with razor blades, cigarettes, candy etc., which I get from the
PX."[1] But Mendelssohn did far more for this popular and highly
regarded author than just procuring some toiletries and candy.
The Jewish-German émigré to Britain was largely responsible
for Kästner being able to resume his former activity as a journalist after the Second World War. Although his books were banned
as "un-German" during the Third Reich, and he had witnessed
with his own eyes, dumbfounded, his works being thrown on
the pyre at the infamous Nazi book-burning in Berlin in May
1933, Erich Kästner (1899–1974) had remained in Germany,
working under a pseudonym as a popular author and script-
writer. At the end of the war, he and his team hastened to the
town of Mayrhofen in South Tyrol, ostensibly to work on the film
Das verlorene Gesicht (*The Lost Face*), which was intended to

encourage German audiences to hold out against the Allies. In reality, though, they were saving their own skin.

On 30th June in Mayrhofen, Kästner had an unexpected encounter. "As we were enjoying the loveliest streusel cake, we got a visit from [US press officer Bob] Kennedy and an English press officer. It was Peter Mendelssohn! 'Long time, no see!' the two of us said nearly in unison, and that was no exaggeration. They asked me if I'd be interested in working on a newspaper they were planning. It was to appear, at the start once a week, in Munich."[2] A short time later Kästner moved to the Bavarian capital, and in September he took up his position as the arts editor of the *Neue Zeitung*.

Even without this bit of help, Kästner—unlike many other writers—would have had no worries about his future. He was already a household name, thanks to his volumes of poetry, polemic commentaries, prose works and the wildly popular film versions of his books. Prior to 1933, he had rigorously opposed Nazism as a satirist and pamphleteer. With his clean bill of political health, no shortage of doors were open to him in the summer of 1945. Before long he received offers to write film scripts and was a candidate for the directorship of the Dresden Staatstheater. But he chose to work for the *Neue Zeitung*, returning to his core profession.[3]

Kästner saw his journalistic work as an urgently needed contribution to the re-education of the German public. In his eyes, Germany's post-war "zero hour" was a chance to reinvent the country. "Someone has to do the everyday work," he argued, since there were too few "willing and able to". He added, "It doesn't help us at all, if the literati now all write long novels about the war."[4] At the same time, Kästner had negotiated very favourable terms of employment, which allowed him time for his literary pursuits as well. He enjoyed a princely monthly wage of 2,200 marks and special privileges from the US military government, including exemption from the nightly curfew.

Still, the meeting in Mayrhofen was a decisive event in Kästner's career, and the "waterfall-like conversation in which we had to catch up on twelve years" also made a huge impression on Mendelssohn.[5] In 1945 he commented: "Driving back that night, I'd rediscovered a world I had considered irredeemably lost, a rational Germany with grown-ups in it. And if it had only been that, it would have been enough to restore my faith and trust after so much homicidal immaturity."[6]

Mendelssohn himself had been particularly exposed to the Nazis' "homicidal immaturity". A native of Munich from a Jewish family, he had started a successful journalistic career and was subject to increasing discrimination from 1933. Because of his famous surname, he initially tried writing under an "Aryan"-sounding pseudonym, publishing an article in the *Vossische Zeitung* under his aristocratic first wife's maiden name. But after the SA ransacked his home, Mendelssohn boarded a night train to Paris and went into exile. In 1939 he began working for the British Civil Service as a member of the Ministry of Information, becoming a British citizen two years later. In January 1944 he was transferred to the Press and Information Division of the Supreme Headquarters Allied Expeditionary Force (SHAEF) under Eisenhower's command. After serving for several months in the psychological warfare department in London, he was sent to the organization's Paris headquarters in late 1944. In April 1945 he accompanied Allied troops into Germany, ending up in a press monitoring office in Munich in April 1945. "That was formally the job," he wrote. "In reality, I was to keep an eye out for people who had been rescued and survivors, with whom a new start could be made."[7]

Ultimately, Mendelssohn's job as a press officer was to prepare the ground for new newspapers to be founded. In Munich he worked together with a handful of German candidates for a licensed paper which became the *Süddeutsche Zeitung* and for which he was able to win over Wilhelm Emanuel Süskind, a prominent writer, journalist and Nuremberg Trial correspondent.[8] He also helped newspapers like *Der Tagesspiegel* in Berlin and *Die Welt* in Hamburg see the light of day. In addition, he acted as a headhunter for the *Neue Zeitung*. "When I learned that Kästner was still alive and where he was staying, I immediately leapt in my jeep," he recalled. The arts section of the *Neue Zeitung* helped set the standards for intellectual forums in post-war Germany—an achievement for which Mendelssohn was partly responsible.

The *Neue Zeitung*

The *Neue Zeitung*—literally "The New Newspaper"—was an ambitious project and a major success for the American occupation authorities. Printed in a largely undamaged building on Munich's Schellingstrasse where editions of the Nazi daily *Völkischer Beobachter* (*People's Observer*) had previously rolled off the presses, it introduced itself as "an American newspaper published in the German language". Eisenhower, then military governor of the American occupation zone, wrote the "Opening Words" for the first issue on 18th October 1945, defining the newspaper's aims as to "sit as an example for the new German press through its objective news reporting, through unconditional devotion to truth in its articles and through high journalistic standards".[9] The publishers defined their mission as making fully fledged politically active citizens out of German readers and teaching them the values and norms of democracy.

With his characteristic brand of irony, Kästner would later compare his first weeks on the job to the "creation of the world". Together with his assistant, Alfred Andersch, he was responsible for the paper's arts and culture section. In contrast to the Nazi press's crass attempts at political and cultural indoctrination, the *Neue Zeitung*'s reporting was largely free of value judgments, and the editorials were well-reasoned arguments rather than harangues. Under the oversight of editor-in-chief Hans Habe, the man who had discovered that Hitler's father was originally named Schicklgruber, Kästner published a wide variety of content and himself wrote polemics, poems, reviews, commentaries, obituaries, birthday greetings, features and portraits. Thematically, he tackled topics including the issue of collective German guilt, the victorious Allies' demolition policies, and house and food provision in devastated post-war Munich. Kästner wrote about everything from the burning of his library during the war to the American documentary films with footage of the Holocaust. His style was direct and full of emotionally charged images and vivid comparisons. Personal experiences and seemingly marginal details, like a derogatory whistle in a cinema, set off chains of association and accrued larger significance.

Along with his own writings, Kästner published an impressive number of texts by famous authors, many banned by the Nazis. The list read like a Who's Who of German literature at the time:

from Bertolt Brecht, Max Frisch, Hermann Hesse and Stefan Heym to Heinrich and Thomas Mann to Anna Seghers, Franz Werfel and Carl Zuckmayer. Kästner also quenched the thirst of his readers for international literature after the deprivations of the Third Reich by including texts by Thornton Wilder, Antoine de Saint-Exupéry, André Gide and Ignazio Silone. Hemingway's *The Old Man and the Sea* was serialized in the *Neue Zeitung*, and Jean-Paul Sartre and John Steinbeck contributed as well. Kästner likened his work to "gardening" and took care to leave room for younger writers to grow. Moreover, he ran reproductions of works by artists rejected by the Nazis as "degenerate" and commissioned articles by scientists like Albert Einstein and Max Planck. The *Neue Zeitung*, with its credo of intellectual freedom, was the most important journalistic forum for literature and political discussion in early post-war Germany, and soon it became the leading newspaper in the country, with a circulation of some 2.5 million. In a speech honouring Kästner's seventy-fifth birthday, Mendelssohn proudly remarked: "You don't always need an act of heroism. Occasionally, it's enough to flick a switch, and something good will come out of it."[10]

It was partly Mendelssohn's high personal esteem for Kästner, nine years his senior, that led him to make the arduous trip to the Tyrolean mountains in 1945 to find his colleague. Like Kästner, Mendelssohn also strived to be an *écrivain journaliste*, applying journalistic criteria to his fictional writings and using literary forms for his journalistic work. Mendelssohn repeatedly suggested that Kästner was a role model. And along with their mutual professional regard and personal affection, the two men also shared the humiliation of having seen their books publicly burned in Berlin in 1933.

In the late 1920s Mendelssohn had worked as a staff reporter for the *Berliner Tagblatt*, to which Kästner had contributed as a freelancer. They first met in 1925. Their Saxon roots— Mendelssohn grew up in the progressive enclave of Hellerau near Kästner's place of birth, Dresden—and the distinct native accent they shared quickly led them to become close. But in 1933, with the start of what Mendelssohn called the "Hitler nonsense", they lost track of one another. "He stayed because despite everything he could stay, and I left because, when worst came to worst, I had to leave," Mendelssohn later remarked. Mendelssohn caught a glimpse of Kästner in a weekly German newsreel in a Parisian cinema amid images of one book after another being tossed on to a bonfire in Berlin. In a close-up, Mendelssohn spied a charred copy of Kästner's novel *Fabian* next to one of his own books. This experience shocked both men, although, no doubt for that very reason, it also had a major role in forming their identities. Kästner, whose literary work was pilloried for its allegedly corrosive influence on the German people, was directly exposed to the ire of the fanatic mob. He chose of his own volition to attend the book-burning. "It was revolting," he would say. "I felt extremely ill at ease [as my books] were burned with cheerlessly ceremonial pomp by a certain Mr. Goebbels."[11]

Change of Language

Twelve years later, Goebbels, who had held a speech at the auto-da-fé in Berlin, was dead. His leading radio propagandist, Hans Fritsche, and other Nazi henchman were in the dock in Nuremberg. And the two men whose books had been consigned to the flames in 1933 were sitting in the press gallery. It was the first time that Mendelssohn had seen Fritsche in person, although as a radio announcer in London he had duelled with him over the airwaves on numerous occasions during the war.[12]

Despite Mendelssohn's idealistic efforts to establish a new German press in the summer of 1945, his work was largely organizational, and he soon longed to do some reporting himself. He had excellent connections to Anglo-American media and had continued to publish occasional articles when time permitted. The Nuremberg Trial, the media event of the century, was a perfect opportunity to focus entirely on his own writing. Mendelssohn was on hand for the opening of the trial and continued covering it until mid-December, serving as a correspondent for the *New Statesman and Nation*, *The Observer* and *The Nation*.

He was writing in a foreign language. As soon as he emigrated, Mendelssohn had begun composing his texts in English. That was unusual. Many German émigré writers found working in foreign tongues too risky. Those who had honed a style of their own in their native language were often unwilling to give it up and start anew. Mendelssohn, however, decided to sacrifice his mastery of German for a simpler writing style in English, even going so far as to write a letter to his wife, Hilde Spiel, a native Austrian, in English. At the 1941 PEN Congress in London he gave a speech titled "Writers without Language" in which he distinguished between two types of authors. Mendelssohn classed himself among those who prioritized content and effect over form, proclaiming: "Any tools will serve."[13]

Kästner took up the fact that Mendelssohn was now writing in English in his reporting for the *Neue Zeitung*. "Hey, do you see the Englishman over there," he had a fictional correspondent say by way of introducing the reporters at the trial. "The one with the horn-rimmed glasses all the way to the right. That's Peter Mendelssohn. Prior to 1933, he was a German writ... oh, of course you know that... Now he writes his novels in English."[14]

Mendelssohn found the atmosphere in the press camp in Stein unusual and irritating and had trouble working there. Although he had generously helped Kästner secure a new professional life, his own was increasingly becoming an issue. Mendelssohn was only employed on a freelance basis in Nuremberg, and on 2nd December 1945, he wrote to a concerned Hilde Spiel: "I have all kinds of ideas about jobs and earning a living in the new year, and something will materialize. I don't think you need to worry... The one thing I've found out in this god-awful press camp where the so-called elite of international correspondents is assembled, is that I'm as good a journalist as any of them."[15] As it turned out, Spiel did not in fact need to worry. In March 1946, while the trial was still going on, Mendelssohn moved to Berlin as an advisor for two papers he had helped get licensed, the *Telegraf* and the *Tagesspiegel*. Later he served as the editor-in-chief for the autonomous Berlin edition of *Die Welt*. Spiel and the children followed him, and soon they were living what Mendelssohn jokingly compared to the pleasant existence of a colonial grandee in a villa in Berlin's posh Grunewald district.

In Nuremberg Mendelssohn only occasionally saw Kästner, who as a German was not allowed to reside in the press camp.[16] Both men had a lot to do, and Kästner was just there for a few days in any case, so there was no chance for anything more than some hastily exchanged words in the corridors of the court build-ing. Moreover, although Mendelssohn and Kästner had both opposed National Socialism and suffered under Nazi rule, they differed in their estimations of the Nuremberg Trial's impor-tance. As he confided to his wife, Mendelssohn was obsessed with the idea that he was living in a historic moment of which he didn't want to miss a single minute.[17] He subsequently com-posed a whole series of articles about it. By contrast, Kästner, who had attended the start of the trial, only filed a single feature for the *Neue Zeitung*, titled "Impressions from Nuremberg".[18]

"Impressions from Nuremberg"

As its title made clear, Kästner's feature offered a cursory, personal overview of the events at the trial. The article was published in the 23rd November edition of the *Neue Zeitung*, three days after the proceedings opened. In it, Kästner focused on individual moments and, to a large degree, on himself. "Autobahn Munich–Nuremberg," he wrote. "We're driving to the start of the trial of the war criminals… Autumn fog hangs over the road and the surrounding hills." Kästner's natural sur-roundings called forth gloomy associations. Crows squat atop "dead fields" amid barren, protruding hop poles. "It looks as though a group of gallows have convened for a meeting."

Kästner introduced the trial without excess pathos. "Tomorrow, charges will be brought against twenty-four men who bear enormous guilt in the deaths of millions of people," he wrote. "Why didn't the peoples of this earth conduct such trials a thousand years ago? The globe would have been spared much bloodshed and suffering." The pacifist Kästner had piously high hopes for the proceedings, presuming that they succeeded in making the defendants answer for their actions. "War might die out. Like the plague and cholera… And later generations might one day laugh at the times in which millions of people killed one another." Kästner, a master of the seemingly offhand remark, knew how to maximize the effect of his words. Bitterly, almost cynically, he mused: "By the way, there are no longer twenty-four defendants. Ley killed himself, Krupp, it seems, is on his deathbed, and Kaltenbrunner has had aneurysms. And Martin Bormann? Did he die en route from Berlin to Flensburg? Or has he grown a beard somewhere in the German pine forest?"

The following day, Kästner abandoned his broad-lens perspective to zoom in on the defendants as individuals. Göring had lost weight, he observed. "When he hears his name, he perks up." "Alfred Rosenberg is unchanged. His skin colour was always sickly." Walther Funk has a "pale, unattractive frog face". Kästner's descriptions of the mannerisms of the accused were very precise: from Rudolf Hess's nervous twitch to the utter ordinariness of the military leaders Wilhelm Keitel and Alfred Jodl, who threatened to disappeared entirely into the background. Otherwise, Kästner filled nearly two pages with the descriptions of the facial expressions, posture, attitudes and dress of the accused. Like a jury member, empiric and detached, he gave his depictions of each of the defendants a personal touch, although because he restricted himself to external characteristics the details took on exaggerated significance. Kästner avoided discussing the context or indeed the sheer horror of what the accused had done. Instead, he recited staccato the list of charges read out by the French chief prosecutor: "Larceny, deportation, sterilization, mass execution accompanied by music, torture, starvation, artificial infection with cancer, gassings, freezing victims alive, limbs torn asunder with machines, usage of human remains to produce fertilizer and soap... an ocean of tears... a hellscape of horror... The midday break comes at noon."

The midday break comes at noon... Kästner seemed grateful for a chance to interrupt his list of nightmares. What followed was a flight of fiction that left the realm of traditional feature reporting and, with it, reality. Kästner sketched an imaginary conversation in the court-building foyer with a colleague, in which he asked the man which famous writers he recognized amid all the "fun-fair buzz of activity". To satisfy the imaginary audience's alleged interest in celebrities ("The readers of our paper... you understand"), the unknown correspondent reeled off names including Dos Passos, Erika Mann and Mendelssohn. In another passage, Kästner again inserted a bit of a fiction as a way of imagining how the trial would be viewed in the future. "Finally, I am standing in the courtroom where the trial will take place," he writes. "The courtroom where, centuries later, a bored old man surrounded by a crowd of curiosity-seeking tourists will recite: 'And now you find yourselves in the historic courtroom, where on the twenty-fifth of November in the year 1945 the first trial of the war criminals commenced. On the wall to your right, in front of the flags of the United States, England, the Soviet Union and France sat the judges from those four nations.'"

It seems as though Kästner used humour, sarcasm and fiction to distance himself from the gravity of a historic moment he could not adequately reflect or capture—as though his emotions were blocked when confronted with insurmountable horrors.

Hence the otherwise extremely inappropriate metaphor of the funfair. Kästner's use of black humour recalled Sigmund Freud's view of humour as a temporary moment of respite from repression.

Speechlessness

A few months after his assignment in Nuremberg, Kästner attended a screening of the film *Die Todesmühlen* (*Mills of Death*), an American documentary containing footage from the death camps. Immediately afterwards, on 4th February 1946, he wrote an article for the *Neue Zeitung* titled "Wert und Unwert des Menschen" (What Human Beings Are and Aren't Worth), in which he described the thoughts and associations that arose while he was trying to compose an account of the film. Kästner, a master of language, was struck speechless at the horrors on display. "My thoughts flee every time they approach memories of the images in the film," he wrote. "What happened in the camps is so terrible that you cannot be silent, and you cannot speak about it."[19]

Kästner's tactic and technique in "Impressions from Nuremberg" was in one sense similar. His report on the trial was also an attempt to shield himself from the horrors wrought by Nazism by journalistically capturing their banality.[20] When the trial recessed, he headed home. "My heart aches after all I've heard," he wrote. "My ears ache as well. My headphones were too small… Driving home on the Autobahn… I look out the window and see nothing. Just stubborn, milky fog." Kästner would never return to the courtroom, although the *Neue Zeitung*

was one of the few newspapers allowed a permanent correspondent and the proceedings went on for almost a year. In his
correspondence, including his almost daily letters to his mother,
he didn't mention the trial at all.

Mendelssohn was likewise left speechless when he first
returned to his former home country after the end of the war.
In a 14th July 1945 article in the *New Statesman* titled "Through
the Dead Cities" he admitted to having no vocabulary to describe
the utter destruction and sea of ruins he encountered. But in
contrast to Kästner's near-complete muteness when confronted
by the crimes of the Nuremberg defendants, Mendelssohn was
struck dumb by the fondly remembered places from his youth
that had been obliterated.

During his time in Nuremberg he worked feverishly on his
book *The Nuremberg Documents: Some Aspects of German
War Policy, 1939–45*, a compilation of documentary evidence
introduced by British and American prosecutors. Mendelssohn
edited these documents and published them, first in English
in 1946 then the following year in German. The tribunal also
played a leading role in the articles he filed.[21] He was a great
defender of the trial, criticizing what he called the "sceptics
and hair-splitters who claimed that it ignored existing law, cir-
cumventing, indeed, to an extent, breaking it, in order to create
a new law, and "disregarded precedent in order to create new
precedent".[22]

But unlike Kästner, whose "Impressions" seemed perfunctory,
Mendelssohn didn't just churn out words. He reflected on the
trial and dived deeper into Nazi crimes when putting together
his book. He also sought moments of respite, for instance by
composing an extensive description of a walk he took through

Nuremberg's old town. But he never sought to evade the gravity of historical events.

German and Foreign Perspectives

Mendelssohn occupied a position of responsibility in his work for the victorious Western powers, and he was committed to the idea of re-education. Underlying that concept was the conviction that Germans were collectively guilty of Nazism, that the entire German people had actively supported fascism's rise to power. But there were two irreconcilable sides to this emotionally charged post-war issue. The "one Germany" argument guided by the notion of collective guilt was opposed by a "two Germanys" thesis that not all Germans had been Nazis. Mendelssohn tended towards the former outlook. He was disappointed above all in Germany's intellectual elites, which he felt had reacted in "typically German" fashion to the collapse of the Third Reich. After initially hoping for a change of heart, he soon became frustrated, writing to Hilde Spiel in August 1945, "My personal disappointment or rather disgust with the Germans, and I mean the so-called good, intelligent and intellectual Germans, has not diminished."[23] His countrypeople were unteachable and indifferent to the wider world. Kästner, Mendelssohn found, was an exception.

But Mendelssohn was kidding himself somewhat about Kästner as an "inner emigrant" during National Socialism—in part because he didn't want to know everything about the past of the man he so greatly admired. Although Kästner's opposition to the Nazis was obvious, and the burning of his books and the ban on him publishing spoke volumes, he did allow himself to be co-opted by the Nazi regime more than he later admitted. The committed pacifist may never have written a word in support of Nazism and have been hauled in for Gestapo questioning on multiple occasions, but he also reportedly applied for membership in the Reich Chamber of Writers. Under a pseudonym, and with special permission by Goebbels, he wrote the script for the film *Münchhausen*. He also wrote comedies and worked in the German film industry, thus becoming a voluntary supplier of the Nazi entertainment industry. For this reason, Mendelssohn's boyhood friend Klaus Mann took a critical view of Kästner. After the publication of Kästner's 1934 novel *Drei Männer im Schnee* (*Three Men in the Snow*), Mann attacked the "jovial Saxon's" malleability and accused him of violating his own moral standards.

The conflict would be revisited in Nuremberg when Kästner encountered Klaus Mann's sister Erika in the press gallery. The two couldn't stand one another. Erika considered Kästner a "German on the inside", an opportunist who had done too little to combat the Nazis and had indeed made his peace with them. In her 1939 book *Escape to Life*, co-written with Klaus, she took her fellow writer to task: "He's given up writing satirical verse; he writes little novels which are so mild that it almost looks like he did it out of spite, as if he wanted to tell the public: 'Look at this. Look at the trash I have to write! Look at what I have come to and you all remember how gifted and witty I was.'"[24] In return, in his "Impressions" Kästner referred to Erika merely as "Thomas Mann's daughter", characterizing her as non-German and unfeminine and reducing her to her external appearance—"the pointy-faced American with the dark, short, slicked-back hair". He wrote in much the same way about the accused.

After the war, Kästner was often asked why he had preferred to negotiate his way through the years of Nazi dictatorship rather than leave Germany. He justified staying on in his home country by arguing, among other things, that he wanted to chronicle events on the ground there. This was also the explanation he proffered when questioned by US military officials. Additionally, he said that he couldn't abandon his mother, with whom he was very close and who was not prepared to leave her native land. After 1945, he depicted the twelve years of the Third Reich as a kind of martyrdom and defended those who had remained in it, as he had.

He was also an early critic of occupation policies. "[Kästner was] one of the first to turn against the planned re-education of the German people," writes contemporary biographer Kurt Beutler, "because he considered decrees and coercion, regardless of from whom and to whom, an affront to humanity."[25] Confined within a solely domestic perspective, Kästner sided with post-war Germans vis-à-vis everyone else. Germans, he contended, "would certainly never forget how many people had been killed in the camps, and the rest of the world would do well to remember on occasion how many Germans were killed". This statement was implicitly aimed at the judges in Nuremberg, who never brought up the issue of crimes committed against Germans. In the end, Kästner believed that it should be up to Germans to remake Germany. "We've changed," he proclaimed in 1947 in a different context.[26] He rejected Adenauer's policies, remarking in retrospect: "For example, there was no independent German diplomacy. On the contrary, American political and other wishes were just dutifully fulfilled... I see the Adenauer era as a kind of democra-dictatorship."[27]

By contrast, the British citizen Mendelssohn was, in the words of his wife, an "uncompromising re-educator", also in a cultural sense. In 1947, in his capacity as a monitor of newspapers for occupation authorities, he addressed the First German Writers Congress in Berlin, presenting his peers with an ideal of a "Western European tone in [German] literature". Mendelssohn explained: "From my own individual perspective and with my personal captiousness, I would simply call it a civilized tone. The point is to write in civilized fashion, as civilized as what I personally consider the tone to be in England."[28] Mendelssohn's ideal was the opposite of the culture promoted by the Soviets in Berlin, which aimed at using literature to change social and economic structures. Mendelssohn's peers weren't thrilled by his suggestions. Many found them presumptuous and arrogant since they implied that most German writers were uncivilized. In 1948 the midday tabloid *B.Z. am Mittag* complained that "our former compatriot" Mendelssohn "treats us much more stringently than the Christian Lord Pakenham", the high commissioner of the British occupation zone.[29]

Thus, as much as Kästner and Mendelssohn shared a mutual loathing of Nazism and its crimes, they differed on how Germans could best be re-educated. Kästner was convinced that, with the help of their own culture, they could liberate themselves from the "Nazi poison". Both he and his assistant editor, Alfred Andersch, rejected the idea of collective guilt, and in 1945 he wrote in his diary that the occupiers who behaved as conquerors had prevented a "transformation of a revolutionary type". Ultimately he wanted to hark back to what he saw as a freedom-loving tradition in German literature and culture. But the Western Allies, and Mendelssohn with them, saw a contradiction between German culture and the value of freedom and blamed the German national character for the rise of National Socialism. If you wanted to liberate the German spirit and change its cultural value system, General Lucius D. Clay once remarked, you had to implement American culture.

Conflicts over the value of German culture were reflected in a debate around the cultural orientation of the *Neue Zeitung*. Kästner gave international authors, American and European, a forum within the newspaper, but he also vigorously supported post-war German literature. In time, his emphasis on German and European culture became a problem for a publication whose mission was to encourage respect for the American way of life. In April 1946 a reader complained to General McClure, the head of media supervision in the American occupation zone, that the elevated position of German culture in the *Neue Zeitung* "involuntarily played the Goebbels' propaganda tune: 'Americans as money-hungry barbarians with no cultural life of their own'".[30] But the assurance of political independence left the publishers of the newspaper little room to manoeuvre, and its success made it hard to justify any major personnel changes. In any case, Kästner, who was mainly responsible for the paper's German-centric approach, was convinced that he was acting in the interests of the American occupiers by teaching German readers to be open to their own culture.

Kästner ran the arts section of the *Neue Zeitung* until April 1948 and contributed scattered articles to it in the five years that followed. All told he published 107 pieces in its pages.[31] He remained friends with Mendelssohn until his death in 1974.

Mendelssohn reacquired German citizenship and moved to Munich in 1970, where Kästner also lived. He had a distinguished career as a journalist and translator and served as a leading literary functionary with organizations like PEN and the German Academy for Language and Literature. His later books—in particular his analysis of totalitarianism *Der Geist der Despotie* (*The Spirit of Despotism*) and his biographies of Churchill and Thomas Mann—were highly regarded. Mendelssohn was the first author to broach, albeit with great discretion, the topic of Mann's homosexuality.

To the end of his days, Mendelssohn maintained an enormous respect for his older colleague Kästner, whom he considered the epitome of reason and a different Germany during the country's darkest years. After his friend's death, Mendelssohn helped found the Erich Kästner Society. And like Germany's leading post-war literary critic Marcel Reich-Ranicki, who once called Kästner Germany's "honorary writer-in-exile", Mendelssohn believed that he had behaved morally and honourably during the Nazi regime. But in retrospect, no matter how influential their encounter in Mayrhofen would prove to be for the *Neue Zeitung* and post-war German culture, Mendelssohn would also come to feel a bit disappointed in his friend. After Kästner's death, Mendelssohn was repeatedly asked what he thought of his decision not to leave Nazi Germany. In one interview it emerged that in Mayrhofen Kästner had promised Mendelssohn that he would write a book about what had happened between 1933 and 1945. Kästner had also justified himself during that encounter by saying that someone had to stay behind, experience everything from beginning to end and describe afterwards what had happened. He had kept a daily journal, Kästner reassured his friend, and made sketches for a major novel. "You have to write that book about the twelve years of Hitler's Germany," Mendelssohn told him. "No one but you can. You have to do it. Promise me that you will. He said: 'I promise you—I have nothing else on my mind at the moment.' We then brought him to Munich, to the editorial staff of the *Neue Zeitung*, in which I was a little involved. From then I saw him regularly, several times a year. I always asked him: 'Erich, what's with the book?' But the book didn't materialize. Of course, he never wrote it."[32]

V

Erika Mann, Her "Beloved Lunatic" and an Unpleasant Reunion

> "Some people say you're combative. What
> else should one be in this century?... Without
> combativeness there is no responsibility."
>
> HANS HABE ON ERIKA MANN'S SIXTIETH BIRTHDAY

I n the first days of the trial, the twenty-one defendants, according to John Dos Passos, behaved more like spectators than
men accused of the most heinous crimes. They were arrogant,
haughty, indeed mildly outraged that they had been hauled up
in front of a court. Rudolf Hess largely ignored the proceedings and passed his time reading a pulpy novel. Hans Frank,
the vicious governor-general of occupied Poland, who had
twice tried to commit suicide, maintained a stony silence. And
Julius Streicher, formerly the absolute master of Nuremberg
as the city's *Gauleiter*, cut a lonely figure among the defendants, following what was happening with an unrepentant glare
of hatred.

Hermann Göring was another matter entirely. He visibly
enjoyed being back in the limelight and was clearly pleased at

being given the first seat in the dock. The ex-Reich Marshal expressed no regrets and seemed to doubt that it could be proven that he had committed any major crimes. Had American officers not lined up to greet him, shake his hand and invite him to dinner when he was arrested? Had Hitler not relieved him of all his positions shortly before the war's end? He had completely broken with Hitler, Göring had claimed at a press conference.[1] Like all the other accused, Göring had pleaded "not guilty". Now he impertinently acted like the star of the show, as Peter de Mendelssohn put it, quasi-sacrosanct and in no need of any enlightenment from prosecutors.

It was difficult for prosecutors to make a case against the defendants. In fact, as late as the summer of 1945, Jackson was sending out teams to feverishly comb through archives and find data that could be used as evidence against the accused. And in fact, within the space of a few months, they compiled 4,000 records, mostly from German sources. Still, power struggles and jealousies, particularly among the British, hampered Jackson's work. The American chief counsel prioritized documentary evidence over eyewitness testimonies, which he believed were inherently biased. Victims, he felt, tended to exaggerate when confronted with perpetrators in court, while Nazi eyewitnesses could be attacked on moral grounds and were largely useless.

Jackson's insistence on facticity led to endless tedium in the courtroom. In the interest of judicial precision, Judge Geoffrey Lawrence had agreed that all evidence presented should be read aloud. Thus those in the gallery had to endure hours of bureaucratic government-speak. A resigned Janet Flanner wrote: "On the whole our lawyers have succeeded to making the world's most completely planned and horribly melodramatic war seen seem dull and incoherent."[2]

From the judges' perspective, tedium was not an issue as the trial was there to get at the truth, but the prosecutors still needed to address the question of how to make comprehensible the full extent of Nazi crimes. Reading aloud from official paperwork or minutes of meetings was scarcely an adequate way of conjuring up emotion or communicating unfathomable atrocities like concentration-camp genocide. After they had collected evidence and determined what had happened in the past, the prosecution in Nuremberg needed to convince the judges, but they ran up against the limits of rational language. In response they utilized the power of moving images, introducing film footage as evidence and thereby prioritizing the optical over the conceptual. In the afternoon court session on 29th November 1945, they showed three rolls of documentary film titled "Nazi Concentration Camps". The material was intended as evidence to be used in conjunction with the charge of "crimes against humanity", but it was brought forward to the early section, which primarily dealt with "crimes against peace".

Showing the footage had a purpose. Spectators watching it in the darkened courtroom were plunged into a horrible nightmare. Those attending the trial had heard about the atrocities committed in the camps, and in October the Allies had begun showing the re-education film *Die Todesmühlen* in German cinemas, but very few of those present in Nuremberg had in fact seen images of conditions within the camps. The footage had been shot immediately after the liberation of those death factories and showed piles of bodies, the remnants of charred corpses in the crematoria and just-freed prisoners with shaven heads and humiliating prison stripes, emaciated and pale, staring emptily into the camera as though they had long since ceased to fear death. Scenes from Bergen-Belsen revealed a liberated prisoner doubled over, unable to stand because of malnutrition, while a bulldozer shovelled naked corpses into a mass grave. The driver of the vehicle held a handkerchief over his nose to block the stench of the decomposing human bodies.

These were devastating images that today, having been reproduced thousands of times, have become what historian Cornelia Brink calls familiar "icons of annihilation". Back then, when shown in the Nuremberg court, they devastated those who viewed them, many of whom wept. Some left the courtroom because they could no longer bear the sight. This sort of extreme emotional response was exactly what the prosecutors intended. The only light in the courtroom came from specially installed fluorescent lamps that illuminated the defendants. It later emerged that this was arranged not for security reasons but so that a psychiatrist and a psychologist, Major Douglas M. Kelley and Lieutenant G.M. Gilbert, could observe the accused while the film footage was being shown. In the opinion of these experts, the images shocked even the men in the dock. For the first time, the accused had difficulty maintaining their arrogant, dismissive postures. Franz von Papen and Hjalmar Schacht averted their eyes from the projection screen, while Walter Funk and Hans Frank completely lost their composure and cried. "All the defendants were obviously affected," wrote the experts, "and the majority felt profound shame at what they realized was Germany's disgrace before the world."[3] Even Göring, otherwise so self-confident, shielded his face with his right arm, particularly during the sequences concerning torture.

For many people in the court, it was clear that the defence faced an impossible task to combat such images. The reality of history completely undermined their case. The screening of film footage from the camps represented a turning point in the trial. In her article for the *Evening Standard*, Erika Mann (1905–69) wrote: "The film, strongly though it affected the accused... left the counsels for the defence all but prostrate and wholly demoralized. Throughout their common dinner there was no conversation and little appetite. Paler than their clients, they went home, if not to sleep, to go on trying to defend the indefensible. After the film one lawyer went so far as to comment: 'The sooner my client is hanged, the better.'"[4]

A Special Reunion

What must Thomas Mann's daughter have thought, sitting in the correspondents' gallery and observing former Nazi Interior Minister Wilhelm Frick as he watched the footage, stony-faced but pale and emotionally stressed, like the other accused? This was an unusual reunion for Erika Mann. Twelve years previously they had encountered one another in exactly the opposite roles, she in the spotlight and Frick among the spectators.

On 1st January 1933, less than a month before Hitler became Reich Chancellor, Erika, her brother Klaus, Therese Giehse and Magnus Henning had just successfully put on their first performance at their political cabaret *Die Pfeffermühle* (*The Pepper Mill*) in Munich. Billed as a "laughing declaration of war on Hitler", public satire of this sort was still possible because the Catholic regional government was energetically fighting for Bavaria to maintain independent authority. But among the audience was one of Hitler's henchmen.[5] "In our always overcrowded space sat Mr Frick, assiduously scribbling notes," Erika wrote. "He was drawing up a blacklist. We performed while the Reichstag burned."[6] Erika was speaking rhetorically, but a few months later, after a fire did in fact break out in the Reichstag, helping Hitler to achieve emergency dictatorial powers, Bavarian autonomy was a thing of the past. The only option left open to the Mann family, the other members of the cabaret and those on Frick's list was to flee. *Die Pfeffermühle* became the first-ever German-language theatre-in-exile in Zurich.

Nazi hate propaganda had long targeted not only Thomas Mann, but even more so Klaus and Erika, who were considered to be of Jewish descent because of their mother, Katja. After Erika performed at an event of the International Women's League for Peace and Freedom on 13th January 1932 in Munich, the Nazi *Völkischer Beobachter* commented: "An especially revolting chapter was the performance of Erika, who dedicated her 'art' as an actress, she said, to the cause of peace. Posing and carrying herself like a smug young dandy, she declaimed her bounteous nonsense about 'the German future'."[7] During the Second World War, with Erika working for the BBC and providing anti-fascist pieces in German in the battle for the airwaves, the newspaper would be considerably more hostile. Erika was a "commonly used political whore", wrote an author identified only as "Lancelot" in the issue of 8th October 1940, adding, "This paradigmatic example only appears where stupidity reigns and philistinism is married to street filth."[8]

Female war correspondents attached to the US Army in the autumn
of 1944. Third from right Betty Knox, first from right Erika Mann.

Another woman reuniting with Nazi functionaries in
Nuremberg was Erika Mann's lover, Betty Knox (1906–63). She,
too, worked as a correspondent at the trial, although that was
where comparisons stopped. Knox's family background could
hardly have been further from the daughter of the affluent,
socially respected Manns. Erika had met the thirty-eight-year-
old from Kansas in France in the spring of 1944. Knox worked
as a journalist for the London *Daily Express* and the *Evening
Standard*, although she would report from Nuremberg for the
American magazine *Tomorrow*. Knox had an adventuresome
past behind her as a burlesque dancer and was considered wild

and crazy. To Erika, she was her "beloved lunatic". As a member of the trio Wilson, Kappel and Betty, which was known for its parodies of classical dance and pseudo-Egyptian costumes, she had travelled the world's metropoles, including Berlin in 1936. During the negotiations of the Munich Agreement in 1938, she and her male-co-performers had been part of the official entertainment programme. Mussolini was charmed by the frivolous performance in the Bavarian capital, but the Nazi leadership, which included Göring, had not been amused by the spectacle of hairy male legs under mini-skirts. Joseph Goebbels found the act and its erotic centrepiece, Betty Knox, positively immoral.[9]

In 1941, in the middle of the war, Knox rather surprisingly became a journalist. The editor of the *Evening Standard* was a fan of her dance parodies and wanted to give his readers a comic perspective on the fighting. So Knox handed over her spot in the dance troupe to her daughter and became a war correspondent, writing a thrice-weekly column titled "Over Here". It proved very popular, among other reasons because Knox's British audience enjoyed her use of American slang. In 1944 she crossed paths with Erika, and the two became inseparable.

Sweet Revenge

For Erika Mann, the main trail in Nuremberg righted past wrongs—and not just because she could triumphantly look Frick in the face. She had already done that. Before Nuremberg, she had been sent to Luxembourg to write about fifty-two Nazi leaders and others who were being held there awaiting prosecution. "My last trip was to Mondorf-les-Bains, where I visited the 'Big 52'," she wrote to her mother. "You cannot imagine a more chilling adventure. Göring, Papen, Rosenberg, Streicher, Ley—*tout de horreur monde*, including Keitel, Dönitz, Jodl, etc—confined in a former hotel used as a prison and converted by its inhabitants into a veritable lunatic asylum."

Erika insisted that the inmates in Mondorf-les-Bains knew who she was. Although she wasn't allowed to speak with them, she inspected their rooms, observed them and had interrogators inform them that she was present. Rosenberg was said to have exclaimed, "Ugh, not you again!" Erika visibly enjoyed her belated triumph and still loathed her enemies. It was no accident that her mother described her as "vengeful",[10] and in a letter from 1939 her then-husband, W.H. Auden, had counselled her, "Don't be so full of hate." On the other hand, she had good reason to detest Nazis and bask in satisfaction at their ultimate downfall. After all, there had been standing orders in the Third Reich to liquidate her, should she ever again set foot on German soil.

Born in 1905 in Munich, Erika described herself as a "militant liberal". Like her siblings, she grew up in the shadow of her world-famous father, and Erika and her favourite brother Klaus, upon whom she had a decisive influence, were anything but obedient children. On the contrary, they were rebellious, insouciant and impolite. Spoiled by her parents, but full of humour and free spirit, she refused to conform to the demands and pedagogic style of traditional German higher education, leading her parents to send her to a reform school. But there, too, she wouldn't bow to authority or any attempts to mould her personality. In the end, she managed to get what she dismissed as a "swine-puke-diploma" from Munich's Luisengymnasium

academy. Surrounded by artists who frequented her parents'
house on Poschingerstrasse in the Bavarian capital, she became
an actress, even though she herself said that she "simply wasn't
very suited to theatrical performance". She married actor
Gustav Gründgens, although she was in love with both Pamela
Wedekind and Therese Giehse. She took part in car races
throughout Europe, changed "countries far more frequently
than outfits",[11] favoured an androgynous look of men's clothing
and a pageboy hairstyle, and worked as a travel writer and author
of children's books.

Erika's high-octane, excessive lifestyle, which included drug
addiction, lived up to the cliché we have about an artist's existence in the Roaring Twenties. Like many at the time, she only
gradually became interested in politics. The "dancing generation", as Wilhelm Emanuel Süskind put it in an essay that was
dedicated to Erika, was both liberal and materialistic. In contrast
to the war generation, they were devoted to a hedonism embodied by the era's many dance crazes. For Süskind, Erika was the
personification of her times.

Thomas Mann's children began to suspect that all was not
well in the late 1920s, particularly with the start of the Great
Depression in 1929. One year later the Nazis' electoral success,
which saw the NSDAP become Germany's second-largest party,
changed everything. Erika was subject to increasingly beyond-
the-pale attacks and had trouble finding roles as an actress.
The Manns' family chauffeur, a man named Hans, turned out
to be a spy who regularly reported to the party's national headquarters in Munich, the "Brown House", about goings-on at
Poschingerstrasse. Hans, whom Klaus Mann described as "das-
tardly but with an occasional soft heart", apparently felt guilty

and warned the Mann children in 1933 that they should flee Germany immediately or risk being arrested. Erika and Klaus went underground and eventually escaped the country, warning their parents, who were spending time in Switzerland, that they should on no account return to Germany.

But Erika Mann wouldn't have been Erika Man if she had refused to take up the gauntlet thrown down by the Nazis. She performed over a thousand times with the *Pfeffermühle* in Switzerland, Czechoslovakia and the Benelux countries. The shows were only indirectly critical of the German regime, but behind their literary façade the message was always cavalierly political. Erika did "ten times more than all us writers together to combat the barbarism", novelist Joseph Roth remarked in 1935.[12] That year, her German passport was revoked in retaliation for her allegedly anti-patriotic activities. She immediately married Auden so that she could obtain British citizenship.

During her exile, first in Switzerland then in the USA, Erika wrote and held lectures about what was going on in her native country. Although she had hoped to evade the "family curse" of writing, she published successful works like *Zehn Millionen Kinder* (*School for Barbarians: Education Under the Nazis*, 1938), *Escape to Life* (1939), *Wenn die Lichter ausgehen* (*The Lights Go Down*, 1940) and *The Other Germany* (1940), sometimes together with Klaus. In all her writings she presented herself as a fearless warrior and moralist. Horrified by Hitler's initial military triumphs, she began working for the US Office of War Information in 1942 before becoming a war correspondent for American and Canadian newspapers in various theatres of the conflict.[13]

It was as a US Army officer that she arrived first in France, then back in Germany in 1944. One of her tasks was interviewing people of various political responsibilities in the liberated territories. She also wrote about the material and psychological situation of the German people and the American re-education and reconstruction efforts. She came to Nuremberg two weeks before the start of the trial and moved into the women's house at the press camp together with Betty Knox.

She hated the conditions there, particularly the inadequate food and heat, and left the camp as soon as she could. "Nuremberg, too, has so far not been any genuine fun," she wrote to her friend Lotte Walter in the USA on 3rd February 1946. "We're doing too much wrong. Revolting living conditions (food completely bereft of vitamins we have to accept… great cold and a lot of unpleasantness) made me flee for the Christmas festivities and a week in Switzerland." She proudly signed the letter "War Correspondent E.M." and gave her contact address as "I.M.T. Press Camp Nuremberg".[14]

Erika didn't mention that she been together with Betty in Switzerland, where they spent the holidays with Klaus and Theresa Giehse. Her partner was in some regards an embarrassment. She had once behaved "rather inappropriately" during a visit to Lotte Walter's father, the famous music conductor Bruno Walter, and Thomas and Katia Mann were also not amused by their daughter's girlfriend. Katia had bad memories of the 1944 New Year's celebrations, at which "The Owl", as she dismissively nicknamed Betty, had failed to show the patriarch Thomas Mann proper respect. Later Erika, who was no doubt head over heels in love with the lively, attractive Betty, ironically remarked to Klaus that she was "not precisely what the doctor ordered".

During her stay in Switzerland Erika fell very ill. That winter in Central Europe was bitterly cold and, as she reported to Klaus, she had not brought along sufficient warm clothing and was always freezing. Alongside an oral infection and the side-effects of her drug abuse, she also suffered chronic bronchitis. In the end, she felt so bad that she had to spend several weeks in a Swiss hospital. "The Owl is at my side and is enjoying similar ailments, albeit milder in form," Erika wrote to her parents on 10th January 1946. "It hasn't been decided whether I'm to be brought to the Höh [the hospital]." Both Erika and Betty feared that they wouldn't be able to support themselves if the illness continued, but they were spared the worst. After Erika's recovery they returned to Schloss Faber-Castell.

The "Head Quarter" in Stein

Hardly any statements have survived from Erika Mann about the press camp and her fellow journalists there, although she re-encountered acquaintances like Peter de Mendelssohn and William Shirer. The fact that she was illicitly living with her lover in the women's building probably encouraged her to maintain distance from her fellow residents and avoid discussing her private life in her correspondence. The press camp was run by the US military, and homosexuality was a punishable crime. In her letters, Erika referred to Betty with gender-neutral nicknames like "Owl" and "Tomski". Moreover, she did little to endear herself to Ernest Cecil Deane. In March 1946 she, Betty and some of the other residents complained about the cramped quarters and inadequate living conditions in the women's building. On the seventeenth of that month she gave Deane a proper dressing-down. The following day the nonplussed camp manager wrote to his wife: "It was one of the toughest 'committee meetings' I've ever attended, and I hope I go to no more of its kind, ever! Women correspondents are a pain in the seat, generally speaking, and several of those in the meeting yesterday, including Higgins, Knox, and Mann, are especially so."[15]

Yet although Erika found it difficult to tolerate conditions at the camp, she considered it very important. In the synopsis of her book project "Alien Homeland", which she began in 1944 but never finished, Chapter 17 was to be devoted to "The press camp, a unique establishment". Unfortunately, that was as far as the chapter went, but the bare fact that she felt the camp deserving of such attention indicates her regard for it as a unique historical media institution. The book was to be a chronicle of the most important events and her most important experiences while in Germany. It's reasonable to conclude that she saw the camp as the centre of a free democratic press and an encouraging example of international cooperation that could serve as a model for Germany and the members of the German media.

Competition for space remained fierce in Schloss Faber-Castell, as Erika knew all too well. Part of the brief description for Chapter 16 of "Alien Homeland" reads: "With other correspondents the author does not dare leave the scene for more than a couple of days lest she find her cot and seat occupied by a competitor." Erika's colleague Rebecca West confirmed the claustrophobic conditions in the women's building, writing: "There was nowhere in the Schloss where one could be alone. Everyone's bedroom became full of people sitting about because their own bedrooms were full of people sitting about because they too had found their bedrooms full."[16]

Erika was on the go a lot during this time. From her "head quarter", as she referred to the press camp, she wrote pieces for the American weekly *Liberty* and, more frequently, Britain's *Evening Standard* between the late summer of 1945 and the spring of 1946. All in all, she penned twenty-one articles for the latter. Yet although Erika Mann may have been a familiar name to everyone in Nuremberg, she was hardly a star correspondent. Almost all her pieces were either not published or ran anonymously and in edited form. Only her report from Mondorf-des-Bains appeared in an edited version under her own name. The *Standard*'s chief correspondent in Nuremberg was the Scotsman Richard Macmillan, who had previously reported from the front lines in Northern Africa and Normandy.[17]

What made Erika unique among the correspondents was the fact that she came from a famous family who had been persecuted by the Nazis. Her journalistic work notwithstanding, she was in great demand as a source of information who gave interviews and could put the historic dimensions of the trial and its place in the re-education process into perspective. In contrast to Rebecca West or Janet Flanner, she didn't find the trial tedious and considered it vitally necessary.[18]

Erika knew Germany and her former compatriots, and her view of post-war Germans could hardly have been more negative. She was convinced that they bore collective responsibility for Nazi crimes and fiercely criticized their lack of self-reflection, "obnoxious self-pity" and subjective inability to acknowledge their own culpability. In a letter to her parents, who were still living in the USA, she urged them not to return: "I beg of you:

don't think of coming back to this lost country for a single minute. It is simply unrecognizable to the human eye. And I'm not talking about its physical condition!!!"

A "Nasty, Unholy People"

Erika Mann's antipathy towards everything German was such that she consciously denied her German heritage and native tongue in Nuremberg. She sometimes presented herself as an American, using the word "we" when she spoke of US actions. Her fellow correspondents, who knew her, didn't fail to notice this behaviour and often found it affected. Erich Kästner was struck by her adopted US patriotism and referred to her as "the American woman with the narrow head and short-cut hair", while for Willy Brandt it was "a little irritating that Erika claimed not to speak German any more".[19] Erika went so far as to pass herself off as a naive American journalist named Mildred to German interview partners in order to conceal her true identity. Erika used this persona, for instance, to appeal to Rudolf Hess's wife, Ilse, in the belief that she would be more forthcoming to an American country bumpkin than to the Nazi-persecuted daughter of Thomas Mann. The trick worked. Ilse Hess freely provided information to "Mildred".

Erika used her acting ability and carefully sculpted her image when carrying out interviews. With her sense of drama and keen eye for affecting stories, she also was not above embellishing her reports.[20] Her pieces were often like short stories focusing on an unusual event or absurd situation—and on numerous occasions her aim seems to have been to illustrate what would become known as the banality of evil. For example, she once described how Wilhelm Frick's wife snuck into the visitors' gallery while the trial was in session and how the two had blown kisses at one another.[21]

Erika's views on Germany and its "nasty, unholy people" were uncompromising, often bitter and disillusioned. Even her brother Golo considered them extreme and accused her of crossing the line in her articles between criticism and untruth. It wasn't correct, he said, that most Germans had enough to eat, as Erika contended.[22] But she stuck to her guns, maintaining her views into the post-war Adenauer era. Germans, she opined, had an automatic proclivity towards repression and self-pity. In her eyes, they had never truly come to terms with the Nazi dictatorship—on the contrary, many former Nazis continued to occupy elevated positions in the judicial system, politics, culture and business. Much to her dismay, she encountered them everywhere, including among her colleagues in the Nuremberg court. The fact that one of those who had sold out to the Nazis was previously a close friend only increased her ire, and she studiously ignored him at the proceedings.

An Unpleasant Encounter

Wilhelm Emanuel Süskind—father of Patrick Süsskind, who would become the bestselling author of the novel *Perfume*—was a special correspondent for the *Süddeutsche Zeitung*. Himself a writer of fiction and a literary critic in his early years, W.E. Süskind, as he called himself, was a close friend of both Erika and Klaus Mann. According to Erika's later biographer, Irmela von der Lüthe, Süskind was in love with Erika and would have liked to marry her.[23]

But when the Manns were forced to flee in the face of fascist terror, Süskind stayed in Munich and bent with the new winds blowing in the Third Reich, establishing himself as a journalist. He became the head of the books section of the *Krakauer Zeitung*, the only German-language newspaper in the General Government of Poland, and the co-editor-in-chief of the *Krakauer Monatshefte*, which, to quote historian Knud von Harbou, was a "foul National propaganda magazine". He also worked for *Das Reich* newspaper, where Goebbels often published editorials, and was fulsome in his praise for the governor-general, Hans Frank, also known as the "butcher of Poland". It no doubt made Erika's ears burn when Süskind called upon her father to return to Germany in 1933, assuring him that everything there was "most amusing, interesting and exciting".

After the war, Süskind again changed his colours with a swift ease that for Erika was so typically German, covering up everything he had done under Nazism and joining the ranks of the politically compromised journalists who nonetheless found employment at the *Süddeutsche Zeitung*.[24] Although he was accused in 1957 of promoting "Nazi culture with all means at his disposal" in the paper,[25] Süskind's career wasn't harmed. In 1963 he published his reports from Nuremberg as a book with the title *Die Mächtigen vor Gericht* (*The Mighty Before the Court*), and it was a hit. The perspective he adopted in it was that of a chronicler, not a historian—a way of avoiding having to mention his own involvement in the recent Nazi past. During the 1950s he even considered legal action against a book by former Nazi journalist Karl Ziesel that mocked him and others for concealing their pasts.

In 1957, together with Dolf Sternberger and Gerhard Storz, Süskind also published a legendary reference work titled *Aus dem Wörterbuch eines Unmenschen* (*From the Dictionary of a Monster*), an analysis of the vocabulary of the Third Reich that purported to be a journalistic critique of the language of the reign of terror. The fact that Süskind of all people was entrusted to write the entry on "propaganda" in a work that dealt with the totalitarian aspects of language doesn't bolster its credibility from today's perspective. But just as the judges at the Nuremberg tribunal rendered their verdicts about the deeds of the defendants, Süskind presumed to judge their words.

Despite all his failings, Süskind was a gifted writer and an intelligent commentator, and he was one of the few correspondents in Nuremberg to address the linguistic difficulties of translating Nazi bureaucratic language. How could terms like *Grosseinsatz* (large-scale operation) or *kolonnenmässiger Einsatz* (platoon-like operation) be rendered into foreign languages, he asked in the *Süddeutsche Zeitung*. Would the judges be able to recognize that what such terms referred to were death squads?[26]

Süskind was quite popular among his German colleagues, among other reasons because he was one of the four correspondents behind the satiric publication *Nürnberger Extra Blatt*. It appeared on 20th September 1946 in an edition of 300 copies. In it Süskind used the distich metre of Schiller's poem "The Walk" to make fun of the inadequacies of the German press room, writing of the "eternally defective, blinkingly asthmatic tubes of the lively neon lighting" and the obtrusive "automotive clinking of the rattling window panes". He also invoked Shakespeare to complain about the bare walls, noting that the only decoration was to be found above the telephones, where there hung "Gaston Oulmàn's portrait—the rest is silence".

Nothing Süskind wrote after the war was politically objectionable. He welcomed the Nuremberg Trial, even if he also argued that strict distinctions should be made between the perpetrators and those who remained passive. He rejected the notion of collective guilt, probably because, among other things, it would have required him to ask unpleasant questions about himself. The aim of the defence, he proposed, should be to "identify a specific circle of truly guilty people from the amorphous many and to limit the guilty verdict as far as possible to these people".[27]

Süskind had retained his idiosyncratic way with words during the Third Reich, and his stylistic peculiarities helped him pass himself off after the war as someone who had gone into "inner emigration". That made him doubly loathsome to Erika Mann. In her eyes, not only did he fail to show any regret; taking on the mantle of "inner émigré" also allowed him to count himself among the victims, although he had never lifted a finger to oppose the Nazi regime.

Erika wrote extensively about Süskind in a letter to novelist Alfred Neumann, who had been forced to flee Germany because of his Jewish background. Neumann had asked her for her opinion because Süskind was accused of attacking Thomas Mann shortly after the Manns had been forced to seek refuge abroad. Her characterization could hardly have been more sarcastic, invoking the posh area around the Starnberger See near Munich: "Even when he took over the books section of the

Krakauer Zeitung, the brainchild of the bloodstained [Hans] Frank, on 1st November 1943, he did nothing wrong in the eyes of the 'inner émigrés'. No matter how much blood his boss had on his hands, no matter that millions of Poles and Jews had been killed horribly under the regime, W.E. Süskind was courageous enough to service the wishes of the 'governor-general' in educated German, and the 'inner émigrés' thanked him for it. It was more than their other 'warriors', more than Molo, Bonsels and Thiess would have been able to do. Meanwhile, Süskind earned a pretty good income and was exempted from the military. Instead, he lived a modest existence in his lovely, new country estate on Starnberger See."[28]

The background to one of Erika's remarks was a stir created in August 1945 by an open letter by the writer Walter von Molo to Thomas Mann. Molo, a defender of the idea of inner emigration, called upon the Nobel laureate to return to Germany. "Come back soon like a good doctor," Molo wrote, seeking to encourage understanding on Mann's part for those "who weren't capable of leaving their homeland" and who thus shouldn't be divided into good and evil. Thomas Mann, who still acutely felt the "coronary asthma of exile", dismissed the appeal as "shallow and shabby". His public answer to Molo, the essay "Why I'm Not Returning to Germany", further stoked the conflict between German cultural figures in exile and so-called inner émigrés. He simply could not understand, Mann wrote, how people could have engaged in culture in the service of Hitler "without covering their faces with their hands and sprinting out of the auditorium".[29]

The Manns were also targeted in a hurtful newspaper polemic composed by author Frank Thiess, another proponent of the inner emigration conceit, who declared that Thomas Mann was guided by a "truly fearsome and terrible hatred, a hatred for Germany".[30] Enduring the night-time air raids and wartime hunger, Thiess added, had given people experience and knowledge far more valuable than that gained from watching "from the loges and balcony seats of abroad".

Ever devoted to her father, Erika sought to defend him and joined the debate. With scornful rage she cut through the pretence of the proponents of inner emigration, "this proud fraternity" who conspired to "dissolve whatever German guilt may conceivably exist in the ocean of human sinfulness". In an essay titled "Inner Emigration", she noted with satisfaction that Thiess, "the club's very founder", had been "recently expelled" after being exposed as a hypocrite. "An article of his, written early in the regime and praising the 'National Revolution' as a great, wonderful and epochal event," wrote Erika, "was re-printed by a number of German dailies—a publication that deprived the 'Inner Emigration' camp of one of its most prominent members."[31]

If it had been up to Erika, Süskind would have been likewise ostracized, but he had a powerful defender in Franz Josef Schöningh, a co-publisher of the *Süddeutsche Zeitung*, whose past was also compromised and who made sure that the newspaper avoided the topic of Nazi crimes. Moreover, most of Süskind's pro-Nazi writings could no longer be found after the war. After all, the past in Kraków, where most of them had appeared, was a long way from the present in post-war southern Germany.

As a German citizen Süskind wasn't allowed to reside in the press camp, but Erika saw him at the court.[32] The first time they encountered one another, years having passed in the meanwhile, Erika stared right through him, and his attempts to contact her—including through her brother Golo—were studiously ignored. On 16th January 1946 Golo, who was at the time reporting from Nuremberg for Radio Frankfurt, wrote to their mother, Katia: "Süskind was sitting behind me and suddenly tapped my shoulder. 'Don't you recognize me any more?' Later he said, in an attempt to be pleasant and conciliatory: 'People mostly forget that your father didn't really emigrate. He simply happened to be abroad when these things happened!' He truly believed I wanted to hear this and was keen on me mediating between him and Erika! What could we possibly have to say to people like this!"[33]

Süskind was persona non grata for the Manns, and Erika in particular. In 1955 he published an obituary of Thomas Mann that also raised the family's hackles. It contained no mention whatsoever of the deceased's opposition to the Nazis and no substantial acknowledgement of his literary creations. Instead, Süskind concentrated on Thomas's guru-like role within the Mann clan and could not resist a jibe at his "uncompromisingly egocentric manner".[34] After the Second World War the Nobel laureate and Süskind had corresponded for a time, with Mann initially supporting the latter's career. Although making it clear he disapproved of Süskind's stance during National Socialism, Thomas had called him a "man of fine gifts" with "charming literary intelligence" in a letter of July 1946, after he had been reluctant to break off contact. But when Süskind's unworthy obituary was published, it was too much for Erika.

Not only did she despise Süskind's disloyalty, moral deficits and lack of political rectitude and responsibility, he was also, in her eyes, a slave to pleasure and entertainment who had used the Nazi movement to fulfil his own desire for amusement and sensual lust. She conceded that he possessed intelligence and literary talent, but that only made his behaviour more despicable in her eyes. "That's just the way he was," she wrote to Neumann, "weak, craven in his need for entertainment and thrill, morally stunted, a hedonistic voyeur who perceived every new spectacle… as a stimulus."

For Erika Mann, Süskind was thus the real personification of the "dancing generation". In his 1925 essay Süskind had written of Erika: "For some reason she finds it inappropriate to put her stamp… politically on the world. She makes no moves in this regard."[35] After the war, this was definitely not true of Erika, who had gone from 1920s hedonist to a political activist. Even the former burlesque dancer Betty Knox became an outspoken critic of National Socialism. By contrast, for Erika Süskind remained forever the apolitical, "epicurean voyeur".

Nonetheless, Süskind kept trying to get back in Erika's and the rest of the Mann family's good graces, including—between the lines—in the book version of his reports from Nuremberg. During the trial, Thomas Mann became the focus of a case of mistaken literary identity when British chief counsel Hartley Shawcross ended a peroration with a literary quote he attributed to Goethe, claiming that fate would someday strike down the German people because they "ingenuously submit to any mad scoundrel who appeals to their lowest instincts, who confirms them in their vices and teaches them to conceive nationalism as insolence and brutality". Shawcross then pointed at the defendants and proclaimed, "With what a voice of prophesy he spoke— for these are the mad scoundrels who did these very things."[36] Süskind, who was present at Shawcross's address, was one of the first to notice that the quote came from Mann's Goethe novel *Lotte in Weimar*, not Goethe himself. (Erika had by this point returned to the USA.) Süskind wrote that the quote was not by Goethe but of him, because it came from "the most resplendent corner of literature", adding that the incident deserved a place in the "anecdotal treasure trove of literary history".[37]

In November 1955, Süskind congratulated Erika on her fiftieth birthday. His exact words weren't preserved, but her response, which alluded among other things to Hitler's early attempted putsch in Munich, has survived. "W.E.S.," she wrote without any preamble. "It was friendly of you not to shy away from this latest attempt. On the occasion of the half-century I have now put behind me, you remind me of 9th November 1923, which would admittedly have stuck in my memory even without your efforts. Years spent together as children or youths are probably binding—or they would be, if that which followed had not necessarily led to the most complete estrangement. I am not to blame for this, and I don't accuse you either. I'm nobody's judge. But I'm convinced to the core that our paths have diverged never to meet again. Yes, even if I had got over 'Kraków', which is scarcely conceivable, your presumptuous 'Dialogue with a Dead Man' [Süskind's obituary for Thomas Mann] would have driven me away again. 'The world rests, notably, on the idea of Fidelity,' you inscribed anno 27 in Klaus's copy of [your novel] *Tordies*. That was Joseph Conrad. You're not worthy of those words. Thanks anyway for thinking of me."

Erika remained likewise revolted by Germany. In May 1946 she left the country of her birth to attend to her father, who was suffering from lung cancer, in California. Six years later, at the height of McCarthyism, when the Manns learned they were being kept under surveillance for potential Communist activities, they left the USA for Kilchberg, near Zurich, where Erika lived until her death in 1969. She became, in Thomas Mann's words, his "daughter adjutant" and the manager of his authorial estate. Not for a moment did she ever consider moving back to Germany.

Betty Knox was different. There is no record of when their relationship ended. In 1949 Katia Mann wrote with a hint of irony that Betty had "hopefully not" arrived yet with Erika in California. That would seem to imply the two were still in a long-distance relationship. In any case, Erika's "beloved lunatic" had stayed behind in Germany and continued to work as a correspondent, covering the subsequent Nuremberg trials. As time passed she became increasingly critical of the proceedings, considering them an example of "victor's justice". In 1948 she witnessed the executions of three condemned men at the prison for war criminals in Landsberg am Lech and protocolled their final words and protestations of innocence. Freda Utley wrote in her critical 1949 study of the Allied occupation policies *The High Cost of Vengeance* that Betty Knox found the experience of the executions deeply shocking.[38] In the early 1950s she headed an international press club in Bonn and later wrote articles for various Canadian newspapers. She lived out her days together with her mother and daughter in Düsseldorf, dying in 1963 at the age of fifty-six.

VI

William Shirer and the
Good Wehrmacht General

"A great book."

GOLO MANN ON WILLIAM SHIRER'S *RISE AND FALL OF THE THIRD REICH*

W ere the inadequate conditions in the press camp an act
of retribution? Was the US military government taking
revenge on correspondents for what it felt was the overly critical
tone of their reporting? William L. Shirer (1904–93) reported
that some of his colleagues at the *New York Herald Tribune*
suspected that this was the case, although he quickly added that
most of his fellow camp residents felt differently. Their view
was that the US Army was much too demoralized and disor-
ganized to take revenge. Whatever the truth of such suspicions,
Shirer's articles were an unusually bleak take on the conditions
at Schloss Faber-Castell. The fact that he made his criticism
public, in the form of a plea for help on 8th December 1945,
shows how desperate he was. Half of the people reporting on
the trial, he wrote, were sick from "vile food" the army wouldn't
have dreamed of serving even to German POWs. Dysentery was
going around. "Packed in eight or ten in a room in a ramshackle

building which serves as a press camp, they are forced to live under sanitary conditions—or rather the lack of them—which the State of New York would never permit in Sing Sing."[1]

Colleagues from other countries were charmed by the castle Shirer dismissed as a "ramshackle building". Xiao Qian called it "enchanting".[2] And opinions also differed on the "vile food"—at least many residents didn't notice it having any adverse effects on their health. While US photographer Eddie Worth found it bad beyond belief, *Pravda* correspondent Boris Polevoi praised the grand dinners in the castle, into which the cooks had invested "proper effort". Although complaining that the cooks prioritized appearance over taste and used too many tinned goods, there were still "the famous American steaks, tenderly grilled, pieces of meat as broad as your hand".[3]

Individual standards varied, obviously, and the man who so vociferously made his discontent known in the *Herald Tribune* was accustomed to better than the press camp. After the 1944 liberation of Paris Shirer had, like many other journalists, lodged in the Hôtel Scribe with its restaurants, mahogany-panelled bars and comfortable rooms with hot baths. Shirer, whose first-hand account of Nazi Germany, *The Rise and Fall of the Third Reich*, would become an international bestseller and serve as the basis for a film, was one of the stars of the press camp in Stein, and he knew it. Sharing sleeping quarters with only a field cot for a bed, as was the rule in Schloss Faber-Castell, was something to which the son of a US assistant district attorney in Chicago was not at all accustomed.

Shirer's article caused a stir, particularly after NBC Radio passed on the suggestion that an epidemic had broken out in the camp. Ernest Cecil Deane had no time for such complaints and put them down to the correspondents' tendency to exaggerate. While some inhabitants suffered from diarrhoea, an irritated Deane wrote to his wife, Lois, on 6th December 1945, no one was seriously ill: "The correspondents magnify facts sometimes out of all proportion to the truth."[4]

For Shirer, conditions in the camp were about more than just bad food and intestinal distress. To his mind, the US Army didn't sufficiently appreciate the work and he and his colleagues were doing. After all, the American military had no problem carting a Broadway impresario like Billy Rose throughout Germany but gave reporters no chance to view major cites for their pieces. This aspect of Shirer's complaints in the *Herald Tribune* was justified, and as a respected personality in the USA his words carried weight. Shirer enjoyed near-legendary status among the correspondents in the press camp as one of the few Western reporters who had actually experienced the Third Reich first-hand. He had reported from the heart of Nazi Germany, first as a newspaperman, later as a radio journalist. As a correspondent initially for the Universal News Service and then CBS New York, he lived in Berlin from 1934 to 1940, battling the German censors and telling his American and British audiences what it was like under Hitler. He also had regular contact with other Nazi bigwigs, whom he interviewed, and was particularly well acquainted with Göring. Before the Second World War Shirer had even served as a mediator for Universal News Service, who wanted to engage the Reich Marshal as a columnist. That never came to pass, partly because of Göring's overblown salary demands.[5]

Shirer had reported numerous times from Nuremberg on the Nazi Party rallies—or, as he called them, "those obscene orgies of the Teutonic herd in which the German men and women had joyously shed their individuality, their decency, their dignity as human beings, and become merged in the putrid inhumane mass that Hitler was shaping".[6] During the German conquest of France, the British evacuation from Dunkirk and the Battle of Britain, Shirer dramatically described the events of the war. His fame was based on his status as a pioneer of live radio reporting. Radio journalism was still in its infancy, and Shirer's voice was broadcast into countless British and American living rooms. His reports, which he invariably began with the words "This is Berlin", established him as one of the world's most immediate newsmen and showed that radio could be more than just transmitted agency copy, headlines and background features. He was literally on the ground when reporting live on events like France's humiliating signing of a ceasefire with Germany in the forest of Compiègne in 1940. His work helped make radio a mass medium in the USA.

In the winter of 1940 he left Germany, where it had become impossible for him to function as a journalist. The Nazis had pressured him to broadcast official reports he knew to be false or incomplete, and when he learned that the Gestapo wanted to put him on trial as a spy he had no choice but to depart. Back in the USA, he published *Berlin Diary 1934–1941*, his reckoning with Nazi Germany, which became a global bestseller. It is still used as a historical source today, even though we now know that he thoroughly edited it for publication, deleting, for instance, passages that expressed his early admiration for Hitler.[7]

In November 1945, the former American voice in Berlin became the American voice in Nuremberg. One reason for Shirer's disgruntlement with conditions in the press camp was that he was ill nearly the entire time he was there. He ran a fever and stayed in bed as much as he could, only dragging himself to the courtroom, the press room and the recording studio when absolutely necessary. His neighbour in the camp and CBS colleague Howard Smith helped Shirer cope with the demands of his work.

Shirer was assigned to cover the opening of the trial and only stayed in Nuremberg for a few weeks. But he still missed one of the key moments, Jackson's opening address, because he was sick in bed. On 27th November Smith brought him some bad news. Shirer's mother had died the day before, and although as her eldest son he should have delivered the graveside eulogy, he was in no shape to travel to her funeral. In his autobiography, Shirer wrote that he had desperately tried to return to the USA but that the army doctors had urged him not to make the trip. So he stayed on in Stein, sending a telegram for the pastor to read aloud at his mother's burial.

During the days that followed, he reported on the trial to a US public weary of news from the war. After the dramatic opening week, the proceedings soon turned tedious. As Smith remarked, this was "a fact that may be unimportant to history, but was vital to a reporter trying to hold the interest of a milkman in Peoria".[8] Shirer had trouble concentrating on the trial. In addition to his dissatisfaction and depressed mood, he was facing private complications. A married man with children, he had begun a relationship with the Austrian ballerina Tilly Lösch, a former solo performer at the Vienna State Opera, whom he had met in 1941 back in the USA. The question of whether he should leave his wife, herself a Viennese photographer, and his children weighed on his mind, and he was wracked by self-doubt and guilt.[9] His only escape was, despite his illness, his almost compulsive devotion to his work.

During his time in Nuremberg he collected copies of trial documents he hoped to use for a planned book-length analysis of the Third Reich. In the press camp, Shirer, who wrote articles for *Reader's Digest* from Nuremberg in addition to reporting for CBS radio, became acquainted with John Dos Passos, whose literary work he admired. The two men's reports could not have been more different. Whereas the Germanophile Dos Passos freely admitted that "the Americans didn't enter the court room with clean hands" either, Shirer was a dyed-in-the-wool Vansittartist.[10]

Vansittart's Faithful

In the 1930s, British diplomat Baron Robert Vansittart had led the opposition to Neville Chamberlain's politics of appeasement. He not only considered Hitler a war-mongering barbarian, he also distrusted Germans collectively as a fundamentally militaristic and aggressive people. In his 1941 pamphlet *Black Record: Germans Past and Present* he depicted Nazism as the most recent manifestation of this aggression which he claimed had been present since the Roman Empire. Once Germany had been defeated, Vansittart argued, the country should be denied any capacity, including heavy industry, that would allow it to re-militarize, and the Germans should be kept under strict Allied surveillance for at least a generation.

A de-Nazification process wasn't enough for Vansittart. He believed that the German military elite, in particular the

Prussian officer corps and the Wehrmacht general staff, had been the ones actually behind the Second World War. Both groups, he urged, needed to be destroyed. The cover of his 1943 book *Lessons of My Life* proclaimed: "In the opinion of the author, it is an illusion to differentiate between the German right, centre, or left, or the German Catholics or Protestants, or the German workers or capitalists. They are all alike and the only hope for a peaceful Europe is a crushing and violent military defeat of Germany followed by a couple of generations of re-education controlled by the United Nations."[11]

With a few notable exceptions, for instance Willy Brandt, who rejected Vansittartism as a kind of "reverse racism",[12] many correspondents in the press camp supported such hard-line ideas. In a letter to Hemingway, Martha Gellhorn expressed her sympathy for this perspective. Erika Mann interviewed Vansittart for *Vogue* magazine in 1942 and defended his ideas in a 1944 article for *The Nation*. The two also corresponded, discussing, among other things, the purportedly essential character of the German people. On the other hand, German émigré circles were sometimes very critical of Vansittart's theses. Communist detractors, for example, accused him of entirely suppressing the existence of a German Resistance to Hitler and Nazi militarism.

Shirer, who was close to Erika and greatly admired her father,[13] was in one respect a moderate. Before he departed Germany in 1940 he wrote in his diary: "There are, of course, a few things that one can take with one from the German land: the love and appreciation of German music—of Bach and Beethoven and the Austrians, Haydn, Mozart and Schubert— and the beautiful things that a few Germans wrote: Schiller and Goethe and Heine and Thomas Mann and the wonderful lyric poet Rilke, who was born in Prague, and Kafka, who was a Czech but wrote in German. Theirs was a German spirit, if you will, that I can live with for the rest of my days in my own Anglo-Saxon native land."[14]

But for Shirer such cultural luminaries were exceptions rather than typical representatives of the German people. What he witnessed when he returned in late October 1945 to the once-proud nation, first to Berlin, then Nuremberg, profoundly disillusioned him: the enormous apathy of the Germans, their regret not at starting but at losing the war, and their complaints about lack of food and the cold combined with their complete lack of empathy for or even interest in the far greater suffering among the peoples Germany had once occupied. Moreover, Germans reacted with boredom to the Nuremberg trials and showed little willingness to accept democracy, which Shirer also found objectionable. "At home, maybe, they will say the German story is not finished, the German problem still not solved, a third German war not too far off," he wrote. "They will be right. The German story will never be finished."[15]

A major part of this "German story", to Shirer's mind, was the fundamental militarism of the German people. In a film report about the Hitler Youth shortly before the end of the war he had informed his American audience about the shocking fanaticism among young German men, who were being trained in war games for future conflicts. It was the barbarism of these youngsters that needed to be eradicated after the war, Shirer suggested, if the Allies didn't want to risk having to take up arms again, sooner rather than later. He followed up these words with deeds. Even before the end of the war, Shirer joined the board of directors of the Society for the Prevention of World War III, whose aim was to rule out once and for all the possibility of a military threat emanating from Germany.

Shirer's characteristic pessimism was related to his view of history. He identified a continuity running through German history that had culminated in Hitler's assumption of power. A tendency towards violence had been present as far back as Martin Luther, who had been a greater influence on Germans than just about any other historical figure, Shirer argued in *The Rise and Fall of the Third Reich*. Along with his positive, revolutionary qualities, the father of the Reformation had been crude, vicious, fanatic, intolerant and violent. Here Shirer followed a line of thought advanced by Thomas Mann in a speech to the Library of Congress in Washington on 29th May 1945, which his daughter Erika had translated into English as "Germany and the Germans". In it the Nobel laureate had said: "The specifically Lutheran, the choleric coarseness, the invective, the fuming and raging, the extravagant rudeness coupled with tender depth of feeling and with the most clumsy superstition and belief in demons, incubi, and changelings, arouses my instinctive antipathy." Mann also pointed out that Luther had supported the idea of putting down the peasants, whose only wish was to be free, like "mad dogs". In contrast to the religious freedom of Christians deep down in their souls, Luther hadn't cared at all about the political freedoms of citizens of the state. Luther's "anti-political servility", his devotion to St Paul's admonition "Let every soul be subject unto the higher powers", Thomas Mann argued, had helped inspire centuries of German subservience.[16]

Shirer added that Georg Wilhelm Friedrich Hegel had been the one to elevate the state into the highest expression of human life, extending Luther's demand for political servility. In Shirer's reading of Hegel, the state enjoyed priority over the individual, whose highest purpose was to be a loyal citizen. War was a great purifier that would ensure the moral health of peoples that had grown degenerate during long periods of peace. One of the leading and most influential proponents of Prussian militarism, Shirer went on to write, was the historian Heinrich von Treitschke, whose extremely popular lectures at Berlin University were attended by general staff officers and civil servants as well as students. "Treitschke outdoes Hegel in proclaiming war as the highest expression of man. To him 'martial glory is the basis of all the political virtues'... War is not only a practical necessity, it is also a theoretical necessity, an exigency of logic."[17]

Military Resistance on Trial

With his fierce aversion to Prussian militarism, Shirer was very surprised when, on 30th November 1945, he encountered a Wehrmacht general who didn't conform to his ideas at all. The first witness called after the charges had been read out was General Erwin von Lahousen, a close associate of Admiral Wilhelm Canaris, the head of the Abwehr, a military intelligence service responsible for sabotage and other acts of war behind enemy lines. Canaris had opposed Hitler and the Nazi regime from the start and had been arrested in connection with the 20th July 1944 assassination attempt against the Führer. Hitler had personally ordered his execution. A tall man with a thin frame, Lahousen had run the Abwehr's II Division before being captured and becoming a POW. Almost no one in the Nuremberg court, including Shirer, had ever heard of him.

When he was called to the witness stand and began to testify about his covert activities, the British and Russians in attendance were shocked to learn that a special Luftwaffe squadron had flown high-altitude surveillance missions over London and Leningrad even before the start of the war.

Lahousen, who was born Austrian, was one of the main prosecution witnesses, and much to their astonishment he had played a dual role in the Abwehr for years. He was being housed in a villa alongside other witnesses, and his hostess, Countess Kálnocky, had immediately noticed that he was different from them. "He kept apart from the others and seemed lost in thought," she would write in her memoirs.[18] Lahousen was a broken man, wracked by injuries suffered in the two world wars. His fellow residents in the witness house, who included several generals, were struck by his fragile nerves. Once, when the aria "Ombra mai fu" from Handel's opera *Xerxes* was playing on the gramophone in the living room, he suddenly burst into tears. The opera was one of his favourite pieces of music, he told the Countess, and he hadn't heard it in months.

Erwin Lahousen Edler von Vivremont, as was his full name, was one of the few people active in the German Resistance who had escaped Hitler's deadly wrath—despite playing a main role in planning the March 1943 attempt to assassinate Hitler using a bomb, which had failed for mechanical reasons. Lahousen had smuggled a silent English detonator and explosives into the main headquarters of Army Group Centre in Smolensk. They were brought aboard Hitler's airplane, but once it was airborne the bomb failed to go off because the detonator malfunctioned due to the cold of the cargo hold. Lahousen only survived because he had been reassigned to the forces fighting on the Eastern Front, where he was badly wounded. When the Gestapo discovered a secret diary kept by Canaris, the ringleader of the Resistance group, in April 1945, he and his followers were executed in horrific fashion. At the time, Lahousen was lying seriously injured in a hospital bed. He was the only one of the Abwehr conspirators who survived.

In Nuremberg, Lahousen continued to demonstrate loyalty to Canaris, whom he idealized. By contrast he loathed the defendants in the dock. "I have to testify for everyone they murdered—I'm the only survivor," he said. During his military service he represented Canaris at meetings with Hitler, Keitel and Ribbentrop. He was thus very much in the know, and in court he didn't mince words when discrediting the lies of Nazi propaganda. Poland's alleged attack on a German radio station, which had unleashed the war? A staged pretence. Lahousen provided numbers, facts and names on the mass executions of Russian POWs, the liquidation of the Polish intelligentsia, the intentional bombardment of Warsaw, and Keitel's order to murder two French generals. Prosecutors could hardly believe their luck.

Like many other observers of the trial, Shirer was struck by the impression Lahousen made, which he considered utterly unlike that of the defendants: "He was a curious figure under the glaring Klieg lights, which made the top of his shiny head look as though it were a part of his shiny perspiring face. And yet there was something sensitive in it, a quality of honesty, of integrity, of just plain human decency that attracted your attention, I suppose, because you suddenly realized that these very things, so common in more normal lands that you scarcely noticed them, were totally absent from the faces of those who had ruled the Third Reich and who now sat uneasily in the dock... Göring, Ribbentrop, and Keitel glared angrily at the witness as he took the stand, and there were moments when you felt that if they could be granted one wish before they died it would be to wring the neck of this courageous Austrian until he was dead. However, their bearing did not intimidate him. He quickly showed that his contempt for them knew no bounds."[19]

Shirer admired the Wehrmacht general's courage in getting up in front of the world to point the finger at the Nazi leaders for the horror they had visited upon others. In his earlier days as a correspondent Shirer had gone to Nuremberg to report on Nazi Party events, and he saw the city as a particularly pregnant symbol of German militarism. He wrote in his autobiography about one such event, a mass march full of military ritual: "It occurred to me that German militarism, of which we in the outside world had heard so much, was not just a product of spartan Prussia and the Hohenzollerns... It was something deeply ingrained in these people, and, obviously, it had not died with the lost war 1914–1918."[20] But in Nuremberg, a Wehrmacht general showed him that one man could in fact preserve his sense of decency and moral responsibility in Hitler's Germany.

Shirer as Cassandra

On 10th December 1945, Shirer left Nuremberg. Later he would remark that, above all, he owed his knowledge of Hitler's diabolic "final solution to the Jewish question" to the Nuremberg Trial. He also self-critically admitted that he had never imagined the extent of the genocide in his time as a correspondent.[21] In 1945 he wrote in his journal that there had to be less ugly, brutal and awful things he could concentrate on during his remaining years. It was bitterly ironic that he owed his fame and wealth to his expertise in Germany and Germans.

Shortly after his return to the USA, personal conflicts and political differences led to him being fired from CBS. Stereotyped as a Communist sympathizer, he withdrew to his farm in Connecticut to devote himself to his books. Politically, his development was the opposite of that of Dos Passos, his former fellow resident in Schloss Faber-Castell. Whereas the latter became a proponent of McCarthyism, Shirer felt he had fallen victim to that ideology. He never forgave Dos Passos for his anti-Communism and support for McCarthy.[22] Shirer never viewed the Soviets as enemies.[23] In the press camp he quickly discovered that he had a lot in common with his Russian colleagues, whom he characterized as cultivated, intelligent, well informed and likeable.

Shirer's main subject matter would remain the country in which he had lived for those pivotal years as a reporter. His novel *The Traitor* was semi-autobiographical, featuring an American correspondent in Berlin as a protagonist. His roman-à-clef *Stranger Come Home* went even further in this direction and had the hero battle against McCarthyism. Shirer's fiction was a failure—his success, financial and otherwise, would only come when he transformed himself from a journalist to a popular historian. He wrote a series of non-fictional works, including books about the sinking of the warship *Bismarck*, Gandhi and Leo and Sofia Tolstoy, as well as three volumes of memoirs. But his biggest triumph was the 1,000-plus-page *The Rise and Fall of the Third Reich*, published in 1960, which sold more copies than any work of history ever in the USA. It won the National Book Award, topped bestseller lists for months, was translated into scores of languages and afforded Shirer, who was in debt after being fired from CBS, a comfortable life.

The book was not without its critics. Academic historians complained that Shirer had neglected major studies on the topic, largely ignored the political opposition to Hitler within Germany and depicted the connections between German philosophical and historical tradition and National Socialism as greater, more direct and simpler than they had been in reality.[24] The book's reception in Germany was especially problematic. When the German translation appeared in 1961, promptly achieving huge sales, the German press tar-brushed it as anti-German. There were even reported attempts to ban its publication by court injunction,[25] and none other than West German Chancellor Konrad Adenauer was said to have lashed out against it in interviews and conversations with influential Americans. According to Shirer, on a visit to New York Adenauer invited the publisher of *Look* magazine, Mike Cowles, to his hotel and railed against him for printing excerpts from *Rise and Fall* as well as Shirer's article "If Hitler Had Won World War II". When Cowles said that he was prepared to run a rebuttal if Adenauer could prove to him that Shirer's claims were untrue, Adenauer allegedly responded: "Mr. Cowles, you do not get the point. The point is not whether it's truthful or not. The point is that it is turning out to be extremely harmful to German–American relations. It is stirring up in America hatred of the Germans. Mr. Shirer is a German-hater, a *Deutschhasser*! You must not publish any more of his trash."[26]

Shirer recounted this scene with obvious pride in his autobiography, and his agenda was obvious. Ahead of the publication of *Rise and Fall* he had sought to ratchet up American anxiety about a revived, aggressive Germany, which, of course, also helped him market his book. To the end of his days Shirer cultivated his image as a Cassandra warning against the German peril. In his later works he relegated positive counter-examples like General Lahousen in *Berliner Tagebuch (Berlin Journal)* to the absolute margins. But on the other hand, there is no denying that the West German government in Bonn did indeed launch a press campaign against *Rise and Fall* and had a twenty-four-page compendium of negative reviews drawn up.[27]

Shirer continued to write with a sharp, hostile analytical eye about Germany until he died in 1993. In 1985 he travelled back to the west of the country in which he had resided for so long to cover a state visit by Ronald Reagan. Shirer was scandalized at the US President laying a wreath in the veterans' section of a cemetery in Bitburg, where SS men as well as regular soldiers were buried. He interpreted the gesture as the result of a German campaign to rehabilitate the Nazi organization. "I left Berlin that bright spring of 1985 in a state of deep depression," Shirer wrote in his autobiography. "I felt worse, I believe, than that snowy December day in 1940, forty-five years before when I departed from Nazi Germany for the last time… It was not as individuals but as a people that I had my doubts and fears about them. Goethe, a great German and a great poet, had this feeling too. As my plane for Paris took off and we flew over the divided city with the abominable wall separating East and West and as I glanced down for what I was sure was the last time at Berlin, Goethe's words came back to me and seemed near to my own thoughts: I have often felt a bitter sorrow at the thought of the German people, which is so estimable in the individual and so wretched in the generality."[28]

Three years later, a rhetorically unfortunate speech by the President of the German Bundestag, Philipp Jenninger, to mark the fiftieth anniversary of the Night of Broken Glass pogroms gave Shirer yet another example of why all other people should remain extremely critical of Germans.[29]

VII

Alfred Döblin's Didactic Deception: The Phantom Resident of Schloss Faber-Castell

"The newspapers go completely crazy sometimes."
ERNEST CECIL DEANE, LETTER TO HIS WIFE, LOIS, ON 9TH APRIL 1946

A mong other things, the Nuremberg Trial saw a proliferation of what we would today call fake news. In April 1946, *Stars and Stripes* published an article whose headline falsely suggested that Soviet prosecutor Roman Rudenko had shot Hermann Göring in the courtroom. It was based on a rumour that Göring had insulted Stalin in front of the court, whereupon Rudenko became so incensed he killed him. This "news" was passed on by several press agencies. And that was only one extreme example of the false, often purposely misleading information given to the reading public. Some misinformation was spread at the behest of the political leadership. The Soviet media, for instance, reported that the Germans had been guilty of the Katyn massacre. Meanwhile, journalists sometimes unwittingly passed on untruths, and mistakes were adopted, amplified and embellished. The American tabloid press had particularly

141

few scruples, often simply making things up. "Americans and British troops battle Germans" read one headline, which was as sensationalist as it was false. Another newspaper wrongly reported that Göring had died of a heart attack in an American military hospital. Some journalists invented stories to bolster their reputation. As we have seen, one US reporter claimed to have run into Hemingway, Steinbeck and Dos Passos in the press-camp bathroom. This was a relatively harmless bit of deception. But others told lies to discredit political opponents. The French Stalinist Elsa Triolet, for instance, once completely fabricated witness testimony in a piece for her Communist audience.

In the case of Alfred Döblin, deception was used to a specific end. A doctor of psychiatry, Döblin didn't produce an article, a report or a monograph, but rather a thirty-three-page didactic pamphlet called *Der Nürnberger Lehrprozess* (*The Educational Nuremberg Trial*). Written in German and aimed specifically at a German audience, it came replete with ten full-page photos of the trial's famous defendants and was published in February 1946 with an initial run of 200,000 copies.[1] This was a text explicitly conceived to reach and re-educate the masses, and Döblin was willing to play a bit fast and loose with the truth in the interest of augmenting his narrative's effect. Indeed, he considered an act of deception crucial to achieving his goal.

At the time of the Nuremberg Trial, Döblin was an officer in the French Ministry of Education working for the French occupation authorities in Baden-Baden. A Jew and a socialist who had suffered greatly under the Nazis and lost family members in Auschwitz, he was one of the first German authors to come back from exile to Germany. After his return he was made responsible for censoring manuscripts submitted for publication. He also worked for the monthly literary magazine *Das goldene Tor* (*The Golden Gate*) and wrote for the *Neue Zeitung* and the Südwestrundfunk radio station, where he enjoyed considerable artistic and moral authority. Naturally, he took a keen interest in the Nuremberg Trial, the biggest media event of the day. "I saw, heard and read a lot," he recalled. "I was often repulsed and disgusted. But I felt worse when I saw the poverty and hunger. You had to gather well-meaning people around you. For starters, I decided to write a short, readable pamphlet I called 'The Educational Nuremberg Trial'. Yes, the idea was that the Nuremberg trial, which was publicly going on at the time, would teach those people something."[2]

The pamphlet took in both the general lessons of the Nuremberg Trial and the lessons Döblin himself wished to impart. In reporting on the trial he hoped to kick-start a process of re-education, and the project was designed to push its readers in that direction. The pamphlet was published under a good old-fashioned German-sounding name, "Hans Fiedeler", that gave no hint of being a pseudonym. Indeed, it would take until 1968 for the text to be attributed to Döblin. And it was written to give the impression that the author had personally attended the trial.[3] "As sombre and grey as judges appear," Döblin, for instance, wrote, "just as business-like are the proceedings, and just as quietly and unemotionally do the judges speak."[4] In fact Döblin wasn't even present in Nuremberg during the trial. We don't know why he chose not to travel there as other reporters did. Perhaps he considered it his duty to write the pamphlet but shied away from seeing the defendants directly. In any case, he didn't hold what he had written in very high regard, noting in his diary on 13th December 1945 that he had "fumbled his way to the end" of the text.

Döblin sometimes took a likewise freewheeling approach in quoting others. The pamphlet opens by citing Tacitus— "Voluntary slaves make more tyrants than tyrants make slaves"— but those words aren't to be found in any of the Roman historian's works. Döblin may well have intentionally put them in Tacitus' mouth because the latter was held in such high regard under National Socialism, which often cited his *Germania* to support the Nazi cult of the Germanic tribes. Indeed, for some Nazi readers *Germania* had been a kind of racist Bible. Yet Tacitus, who praised the Germanic tribes—in contrast to the decadent Romans—for their courage, honesty and simplicity, also identified a latent Germanic tendency towards servility. This could be how Döblin wanted people to read his false quotation about slaves creating tyrants. Perhaps it was his attempt to discredit racist Nazi propaganda using its own logic—and the very man German racial supremacists invoked to support their dreams of superiority. In fact, the quotation was not from Tacitus but from one of the fathers of the French Revolution, Count Honoré Gabriel Riqueti de Mirabeau.

Döblin may have had good reasons for his minor deception with Tacitus, but why did he feel it necessary to publish the pamphlet under an assumed name? The author of the Weimar Republic novel *Berlin Alexanderplatz*, with its innovative, Dos Passos-like montage technique, Döblin had been forced to flee Germany with his family for Switzerland in 1933. He later went to France and, when Germany invaded that country, to the USA. His pseudonym was unmistakably German, and the pamphlet was written from the ostensible point of view of someone who,

unlike himself, had remained in Germany during the Third
Reich. Döblin probably felt that his real name would have elic-
ited hostility in some readers, and he was determined not to be
seen as a know-it-all passing judgment on those who had stayed
in their home country. At the very start of the pamphlet he
addressed "those who have spent the last decade in Germany"
and who were confronting the extraordinary spectacle of "what
used to be most powerful names" in the country sitting like
common criminals in the court dock. Döblin was careful not to
cast his readers themselves in the role of defendants. Instead,
at the end of the pamphlet, he has an emblematic figurehead,
an anonymous "remorseful man", say: "They subjugated us and
drove us to do horrific things so that shame will rest upon us for
a long time to come." Such well-meaning people of conscience
were the target audience Döblin wished to address.

Educational Theatre Versus Nazi Theatre

The use of the word "we" in Döblin's pamphlet refers to "Hans
Fiedeler" as a member of the German people, and both are put
in the role of spectators at the "grand theatre" of the Nuremberg
courtroom. The first part of the "drama", a kind of exposition,
sets the scene and introduces the accusers—not the Allied prosecutors, but the millions of dead killed because of the Nazis. The
criminals in the dock had never imagined that there would be a
second half of the play, one that would be about sin, punishment
and the "restoration of humanity". And the significance of the
theatre metaphor goes beyond the audience's perspective in the
courtroom. The theatre is also a stand-in for the Third Reich,

in which the Nazi "actors" deceived and bewitched the German people with proclamations that they were a master race. "Their trick succeeded," Döblin noted succinctly, drawing a contrast to Shakespeare's *The Taming of the Shrew*, in which a drunken peasant is convinced that he is a wealthy, majestic lord. Nazi rule didn't produce a comedy, Döblin pointed out, but rather a "barbaric orgy of murder and destruction".

The trial in Nuremberg confronted Nazi delusions with reality, something "called morality and reason", which takes the stage and "sits down in the judge's seat". In other words, a morally didactic theatre was depicted as displacing the perverse theatre of twelve years of Nazi megalomania. Döblin, a fierce critic of moral relativism who had converted to Catholicism after a revelation on 30th November 1941, played upon the allegorical richness of Jesuit theatre. He didn't exonerate the former citizens of the Third Reich. He sought to simultaneously motivate, criticize and teach them. He freely acknowledged the defensive, hostile attitude of many Germans towards the Nuremberg Trial. "Why all the talk about justice?" he depicted one disgruntled German muttering under his breath. In another passage, Pastor Martin Niemöller was criticized and dismissed as a German "of yesterday" for patriotically volunteering for the war despite his opposition to the Nazis and his previous imprisonment in a concentration camp. The pamphlet's other motto was a (genuine) quote from the French democratic poet and statesman Alphonse de Lamartine: "Woe to the cowards. Those who have not the courage to embrace their own courage will become terrible!" This was a slap in the face of readers who had opportunistically profited from the Third Reich. Precisely because Germans had so abjectly failed to show courage, Döblin rejected the idea that the trial should have included a German judge, as Willy Brandt and others suggested. The Germans had not taken the opportunity to condemn the criminals, Döblin felt, so now the entire world would resist their post-war claims of the right to do so.

Döblin included an excursus about the history of the Third Reich and a section about the German historical faith in power. The pamphlet ended with the anonymous man of remorse levelling an accusation at his compatriots. This was Döblin's method of suggesting that the trial should be understood as the embodiment of hope for a better future. He was very concerned with ethically legitimating the trial in order to encourage German acknowledgement of the crimes committed and their conversion to democracy—the aforementioned "restoration of humanity". To that end, he contended, the authorities in Nuremberg had erected a "legalistic skyscraper" the like of which had never been seen. *The Educational Nuremberg Trial* was warning, sober analysis and passionate encouragement all rolled into one.

The Long Life of a White Lie

What effect did the pamphlet have? "It seems to me hardly any," Döblin conceded in 1953. Moreover, contrary to the author's intention, the pamphlet's sales depended to an extent on sheer voyeurism, since it contained "images, photos of the main figures on trial".[5] Readers were able to gawk at large-scale pictures of the defendants in their cells and the courtroom. Döblin wasn't entirely innocent of exploiting their sensationalistic value, himself composing the drily cutting descriptions of the photographs. The caption for Göring, for example, read: "Hermann Göring,

Reich Aviation Minister, Reichstag arsonist, architect of the hells
of Buchenwald and Dachau, expert thief, bon vivant and ballet
enthusiast."

Until recently, no one called Döblin's bluff about having been
present in Nuremberg during the trial. His deception was even
backed up by the erroneous attribution to him of a signature
at Schloss Faber-Castell. The Faber-Castell company still lists
Döblin on its home page as an observer of the trial and a house
guest, while a number of national newspapers and magazines
have passed on the misinformation that he stayed at the castle.[6]
Theoretically, as a French citizen, Döblin would have.

The issue came to a head in the wake of a 2016 German television documentary, *Der Jahrhundertprozess. Das Nürnberger
Tribunal aus prominenter Sicht* (*The Trial of the Century: The
Nuremberg Tribunal in the Eyes of the Famous*). It featured a
press accreditation, dated 5th March 1946, as well as a court
illustration depicting Döblin wearing headphones, along with
two other observers—seemingly evidence that Döblin did
indeed attend the trial. [7] But the notion was not backed up by
anything in Döblin's well-researched biography. When asked
where Döblin's accreditation had been obtained, the history
editor of the public German broadcaster ZDF, which ran the
documentary, responded that wherever possible original documents had been filmed and that he thought he could recall,
for example, "Markus Wolf's wife providing his accreditation".
But he conceded that this may not always have been possible
and that graphic reconstructions might have been made in
order to "personalize" the story: "They were supposed to serve
primarily as graphic signposts and images that introduced the
protagonists."[8]

Christina Althen, the editor of the critical edition of *The Educational Nuremberg Trial*, was uncomfortable about the uncertainty, particularly since the putative accreditation used by the documentary was featured in Döblin's Wikipedia entry. After further research she found that the photo of Döblin used for the "accreditation" came from the German Historical Museum in Berlin, was taken by the Schirner press photo agency and dated back to 9th July 1947, months after the Nuremberg Trial was over. When Althen confronted the ZDF editor responsible for the documentary with her discovery, he wrote apologetically in an email on 19th May 2021 that unfortunately "mistaken information" had been used. The documentary is no longer accessible in ZDF's media centre, and the broadcaster has expunged all misleading traces of the error from the Internet. Döblin would no doubt never have imagined that his "bumbling" would still be the topic of debate so many years after the fact.

VIII

Janet Flanner and the Cross-Examination of Hermann Göring

"There are two sights in Germany which seem
equally to give dramatic proof that the Allies won
the war. One is the vast spectacle of any ruined
German city, open to the skies, and the other is the
small tableau of the Nazi-filled prisoners' box."

JANET FLANNER

The American journalist Janet Flanner (1892–1978), the
daughter of a Quaker funeral director, escaped from an
unhappy marriage and a middle-class existence she despised
by moving to Europe, eventually settling in Paris in 1922 with
her lover, Solita Solano. She later commented on this decision
with the words: "I wanted beauty with a capital B. I was consumed by my own appetite to consume—in a very limited way,
the beauties of Europe, the long accretions of architecture and
poetry and civilization and education, the beautiful gardens, the
beautiful palaces."[1] Flanner and Solano became part of a wave
of artistic and intellectual émigrés to Paris, and soon they began
writing novels. Flanner had already gained some initial literary

151

experience as a culture columnist in the USA. But although she was later deluged with awards, including membership of the French Legion of Honour in 1947 and the 1966 National Book Award in the USA, she doubted her own abilities and always considered herself a journalist, not a writer.

True to that self-estimation, and despite positive reviews for her 1925 debut autobiographical novel *The Cubicle City*, she soon gave up fiction for journalism, feeling that she lacked the necessary imagination. As a journalist, by contrast, she had more than enough material, although that didn't lower her literary standards in the slightest. Soon she became famous for a mixture of New Objectivity and pointedly humorous conclusions, mood-setting images and fragmentary sentences. Often, she would jump from one topic to another in a single sentence, creating unconventional connections between opposites. In 1925, after founding *The New Yorker*, Harold Ross and Jane Grant hired her to write regular articles from the French capital. In her previous private correspondence with Grant, Flanner had so vividly described European artistic and cultural life that Grant suggested the column to her husband. Published under the androgynous pseudonym Genêt, which Flanner initially thought was French for Janet, her semi-weekly "Letters from Paris" were a constant feature of the magazine for a half century, until 1975.

One reason the column became such an institution was Flanner's ability to deliver, with inimitable flair, a fly-on-the-wall perspective on Old World society. Frequently depicting herself as sitting outside Parisian cafés, cigarette in hand, Flanner commented with American expatriate distance on whatever she saw: everything from politics to haute couture, new music, ballet, Chaplin films and Dadaism and surrealism. It's no exaggeration to say that Flanner's columns helped establish the genre of essayistic journalism.

Flanner resided with Solana in a *pension* in rue Bonaparte in the bohemian epicentre of the French capital. She actively participated in much of what she wrote about and was friends with many important cultural figures, including Gertrude Stein, Ernest Hemingway, Alice B. Toklas and Djuna Barnes. She was also part of a group of bold, independent, highly educated women—painters, poets, publishers, journalists, photographers and patrons of the arts—who had sworn to defy social convention. Among Flanner's lovers were the beautiful singer Noël Murphy and Oscar Wilde's extravagant niece Dolly. She and Solano, with whom she had an open relationship, were immortalized as Nip and Tuck in Djuna Barnes's travel guide to lesbian Paris, *Ladies Almanack*.

"As American women in French society, they enjoyed the best of both worlds," writes Flanner's biographer, Brenda Wineapple, of this glamorous circle of women in 1920s Paris. "At home they felt they were living a shadow life—ignored, censured, condescended to or despised because of their sexual preference; here they were suddenly a minority of a different kind: they were American women abroad. That they lived together, worked together, were openly sexual with one another was no longer the concern of friend or family."[2] This unusual clique was known as the "the women of the Left Bank", who sought to quench their thirst for a life without constraints by writing, partying, debating and constantly swapping partners.

Flanner and her friends didn't know what was eventually in store for them when they arrived in Europe. Their life of liberation ended in 1929 with the start of the Great Depression and the rise of fascist movements throughout the continent. Very much in the spirit of the Roaring Twenties, Flanner bemoaned the change of times by describing how pretty women now had to pay for their own cocktails at the luxurious bar in the Ritz Hotel, a favourite expatriate haunt. With similar frivolity she referred to the US stock market crash as "the recent unpleasantness on Wall Street".[3] But the following year, as France started building the defensive Maginot Line along its German border in fear of being invaded by its neighbour, the dark clouds became impossible to ignore.

Flanner wanted to expand her perspective and get a view from the ground, so in 1931 she travelled to Berlin. She titled the laconic but pointed column that resulted "Uber alles". But she also marvelled at the culture and nightlife of the still-lively, multicultural German capital, which radiated freedom and "Semitic chic". Flanner wrote: "Though perhaps otherwise unemployed, the Berliners are busy making a new race. It may be that the fat-necked pre-war German was killed in the war and the fat wife who matched him died of grief. In any case, they have disappeared from the capital city. They are only seen in cartoons there."[4]

Along with many others, Flanner began to realize just how serious a threat the Nazis posed to the world. Nonetheless, her snobbish 1936 portrait of Hitler was a largely anecdotal piece of writing, devoted to his culinary tastes, provincial manners and celibacy. Flanner's "Führer" was more laughable than frightening. "Adolf was born in the Austrian border village of Braunau-am-Inn on April 20th, 1889 in a house, now a cheap hotel preposterously pink-plastered" was how she described the start of his life.[5] Retrospectively she justified her inability to appreciate the terrors to come by claiming that her situation first became worrisome in the mid-1930s. The transition was too gradual for most people to notice, and no one had predicted such a dramatic explosion of horror.[6] But by the autumn of 1939, when her "Letter from Paris" was censored, Flanner knew the time had come for her to leave France. She departed the French capital on 16th September and arrived via Bordeaux in the safe haven of New York amid an exodus of former expats in early October. By the time German troops occupied Paris in December 1940, the community of women from the Left Bank had ceased to exist.

Flanner didn't feel at home in New York. The central pillars of her existence were gone: the intellectual playground that was the French capital, her letters, her work routine and her friends. She was alienated by most Americans' view of Europe as somewhere hopelessly exotic. Conversely, she increasingly found her homeland confining, philistine, materialistic and largely uneducated. During the Second World War, she lived with Natalia Murray from Rome and worked for *The New Yorker*. She gave lectures, wrote a portrait of Thomas Mann and supported Klaus Mann by contributing to his newly founded magazine for German exiles. In the months following the liberation of Paris in August 1944, she made a series of radio programmes titled "Listen: The Women" for the Blue Network, the forerunner of American broadcaster ABC.

Official War Correspondent

When Flanner returned to Europe on board a US military aircraft to take up her work as an official war correspondent, she was not the same person she had once been. Her journalistic style, too, had changed. No longer was she an all-knowing, self-confident, ironic writer contemptuous of convention and immune to being shocked. Flanner's reporting on the Second World War was truthful, unsparing and genuinely affectionate towards Parisians, whom she had lightly mocked in the past.

Her first destination was liberated Paris, which she reached in the middle of winter 1944–45 after a stop in London. She hardly recognized the now-emaciated, traumatized and mistrustful French. With a veritable hunt for collaborators with the Nazi-sponsored Vichy regime under way, Paris was no longer the delightful city she remembered. It was restless, nervous and bitter. Ever the sensitive aesthete, Flanner chose to reside in an international press camp in Hôtel Scribe together with other correspondents, including Hemingway and Shirer, the latter of whom she would re-encounter in Nuremberg. The hotel at least offered a warm bath every morning between eight and ten— reason enough to stay there for a while. Little did she know that she would soon be quartered in a press camp in Germany where even a short walk to a sink entailed fierce competition.

After trips to Lyons, La Rochelle and the liberated Rhineland, where she was revolted by what she perceived as Cologne residents' inability "to think rationally or to tell the truth", she returned to Paris, where she batted about and quickly discarded ideas for portraits and features.[7] On 16th April 1945 she visited the Buchenwald concentration camp, which, as she wrote to Solano, was beyond her comprehension. She would publish no report on that trip.

Ahead of Christmas 1945 she travelled to Munich, where she intended to write a column for *The New Yorker*. But Nuremberg beckoned, and on 13th December she set out from the Bavarian capital to take in the afternoon court session. She left Nuremberg the following day after the morning session, but her short stay became the basis for her 17th December "Letter from Nuremberg" in *The New Yorker*. She presented a panorama of the city, from the sea of ruins in the old town to the defendants, prosecutors and judges to the reports in the *Nürnberger Nachrichten* and the daily proceedings inside the courtroom. Among the many facets of her report, Flanner described the court being shown film footage and photos of German soldiers in the Warsaw ghetto that documented members of the Wehrmacht behaving with sadistic brutality. An officer, for instance, helped an emaciated Jewish woman lying on the pavement to her feet, only to knock her back to the ground again. The footage, which had been damaged in a fire, also showed "naked Jews, male and female, moving with a floating unearthly slowness and a nightmare-like dignity among the clubs and kicks of the laughing German soldiers".[8]

She also told her lover, Natalia Murray, what she had seen, using the trial as an occasion to criticize men and male egotism. Like the Argentinian writer Victoria Ocampo, Flanner found the Nuremberg Trial far too male-dominated. Having already likened Germany to "a big male that has been finally knocked down, his ugly face bleeding while he whines", she turned her ire towards her compatriots. "At the Nuremberg trial where I went for an afternoon and next morning session, I thought of you and the Pétain trial," she wrote to Murray. "This trial is also important, and is also weakened by the tiresome egotism of individual professional men, so far among the Americans, who want to drag out their time in court and make personal, cheap history by their talkativeness."[9]

In late February 1946, shortly before her fifty-fourth birthday, Harold Ross made Flanner *The New Yorker*'s dedicated
correspondent at the trial. Ernest Cecil Deane, an avid reader
of the magazine, was thrilled when he learned that the woman
behind Genêt would be joining his charges. On 5th March he
wrote to his wife: "By the way, Janet Flanner, a *New Yorker*
correspondent, is now in the camp. She's a little grey-haired old
lady, full of spirit, and a damn good writer... She was surprised
when I told her that people in Arkansas liked the magazine."
But Deane's elation would be short-lived. Before long, Flanner
would be one of several female thorns in his side.

The contrast between the press camp and the Hôtel Scribe
couldn't have been greater. Thirty women were lodged in Schloss
Faber-Castell's villa, and Flanner was outraged at the miserable
inadequacy of their single bathroom. Those who ran the facility
under Deane had provided them with one bathtub and two urinals, then complained that the women were being difficult. If you
give them urinals, you must really find them difficult, Flanner was
alleged to have sniped when she, Erika and Betty Knox protested
to Deane on 17th March. She was also dismayed by the Russian
residents who visited the facilities half a dozen at a time and left
behind a "pigsty". Flanner humorously attributed this to the East–
West divide in the camp. "We Democrats have no chance against
them: we want to go in one by one and be alone. The Russians
seem to love functioning even with plumbing in community
groups." The only positive was the presence of a refugee masseuse
from the Czech spa town of Karlovy Vary who lived in Stein. "She
has helped my sciatica somewhat," remarked Flanner.[10]

Flanner's scabrous sense of humour amused her colleagues.
One morning, she shocked her breakfast table by asking the

women there which of the accused they would choose to sleep with if they were forced to pick one.[11] The defendants were a favourite topic of conversation, and Flanner was particularly fascinating by Hermann Göring, not sexually, but because of his personal contradictions and bearing. As soon as Flanner entered the courtroom her eyes were immediately drawn to the former Reich Marshal, the man she called "Prisoner Number 1".

Göring's Questioning

When Hermann Göring was captured by US soldiers at the end of the Second World War, he immediately demanded to see General Eisenhower—thinking that the Americans would accept him as a representative of Germany. He was subsequently allowed to hold a press conference, but otherwise he was left disappointed. Eisenhower had no intention of meeting him. In fact, the military governor of the US occupation zone considered him a war criminal and nothing more. Soon Göring found himself back in a cell in Nuremberg, where the only leadership role to which he could aspire was over his fellow defendants.

Shortly after he was taken into custody, doctors ordered that he undergo detoxification. Göring had a habit of taking twenty pills of the opiate Paracodeine every morning and evening, a dosage that was now reduced to a medically responsible level. At the same time, physicians put him on a strict diet to combat his morbid obesity. By the time the Nuremberg Trial started he was in decent physical shape, and many people found him livelier and sharper than he had been for years. Most of his fellow defendants accepted him as their superior, although a few, including Schacht and Papen, sought to ignore him completely. The Allies certainly saw him as their highest-ranking prisoner, as was indicated by his seat, the first one in the first row of the dock. There he sat in his faded Luftwaffe uniform, surveying the courtroom, with his right elbow leaning on the low balustrade while he jotted down notes.

Ever power-hungry and vain, Göring tried to wield the sort of influence he had possessed during the Third Reich over his fellow accused, whom he instructed to follow his line of defence. They were not to toe the Nazi line and treat the proceedings as a "political trial by the victors". Joint meals gave him an opportunity to issue orders, motivate his followers and punish rebels with expressions of contempt. He did this so brazenly that the prison warden eventually ordered him to be kept apart from his fellow defendants.

Göring was both a good actor and a good manipulator, rhetorically gifted and quick-witted. He carefully followed every word said in the court, responding with quarrelsome intensity and scribbling notes for his lawyer when not in the witness stand himself. To a large measure, he assumed responsibility for his own defence. He made no bones about having used brutal violence, having been involved in the Gestapo or having helped to rearm Germany. For him, the trial was not about Germany's former political leadership, but the entire country. He also disputed the tribunal's legitimacy, arguing that many accusations levelled at him were domestic policy matters and thus not subject to international sanction. He also generally justified his actions as expressions of patriotism and loyalty to Hitler. "If I cannot convince the court, I shall at least convince the German people that all I did was done for the Greater German Reich," he had told interrogator and psychologist Major Douglas M. Kelley on 12th August 1945.[12]

Göring argued that the question of German guilt could not be resolved by making an example of the Nazi leadership. That issue remained open, he claimed in his final words to the court, proposing that the German people would someday find a saviour and seek revenge: "Who knows but that in this very hour the man is born who will unite my people—born of our flesh and bones, to avenge the humiliation we suffer now."[13] Others, chiefly Himmler and Bormann, had been responsible for the atrocities and "racial persecution" committed during the Third Reich. Despite having appointed Reinhard Heydrich in July 1941 to find a "final solution to the Jewish question", he disputed that either he or Hitler had known about the "mass murders" carried out by the SS, who took the words "final solution" entirely literally. With breathtaking cynicism, he also declared that epochal historical events had always been always accompanied by great crimes.

Many observers found Göring incorrigible, insouciant, even cavalier. But his "courage" was as much the product of his intelligence as of any personal bravery. Göring knew that his fate was sealed. He had nothing left to lose. His leadership role in the Third Reich was all too obvious. And he didn't want to go down in history as a coward. In his memoirs, Göring's fellow defendant Albert Speer wrote: "I had a certain insight into Göring's real motives when he observed that the victors would undoubtedly kill him but that within fifty years his remains would be laid in a marble sarcophagus and he would be celebrated by the German people as a national hero and martyr. Many of the prisoners had the same dream about themselves. On other subjects Göring's arguments were less effective. There were no differences among us, he said; we were all sentenced to death from the start and none of us had a chance. It was pointless to bother about a defense. I remarked: 'Göring wants to ride into Valhalla with a large retinue.' In actuality, Göring later defended himself more stubbornly than the rest of us did."[14]

The long-awaited cross-examination of Göring began on 18th March 1946, with Jackson, who had won international acclaim for his opening speech, insisting on leading the questioning himself. It was a direct face-off between the trial's two leading protagonists. But the cross-examination of the highest-ranking defendant didn't go to plan for the US chief counsel, who suffered from atypical lapses in concentration, was poorly prepared, misunderstood one of the documents and allowed Göring to get under his skin. When he once tried to surprise the defendant with a compromising statement, Göring demanded to be shown the entire document and managed to find another passage that partially undercut Jackson's argument.

Göring cleverly brought up obvious contradictions and examples of negative actions in Anglo–American history. For instance, when Jackson questioned him about Germany's mobilization for war, stressing that it had been kept absolutely secret from other countries, Göring shot back, "I do not believe I can recall the publication of the preparations of the United States for mobilization." Jackson never got a handle on Göring's sarcastic, unrepentant posturing and calculated nit-picking. At the high point of the cross-examination he tossed his headphones down on the table in aggravation, repeatedly asking the court to call the defendant to order, which was generally seen as a sign of weakness.

The two men's verbal jousting was a media spectacle, and numerous correspondents came to Nuremberg especially to cover it. Many observers felt that Jackson had underestimated his adversary and ultimately lost the battle. Conversely, Göring earned respect even from lawyers in attendance. British judge Norman Birkett, for instance, believed Göring had made a positive impression as intelligent, quick-witted and imaginative. Meanwhile, Boris Polevoy, who was required to submit his reports to Soviet censors for approval, wrote that this "archvillain" was a commanding personality, if "admittedly in the sense of the repulsive, inhuman system National Socialism represented".

Janet Flanner went beyond merely expressing respect, lending Göring—the man Birkett called one of "the last important surviving protagonists of evil"—an aura of demonic genius. In her "Letter from Nuremberg, 15th March 1946", she wrote of the intellectual she and others had witnessed in the courtroom: "What he offered his judges was no *mea culpa* but a dissertation on the technique of power. On the witness stand, he didn't wait to be asked questions by the Allied prosecution; he told them the German answers first. The Reichsmarschall made Machiavelli's Prince look like a dull apologist: Göring was decidedly more amoral, and funnier."[15]

Quoting an alleged remark by an unnamed British lawyer, Flanner stylized Jackson and Göring's confrontation into a pseudo-cinematic "duel to the death", a showdown between good and evil, between the civilized world and a brilliant demon, which could only be won after the fiercest of battles. She outdid all her colleagues in her words of praise for the latter, comparing Göring to a "gladiator who has just won his fight". Flanner

added: "He even won it noisily, which added to the blaring
triumphal note… He displayed… a phenomenal memory and
a remarkable gift for casuistic maneuver, and he was naturally
more knowledgeable about Nazi and other European history."
He also showed a "diabolical skill" in citing embarrassing prec-
edents from Anglo–American history and possessed a "fantastic
and formidable personality".

As much as Flanner built Göring up, she tore Jackson down.
While acknowledging the "high humanitarianism which marked
his fine opening address in November", she depicted Jackson as
a man completely out of his depth: "Even physically, Jackson cut
a poor figure. He unbuttoned his coat, whisked it back over his
hips, and with his hands in his back pockets. Spraddled and tee-
teed [sic] like a country lawyer. Not only did he seem to lack the
background and wisdom of our Justice [Oliver Wendell] Holmes
tradition, but his prepared European foreground was full of
holes, which he fell into en route to setting traps for Göring."
Ultimately, Flanner concluded, "there had been no 'battle of
ideas' because Jackson seemed not to be able to think of any".[16]

Fateful Anti-Americanism

The editorial bosses at *The New Yorker* were less than thrilled
by Flanner's depiction of events. Not only had she criticized
Jackson, a national hero, and glorified the highest-ranking Nazi
on trial in one fell swoop. She had also portrayed the entire
American prosecutorial staff as naive and inferior to their counterparts. "On the whole, the American team has consisted of
simple Davids sent in against the Nazi Goliaths on faith rather

than with equipment—Davids entitled, symbolically, to their small stature because their cause was great." The European prosecutors, in Flanner's opinion, had done a far better job. "The Russian Chief Prosecutor, Roman Andreyevich Rudenko and the British Chief Prosecutor, Sir David Maxwell Fyfe, had to be sent in as cross-examiners to master Göring," she claimed. It was thanks to them that the prosecution had obtained a first confession. "Perhaps the American domination of the court will from now on decline," Flanner speculated.[17]

This was hard for American readers to swallow. When Harold Ross originally hired her in the 1920s, he famously instructed her to report what the French thought, not what she thought about France, and he occasionally took Flanner to task for sounding "like a damned columnist… of which we have enough in the newspapers, and ours is a magazine founded for REPORTING".[18] Ross's target audience consisted of urbane, educated members of the upper class or people who aspired to be, whom he felt could make up their minds on their own. Flanner's job was to entertain, inform and keep them happy, not to change their political views. Flanner had always used her style—ironic, dry, witty, pointed and occasionally venomous—to express her own opinions, but now she was explicitly presenting her own evaluation of how the trial was proceeding. The graveness of what was being adjudicated in Nuremberg had changed the way she wrote. Her letters from the trial passed judgment and critically commented upon what she experienced, thereby violating Ross's initial orders.

Flanner did receive some positive response to her "Letters from Nuremberg", but all in all her criticism of America rubbed up urban elites in the USA the wrong way. And her criticism of the ostensible naivete of her compatriots and her opinion that the Europeans were doing a better job would have consequences, as Ross decided to reassign her.[19] That caused serious resentment, in part because he justified the move by citing her constant complaining about the press camp. Flanner was insulted and departed Nuremberg in a huff on 5th April, claiming she was going on a research trip to Cracow.

Ross replaced her with the grand dame of British journalism, Rebecca West, who arrived in Nuremberg in the summer of 1946. Much to the delight of patriotic American readers of *The New Yorker*, she immediately set about correcting Flanner's depiction of the trial. Always a fan of drastic words, West dismissed the Russian cross-examination of Göring as "childish", although she hadn't actually witnessed any of it in person. Gone was Flanner's intellectually brilliant and Machiavellian Göring. Whereas Flanner elevated Göring into a pantomime demon, West treated him as a joke. Her reports amounted to a verbal evisceration of the former Reich Marshal: "He is, above all things, soft. He wears either a German air-force uniform or a light beach suit in the worst of playful taste, and both hang loosely on him, giving him an air of pregnancy. He has thick brown young hair, the coarse, bright skin of an actor who has used grease paint for decades, and the preternaturally deep wrinkles of the drug addict; it adds up to something like the head of a ventriloquist's dummy."[20] In her 26th October report for *The New Yorker* on the sentencing of the defendants she called Göring, who had just committed suicide, an "enormous clown". She was also not above mocking him as effeminate: "It is a matter of history that Göring's love affairs with women played a decisive part in the development of the Nazi Party at various stages, but he looks as one who would never lift a hand to a woman save in something much more peculiar than kindness. Nevertheless, he does not look like any recognized type of homosexual."[21] She almost completely eschewed any criticism of the US team—she would soon commence a romantic affair with the lead American judge. By contrast, she adhered to the Anglo-American political line of the day and belittled the Soviets as actors in a transparent show trial no one took seriously. All in all, she turned Flanner's judgments completely on their head.

Flanner had fallen victim to her own love of Europe, her cultural and intellectual identification with the Old rather than the New World, and she immediately vented her spleen, telling Natalia Murray that Americans were "preoccupied with making money, and at their worst merely paid lip service to their heritage, which they did not really understand, being uncultivated and mentally unformed". She didn't want to return to that kind of environment, she added, or live among those kinds of people.[22] She returned to her former home, Paris, despite the depressive, paranoid mood there, and continued to write for *The New Yorker*—despite their quarrels, Ross didn't want to lose his star correspondent in the French capital. Returning to Paris also meant going back to her former lover, Noël Murphy, the successor to Solita Solitano, who had managed to survive the German occupation in trying circumstances on her country estate. From then on, Flanner would shuttle between Paris and New York, Noël and Natalia. This love triangle would continue for decades.

She remained fascinated by Göring and his eccentrically criminal lifestyle—an interest that was only bolstered by the Reich Marshal's spectacular suicide. His death by cyanide pill not only made fools of his prison guards but also allowed him to avoid being executed. With grudging admiration, Flanner saw Göring as the resurrection of an archetype of European cultural history: the amorally cunning, vicious but art-loving Renaissance Prince beloved by Machiavelli.

After coming into contact with the Monuments Men between March and May 1946, Flanner worked on her "Annals of Crime", a series of articles about art and cultural artefacts looted by the Nazis. After an instalment about the art museum Hitler had planned for his home town of Linz, she turned her attention to Göring's art collection, which he had kept largely at his Carinhall estate north of Berlin. She gathered so much material for the article "Collector with Luftwaffe" that she had trouble finishing it and openly admitted her difficulties in mastering everything. It was another instance of her fascination with Göring getting in her way. She later told *The New York Times* that Göring had planned a collection devoted specially to northern German art and that he had possessed excellent taste, particularly for stolen Cranachs. In 1948, when she reported from Königstein on the de-Nazification proceedings of industrialist Fritz Thyssen, who was classed a lesser offender, she devoted part of the article to an anecdote Thyssen had related about a hunting trip with Göring. Göring had sent Thyssen and his forester out to kill deer but, intentionally or not, Thyssen kept missing his prey. Finally the forester shot an animal for him, explaining that "the marshal raged so loudly if guests returned empty-handed".[23]

Flanner didn't usually pass on such anecdotal, entertaining details about Germany. Like many of her colleagues, she didn't believe Germans were learning anything from their recent past. "The Nuremberg Trials put the spotlight on the brilliant foul complexities of the big Nazis' master plans, but the average

German can truthfully state that such remarkable ideas never occurred to him," she wrote in 1947. "The significant Berlin catch-all phrase is 'That was the war, but this is the peace.' The cryptic remark means, in free translation, that the people felt no responsibility for the war, which they regard as an act of history, and that they consider the troubles and confusions of the peace the Allies' fault."[24] But despite Germans' repression and lack of guilty conscience, Flanner never doubted that they were collectively to blame. She always described Allied troops as battling Germany and the Germans, not Hitler or the Nazis, and she made no distinctions between the county and its people.[25]

What separated Flanner from many fellow correspondents in Nuremberg, many of whom also believed in the notion of collective German guilt, was her analysis of the problems of masculinity. A staunch feminist, Flanner believed that the male-dominated world with its attendant militarism—whether in Germany, the Soviet Union or the USA—made it impossible to maintain human rights and legal guarantees for all. In her eyes, Nuremberg was a failure because of the fallacy that the principles of democracy and basic human responsibility upon which the trial was based could be brought about by exclusively male personnel. As a result of this failing, there could be no moral and political new beginning after the Second World War.

But there was no way Flanner could submit such sentiments to Harold Ross. In her private correspondence she complained to Murray about "the slow spread of stupidity, of mass confusion and an instinct only to choose to do the wrong thing, never the right, to complicate all issues under red tape, masculine vanities, jealousies, so that what was meant to be done is lost, stifled, under men's army uniforms, their moustaches, their ridiculous arm patches, like football teams, their drinks, their mistresses, their ambitions, their misconceptions of Europe". Such masculine obstacles gave Flanner a dim view of Europe's future, and she exclaimed in frustration: "I am tired of talking on the male level. I am tired of their levels, which are indeed all flat, some being higher than others, but all platitudinous."[26]

IX

The French Stalinism of Elsa Triolet

"I am Scheherazade, the great teller of stories. I am the muse
and curse of the poet. I am beautiful and I am repulsive."

ELSA TRIOLET

When Elsa Triolet (1896–1970) began reporting on the
Nuremberg Trial in May of 1946, she didn't suspect that
the fame she enjoyed at the time would fade in the not too
distant future. In 1945 she had become the first woman ever
to win France's highest literary honour, the Prix Goncourt—an
astonishing achievement for someone born in Moscow in 1896
as Ella Yuryevna Kagan, who had mastered French as a foreign
language. "Only a short time later, I had enough money to buy
a country house," she would recall. "People began to like my
books. Indeed, they were wild for them. Theatre, cinema, newspapers and magazines were open to me." But despite her literary
reputation and moral credibility as a French Resistance fighter,
Triolet would become an outcast and the target of personal and
political attacks.

Whenever scholars and critics write about Triolet, they always
mention her partner, Louis Aragon (1897–1982). This is not just
down to the male domination of literary history or Triolet being

degraded to an appendage of a famous male author. Aragon was a true living legend. And he and Triolet portrayed their relationship as the latest in a long tradition of symbiotic French literary partnerships: from the patron saints Abelard and Heloise to George Sand and Alfred de Musset to Jean-Paul Sartre and Simone de Beauvoir. The former mill near Paris where they made their home, retreated from the world and chose to be buried bears the words: "And if we rest side by side next to one another, the connectedness of our works will unite us for better and worse in the future that we dreamed and worried so much about. Thus, our united books, black on white, hand in hand, will defy that which would tear us asunder."[1]

Starting in 1964, their works would be published alternatingly over forty-two volumes in the *Oeuvres romanesques croisées*. It was a literary dialogue of monumental size. Aragon's Triolet-inspired love poetry, set to music by famous chansonniers like George Brassens and Leo Ferré, became staples of French national culture. The defiant tone of their epitaph at the mill reflected their life philosophy. When Triolet and Aragon met in 1928, it was a union of two social outsiders. They wed in 1939 and remained inseparable for forty-two years until Aragon's death in 1982. The "lovers of the century", as they were later idealistically known, were soulmates joined by the activity of writing and their love of Russian literature, as well as by their political views and above all by their strength of purpose.

Triolet lifted the sensitive Aragon, a bisexual, out of a deep emotional hole when they met. A few months previously he had tried to commit suicide after unhappily falling in love in Venice. He was part of the literary avant-garde, initially a Dadaist, who later became known with his friend André Breton as a leading surrealist. On the evening of 6th November 1928, he was sitting in the Café La Coupole on Boulevard Montparnasse. "Suddenly, someone called my name," he later recalled. "'The poet Vladimir Mayakovsky asks you to join him'… The next day, at a somewhat later hour, when the café was almost empty, I met Elsa Triolet again. We've never been apart since."[2] Triolet had read Aragon's montage-technique novel *Paris Peasant*, one of the landmarks of French surrealism and a hymn to sensuality and fantasy, and wanted to meet the author. So she seized the chance to make contact with Aragon when her friend Mayakovsky asked her for an introduction.

At this point in her life, Triolet already had one unsuccessful marriage behind her. In 1919 she had wed the French cavalry officer André Triolet, living with him in Tahiti until 1921. But Elsa had intense literary and intellectual interests. Before studying architecture in Moscow, she had been part of a group of formalists around Roman Jakobson and for a time Mayakovsky's lover, and she soon tired of her decidedly unintellectual husband. "You have to be connected to a man by more than just love," she once remarked. After the Triolets separated, Elsa led an unsettled existence between Moscow, where she was a member of the *intelligensiya*, and various European capitals she repeatedly visited to escape the hardships of Soviet life. By that time, her older sister Lilya had replaced her as Mayakovsky's lover and muse, but Elsa remained loyal to the dissolute man she so greatly admired, translating his poems into French and writing a biography of him after his suicide in 1930.

After stays in Berlin, the centre of the Russian diaspora, and London in 1921 and 1922, Triolet settled in Paris, where she became part of the French capital's art scene. Her literary career began with an indiscretion. In Berlin, literary critic Viktor Shklovsky, who had fallen in love with her, began writing her daily letters, a practice she accepted on the condition that he avoid the topic of love. He later included some of her replies, without her knowledge, in his book *Zoo, or Letters Not About Love*. When Maxim Gorky read that work, he considered Triolet's unwitting contributions the most literary thing about it and encouraged her to start writing. In 1926, after composing an account of Tahiti, she published the autobiographical novel *Wild Strawberry*, both in Russian. She was already an established author when she switched to the French language in 1938 with the novel *Bonsoir Thérèse*, though she never considered herself a French author, but rather a Russian who wrote in French.

As had been the case with Mayakovsky, Triolet was fascinated not only by Aragon's literary talent but also by his nonconformism. Both men were theatrical dandies who talked as if their lives depended on it. Both had a dual passion for literature and politics, cultivated an image as scourges of conventional morality and courted notoriety with targeted acts of provocation. Aragon, for example, filled his 1928 book *Traité du style* (*Essays on Style*) with the rudest of insults. Aragon knew that Triolet saw him as an extraordinary master of language, a kindred spirit and, in a sense, an intellectual and artistic heir to Mayakovsky after the latter's death. "Vladimir Mayakovsky, whom Else met at the age of fifteen when he was more or less unknown, not only made a deep impression on her life," Aragon wrote. "He remained for her an image that tortured her for years, an image that inspired the subject matter which became her obsession and which you repeatedly encounter from book to book."[3]

Stalinism

Stalin liked Mayakovsky as a poet despite his eccentricity and his dissipated lifestyle; although his relationship to the Communist Party was not entirely unproblematic, Mayakovsky was altogether willing to serve as a propagandistic agitator. In his memoirs, Dmitri Shostakovich was very critical: "I can readily say that Mayakovsky epitomized all the traits of character I detest: phoniness, love of self-advertisement, lust for the good life, and most important, contempt for the weak and servility before the strong." The composer added: "It was Mayakovsky who first said that he wanted Comrade Stalin to give speeches on poetry at Party Congresses." Such fawning allowed Mayakovsky to become something of a court poet in Stalin's cult of personality.[4] He was well acquainted with Yakov Agranov, a ranking officer in the Soviet secret police, the GPU, a forerunner of the KGB, which was responsible for keeping tabs on the cultural scene. One of Agranov's informants was Mayakovsky's lover and Triolet's sister Lilya. Elsa was also a Stalinist, and she too was closely connected with the GPU.[5] On Mayakovsky's visit to France, during which he asked Triolet to arrange a meeting with Aragon, she was the one tasked by the secret police with ensuring that the capricious poet would eventually return to the Soviet Union.[6]

When Triolet arrived in Nuremberg in 1946, her advocacy of Communism was still mostly viewed as something positive. The French Resistance to Nazism, of which Triolet and Aragon were literary figureheads, mirrored the organizational structure of the Communist Party, and many French people equated Communism with the successful campaign against Hitler and

Germany. Triolet was a heroine and an icon. She was also Jewish, and Aragon was classified as half-Jewish; in 1940, after France's defeat by Germany, they fled to the non-occupied south of the country. In Nice they served as couriers for the Resistance, a function that required them to cover long distances on foot. For a time Aragon even led a Resistance group consisting of writers. After the Italians occupied Nice, the couple went underground and published works under pseudonyms.

Aragon worked intensely during these years on the literary journal *Les Lettres françaises*, originally established as an underground Resistance magazine. The period of French occupation was a productive one for both him and Triolet. They wrote conspiratorial pamphlets and tried to use words to combat the occupiers. Aragon's poem cycle *Les Yeux d'Elsa* (*Elsa's Eyes*) contains several more or less direct calls for resistance and revolt, referring, for instance, to "Paris, which is only a Paris in a hail of cobblestones". Triolet's short story "Les Amants d'Avignon" (The Lovers of Avignon), published under the pseudonym Laurent Daniel, described the hardships of living underground. And the title of the collection of short stories, *Le Premier accroc coûte deux cents francs* (*A Fine of 200 Francs*), for which she won the Prix Goncourt, cited the code name by which the Allies' landing in Normandy was announced in Provence. Meanwhile, after the war, Aragon's verses—particularly "Il n'y a pas d'amour hereux" and the poem "Les Yeux d'Elsa", in which he compares his wife's eyes to his battered homeland—were considered classics of the Resistance.

Nonetheless, as sacrosanct as Triolet had become as a writer and moral authority, despite the Prix Goncourt she was also criticized for her political views. The criticism came, ironically, from French surrealists, who blamed her for alienating Aragon from them and for convincing him to toe the Soviet Communist Party line. To understand why, we must look back briefly.

Starting in 1927, some of the French surrealists had joined the French Communist Party, the only anti-war party in the country, but conflicts soon arose between the artists and party functionaries. Prompted by Triolet, Aragon accompanied her to the Second International Conference of Revolutionary Writers in Kharkov in 1930. He returned from the conference a different person politically and artistically, breaking with Breton and his ideas of surrealism. In a programmatic essay, Aragon demanded that surrealists "recognize, understand and unconditionally adopt dialectic materialism as the only true revolutionary philosophy".[7] He himself had signed a declaration in support of putting art fully under the control of the party in future. That was anathema to Breton, who considered Communist Party bureaucracy the natural enemy of his radical concept of freedom and rejected the sort of obedience and conformity demanded by the Stalin regime as incompatible with surrealism.

Breton blamed Triolet for making his former friend into an apostate, complaining in a 1952 radio interview: "Remember that this trip [to Kharkov], which was full of surprises and consequences, did not take place by any means on Aragon's initiative. Rather it was on the initiative of Triolet, whom he had just met and who demanded that he go along with her. From a distance, and based on how she later behaved, there is every reason to assume that she insisted on this and got what she wanted... If the circumstances had been different... the Aragon I knew would have never done anything that would risk a split with us."[8]

Be that as it may, after his trip to Kharkov Aragon hewed to Stalin's party line while Breton remained a Trotskyite, co-authoring a manifesto, "Towards a Free Revolutionary Art", which called for artistic autonomy vis-à-vis the state, even in revolutionary circumstances. Aragon's literary style also changed. Whereas Breton stuck with the ideals of literary surrealism and its renunciation of logic, syntax and aesthetic forms, in a 1935 article Aragon called upon French authors to follow the lead of Socialist Realism, which the previous year had been made the only legal style in the Soviet Union—although Aragon did allow himself some linguistic leeway on the margins of this doctrine.

Triolet, too, stressed the importance of linguistic "artisanship" while remaining faithful to the principles of the Russian avant-garde, particularly Mayakovsky.[9] And both Aragon and Triolet's Resistance activity would show that language offered plenty of space for political activism. Their easily understood texts had moved the French masses; their literary endeavours had real social effects. That no doubt further convinced them that surrealism was an ivory tower of social and aesthetic exclusivity.

There has been much emotionally charged discussion in recent years about whether Triolet steered or even manipulated Aragon, and there is no dismissing the fact that her influence was one reason why he became a Stalinist. In 1931, Aragon went so far as to write a poem, "Vive le Guépéou" (Long Live the GPU), originally known as "Prélude au temps des cerises" (Prelude to the Cherry Season), that called for a French version of the Soviet intelligence service and justified the persecution of enemies as a necessary evil.

"The Judges' Waltz"

Over time, the journal *Les Lettres françaises*, which Aragon edited after the liberation of France, became his and Triolet's main literary and political organ. Like many respected journals, it sent a correspondent to the Nuremberg Trial. The task fell to Triolet, who accepted the assignment, among other reasons because she wanted to see the criminals who had subjected her family and many friends to such indescribable suffering. She attended the trial in late May 1946, and on 7th June and 14th June 1946 she published "La Valse des juges" (The Judges' Waltz), a two-part field report illustrated with caricatures.[10]

Triolet stayed in the Grand Hotel, but she did visit the press camp and even devoted a section of her article to it. Ever critical of the products of capitalism, she was less than impressed by Schloss Faber-Castell, which she saw as a place of both gloom and megalomania, replete with "a veritable throne for the Faber boss". She was also struck by the militarism of the wall fresco in the dining room: "In this painting one can see two knights in full armour with pencils for lances. Apparently, the knight with the Faber weapon is goring the other one... How many pencils were needed to give the Fabers the means to build such a thoroughly ugly castle?" Triolet did, however, like the "wonderful" park, remarking that "even at the Fabers' estate trees remain trees".

The article, which was shot through with discomfort and outrage, was many things at once: an idiosyncratic report on the trial focusing on the cross-examination of Baldur von Schirach, an autobiographical account of the difficulties she had travelling to Nuremberg, and a collage emphasizing, among other things,

Jacques Decour, a Resistance fighter killed by Germany. Triolet was particularly repulsed by Schirach's testimony, but she was also nauseated by what she considered the frivolity of the judges and other main figures at the trial, exemplified in their pursuit of post-work amusements. In the evening, she complained, you could see the judges dancing in the marble ballroom of the Grand Hotel. Triolet found the sight so objectionable against the backdrop of the horrors adjudicated in court during the day that she chose the image as the title for her article.

Triolet divided her report into various sections: "The Tribunal", "In the Press Camp", "The Job", "The High Court", "The Monster Trial", "After Work", "Naked Reality" and "Destinies". Her style was highly metaphoric and rhetorical, avoiding explicit statements and engaging in surrealist flights of fancy. Nuremberg, for example, was a "city like a squashed brain, pink and grey in well-heated butter". She frequently used paralipsis, emphasizing a topic by claiming to skip over it, and her tone was sarcastic and mocking. In essence, Triolet was putting the trial itself on trial.

The cross-examination of Schirach, which she personally witnessed, had a direct connection with Triolet's social circle in the person of Pierre Daix. A long-time friend, who described their 1945–71 relationship in a memoir published in 2010, Daix was a fellow former Resistance fighter and a Communist. In 1944, having been captured by the German occupiers, he was sent to the Mauthausen concentration camp. In his book he recalled a conversation with Triolet immediately after her return from Nuremberg. Triolet remembered that he had been imprisoned in Mauthausen, and the camp had also played a role at the trial, so she sought him out.

During the trial, Schirach had testified that he knew nothing about the atrocities committed in the camp and that what he had found when he visited was a model prison. "I saw the building in which there was an admirably well-organised dental station," Triolet quoted him saying in her article. "Then I was taken to a room where the internees were making music. There was a whole symphony orchestra and I was told that in the evening, after work, the internees had the opportunity to occupy them- selves however they liked, and there the internees were making music. I had the opportunity to hear a tenor."[11] Schirach, the former Hitler Youth leader, tried to present himself to the court as a man of culture. In his defence, his lawyers put forward a letter by the poet Hans Carossa, in which the latter expressed his surprise at Schirach's cultural knowledge and testified that he had tried to help the writer Rudolf Kassner, whose wife was Jewish. Triolet found it an "enormous blasphemy" that Carossa was introduced to the court as a poet. Her friend Jacques Decour, the founder of *Les Lettres françaises*, who had been executed by the Nazis, had been Carossa's French translator before the war, but Carossa had not testified on his behalf. "Perhaps," Triolet remarked bitterly, "because he had no con- tact with him, and Hans Carossa knew nothing of his culture, the same culture he marvelled at with Mr von Schirach, who, however, came from a genteel and affluent family."

Daix told Triolet that Schirach's testimony may indeed have been honest. The authorities at Mauthausen had forced the prisoners to erect a Potemkin village to conceal the true condi- tions in the camp. During a Red Cross inspection, he said, he had been made to give a positive description of camp life to a Swiss delegate. Geraniums had even been planted to help prop up the illusion, and the Red Cross had fallen for the carefully staged deception.

Her direct experience of Schirach's testimony led Triolet to question the entire Nuremberg Trial enterprise. To her mind, the proceedings gave men like Schirach the chance to act out a charade in front of the entire world, like what the Nazis had arranged in Mauthausen. Worse still, the accused had the opportunity to defend their view of the world. "Nuremberg makes me see red," she told Daix. "You won't believe it, Pierre, but the whole trial, everything in Nuremberg, is there to allow [the war criminals] to justify their ideology."[12]

Triolet used almost exactly the same words in her article for *Les Lettres françaises*. Blame for the botched procedures of the Nuremberg "Monster Trial", she wrote, rested with the Anglo-American organizers. "You don't need evidence for the existence of Auschwitz, Dachau, etc… There are enough witnesses to confront an ideology and a regime [like this one]," she argued. "The Nuremberg Trial could have been a sledgehammer against Nazism, an immense help in the denazification of minds… [but] it gives these men, who are so well versed in propaganda, a chance to exonerate their ideology."

Other Western correspondents, for example Hans Habe, also criticized the trial's shortcomings, but not in the way Triolet did. Her vantage point was markedly anti-Anglo-American, and she rejected the entire ideal of the trial. Indeed, she saw it as part of a pernicious conspiracy. Without ever coming out and saying as much directly, Triolet wondered why the defendants hadn't just been executed. "Here we have a world that is already at the bottom of an abyss, and which seems to be doing everything it can to sink even deeper, more completely… I know, more clearly than before my trip to Nuremberg, that we are in the middle of a war." She was referring to the incipient Cold War, which she blamed on the Anglo-Americans, who had also given the Nazis a stage and aligned themselves with them in Nuremberg.

Triolet's article was an edited text, later republished by Aragon in his 1960 book *Elsa Triolet choisie par Aragon*,[13] and research has shown that the most controversial political barbs were deleted from the handwritten manuscript. Triolet accused the Anglo-Americans of having anti-democratic tendencies, being infected by Nazi ideology, showing criminal levels of empathy with the defendants and even collaborating with Nazis. "Nazi septicaemia is in full vigour, it only grows and becomes more embellished," she originally wrote. "All the anti-democratic forces recognize each other, stretch out their hands, comforted by the criminal clemency." In the published version this passage simply read, "It shows how strong the Nazi poison is." But where Triolet's words were softened, the images she used were allowed in the name of satire, and

— *Et maintenant la parole passe à notre bon camarade von Schirach.*

Illustration for Elsa Triolet's "La Valse des juges" in *Les Lettres françaises*, 14th June 1946.

they spoke volumes. The caricatures accompanying the article as published in *Les Lettres françaises* were extreme, monstrous depictions of the Anglo-American judges. One of them showed a defendant sitting in the dock while a friendly judge points at him and says, "And the word goes to our fine comrade von Schirach."

When she wasn't directly attacking the Anglo-Americans, Triolet used exaggeration and polarization to undermine their credibility. On three occasions, she wrote of the trial being conducted in the "Nazi-built" Palace of Justice, the intent being presumably to establish a sense of continuity between the non-Soviet-occupied part of post-war Germany and the fascist past. In fact, the building was constructed in 1916—before the Nazi Party even existed. This was typical of the half-truths, falsehoods and fictions Triolet engaged in to mock the authorities at the trial. For instance, she wrote of Schirach being questioned "as a witness in the trial of Höss (not to be confused with Hess), of Höss, the executioner of Auschwitz", adding that "the testimony of a man who has also been tried as a criminal will be accepted as valid". This was manifestly untrue. The commandant of Auschwitz, Rudolf Höss, was tried in Warsaw in 1947, not in Nuremberg, so there was no way Schirach could have testified against him, as a witness or otherwise. Höss himself was summoned as a witness for the defence by Ernst Kaltenbrunner's lawyers, and he testified on 15th April 1946. But it is impossible that Triolet saw him in person, as she suggested by using the word "today" in her text, since she herself only arrived in Nuremberg in late May.[14]

Triolet's article was intentionally manipulative, distorting the truth to lend weight to her depiction of the trial as something "unhealthy". Like the Potemkin village constructed in

Mauthausen, she saw the proceedings as a charade concealing the reality of an Anglo-American/Nazi collaboration. But Triolet set little store by a trial conducted according to the rules of law. "Laws are powerless is such a case," she remarked. "Emotion is a thousand times more just than the law."

Aragon also argued emotionally, and he, too, wasn't particularly interested in laws and judicial principles. Shortly after the end of the war he published a seventeen-page pamphlet called *L'Enseigne de Gersaint* (*The Shop Sign of Gersaint*). The title was taken from a painting by Watteau in Schloss Charlottenburg in Berlin. Aragon called for the artwork to be returned to France, although it had not been looted by the Nazis but commissioned by the Prussian King Friedrich the Great in 1744. Aragon's text was an emotional appeal to avenge the German humiliation of his homeland, with the return of all French works of art as a way of assuaging the immeasurable suffering caused by Germans to the French. "That's why I suggest that no French book, no French painting, no French sculpture be left in German hands. Let it be anchored in the peace agreement that all French artworks in whatever form be brought from German museums and private galleries back to France. The art of France must be brought back to France. The war cannot be over as long as our prisoners and kidnapped remain in Germany. French art, which is a part of France, cannot be allowed to stay in Germany. It has a part to play here, in our rebirth. We need this cultural blood transfusion. This coursing blood, this hot, red blood, should not be pulsing in Berlin, Munich or Dresden. I have said that we will demand a terrible, tragic penitence from this criminal people. We will burden this German people with a heavier, more oppressive yoke than history has ever seen."[15]

German writer Stephan Hermlin—Communist, German émigré and an admirer of Aragon—publicly rejected such extreme demands, arguing that works of art served a crucial didactic function in a Germany that had entirely lost its moral compass. But Aragon published a follow-up essay in which he stubbornly insisted on the restitution of French artworks. The two articles were then combined into a luxury edition published for bibliophiles in Switzerland.

Combatting the Pact with the Nazis

Aragon and Triolet's missionary and militant radicalism appears all the more astonishing when compared with their Soviet colleagues, contemporaries and fellow devotees of Stalin. In Nuremberg, Triolet encountered Ilya Ehrenburg, the famous Soviet writer who covered the trial from the Grand Hotel. Ehrenburg was a point of reference for French Communists, with *Les Lettres françaises* publishing excerpts of his novels in translation. The 7th June 1946 issue, for instance, featured a passage from his novel *Storm* directly after Triolet's report from Nuremberg.

A supporter of Stalin, Ehrenburg had written for the military newspaper *Red Star* during the war, where he published a series of hateful tirades against Germans. As a journalistic rouser of emotions, he was a fervent adherent of the Stalinist slogan "Kill the German". Alexander Werth, who reported from Moscow for the BBC, wrote of his "genius for putting into biting, inspiring prose the burning hatred Russia felt for the Germans", while Willy Brandt, who also met Ehrenburg in Nuremberg, took him to task for his tendency towards agitprop and "exaggerated scrib-blings". But even Ehrenburg never questioned the legitimacy of the Nuremberg Trial or levelled the sort of criticism Triolet did at the Anglo-American judges. For him, there was no doubt that the trial was both necessary and just. "No one can deny us this right [to render judgment]," he wrote. "We have transferred it to judges because we believe that the law and human conscience go hand in hand."[16]

Nor did it occur to the Soviet-Ukrainian correspondent Yaroslav Halan to question the trial as such. On the contrary, in his article "How We Accuse" he wrote of his pride at the performance of Soviet prosecutor General Roman Rudenko.[17] And in his final commentary, the later head of the secret police in Communist East Germany, Markus Wolf, called the court's work "exemplary".

Triolet's view of the trial thus diverged from that of her Soviet contemporaries. Her tendency towards conspiracy theories about the Anglo-Americans secretly collaborating with Nazis was unique. She saw her hostility towards English-speaking countries, especially the USA, as the continuation of the battle against fascism. Following Churchill's "Iron Curtain" speech in Fulton on 5th March 1946, she worried that the defendants in Nuremberg might triumph after all. She felt that it could fuel the hopes of the accused that the Western Allies and USSR would fall out, leading to a new war in which Germany could partner with the Western powers.

Triolet's demonization of the Anglo-Americans was also based on her fear that, in the wake of French joy at being liberated, her adopted country would orient itself towards American, not Soviet politics. That fear was not unfounded. After the euphoria about liberation had dissipated, familiar fault lines re-emerged in French politics. In the initial post-war period there were Communist ministers in government, but in 1947 France's socialist Prime Minister dismissed them. Whereas the socialists and the democrats adopted the American policy of containing the Soviet Union within a Western defensive alliance, the Communists toed the Stalinist party line without reservation, including the demand for solidarity with the extreme left wing.

Aragon and Triolet long ignored the pitiless cruelty of the Stalinist regime, although there was no overlooking its crimes. A March 1953 special issue of *Les Lettres françaises* immediately after Stalin's death reaffirmed the publication's admiration for the Soviet dictator. The front page featured a fawning essay by Aragon and a portrait of Stalin by Picasso.

Many of Triolet's former admirers could not understand how a former Resistance fighter could take Stalin's side so uncritically. But she had a sentimental attachment to Communism, which she regarded not as a doctrine but rather, in the words of one biographer, as "a para-religious constitution of the soul".[18] In this vein she heaped praise upon Stalin as the supreme leader of the Communist movement. But the integration of Europe, particularly via the Marshall Plan, increasingly marginalized the French Communist Party, and Triolet and Aragon with it. And the further France moved in the Western direction, the more radical the former heroes of the Resistance became.

Meanwhile, Aragon and Triolet's peers increasingly began running them down behind their backs, criticizing Triolet's Prix Goncourt as a "Red machination"[19] and dismissing them, often unfairly, as being salon Communists. Triolet, who always dressed elegantly, had for a time in the 1930s made Parisian haute-couture jewellery that catered to wealthy French people's demand for luxury. Aragon was famous for wearing Yves Saint Laurent suits. The fact that Triolet chose to reside in the Grand Hotel and not the press camp, where the other French correspondents stayed, was seen as further evidence of her penchant for the finer things in life.

In 1953 Triolet published the dystopian novel *Le Cheval roux* (*The Roan Horse*), a nightmare vision of World War Three and the Apocalypse. Critics considered it a work of objectivism, the philosophy advanced by Ayn Rand. "It wouldn't have changed anything no matter what I wrote," Triolet later complained. "People's opinion about us was set in stone, and our books were rejected in advance."[20]

It took years for Triolet and Aragon to change their political viewpoint and recognize that the uncompromising Communism of their years in the Resistance had little to do with socialism as it actually existed in the world. In a 1962 letter to her sister, Triolet claimed that she had made mistakes due to her "credulity".[21] But she didn't position herself in public until the late 1960s, when she called Alexander Solzhenitsyn's expulsion from the Soviet Union a "monumental mistake". In 1968 Triolet and Aragon condemned the Soviet invasion of Prague, whereupon the Communist Party discontinued its financial support for *Les Lettres françaises*. The journal ceased publication in 1970.

Triolet was a celebrated icon when she came to Nuremberg in 1946, but her dogmatic loyalty to the Stalinist line pushed her to the margins during the Cold War. She was politically stigmatized, but she also suffered under the weight of Aragon's mythologizing of her as his "Elsa". In later life, beset by health problems, she and Aragon withdrew increasingly often to their mill outside Paris, where she died in 1970, twelve years before her husband.

Although she appreciated German Romantic literature, Triolet retained a negative, indeed pessimistic view of Germans until the end of her days. In her 1965 novel *Le Grand jamais* (*The Big Never*) she concluded that the Allied efforts to de-Nazify Germany had failed. The Germans, she maintained, had remained true to themselves. Behind the beauty of the natural landscape of Germany, the Nazi pestilence lurked forever.[22]

Cassandra, pessimist and outsider—with all her contradictions, Elsa Triolet embodied the ambivalence of being foreign. She never felt as though she belonged anywhere. She realized that those who knew her sensed her uncertainty, and that pained her. Demoralized in her later years, she wrote: "I have Elsa's eyes. I have a husband who's a Communist. And I am at fault for everything. I am a tool of the Soviets. I am a creature of luxury. I am a *grand dame* and a blemish. I am acquiescent to Socialist Realism. I am a moralist and a frivolous, knitting, imaginative creature. I am Scheherazade, the great teller of stories. I am the muse and curse of the poet. I am beautiful and I am repulsive."[23]

X

Willy Brandt, Markus Wolf
and the Katyn Massacre

"After this trial, who would stoop... to
robbing others of their freedom?"

MARKUS WOLF

G ünter Guillaume was veritably captivated by Markus Wolf's
strength of personality. "Whenever we met, Markus Wolf
was also Mischa, a friend, the 'comrade general' and the boss,"
Guillaume, a West German government official who spied on
his country, recalled about the head of the foreign intelligence
division of the secret police in Communist East Germany. "He
had a keen sensitivity for the baggage others carried around with
them. He always asked about our personal lives... and asked if
he could help when difficulties arose." Guillaume always felt
Wolf's "natural, heartfelt connection with his scouts".[1]

Guillaume would become the most famous of Wolf's "scouts",
as the informants working for the East German Ministry for
State Security, the Stasi, were known—the German term
Kundschafter was intended to stress their idealism in contrast to materialistic Western "spies". At the behest of Wolf

(1923–2006), Guillaume became the centre of the most spectacular espionage affair in West German history. In 1956,
having received Stasi training in how to pass themselves off as
defectors, Guillaume and his wife arrived in West Germany as
putative East German refugees. There they established themselves within the Social Democratic Party (SPD) in Frankfurt.
After successfully organizing Transportation Minister Georg
Leber's election campaign in 1969, Guillaume—while secretly
an officer for special missions in the Stasi—joined the team at
the West German Chancellor's office, where he earned the trust
of his superiors. In 1972 he became Chancellor Willy Brandt's
personal assistant for party matters.

That meant East Germany had a mole at the heart of the
democratic Federal Republic of Germany, although it remains
disputed even today how valuable the material Guillaume passed
on actually was. It was by no means expected that this spy, who
ran a Frankfurt photocopy shop after emigrating, would be
able to penetrate the inner circles of power in Bonn, the West
German capital. His mercurial, undetected rise was a triumph
for Wolf. Guillaume regularly reported back to East Berlin via
radio transmission and dead-letter drops. In the end, he was
only revealed when one of his messages was decoded.

West German intelligence received indications that Guillaume
might be a spy in May 1973, but Brandt initially saw no reason to
fire him; following a trip to the Middle East, the Chancellor was
shocked by the news that his advisor had been arrested. Brandt
was not informed in advance of the arrest and did not realize
at this juncture the political waves it would cause. Brandt had
been the hero of the SPD, having led the party to its greatest
triumph ever in the 1972 national election, in which it took 45.8

per cent of the vote. But his once-sterling reputation was in tatters. He suffered from chronic depression and drank heavily. Worn down by defeats within his own party and estranged from SPD parliamentary leader Herbert Wehner, he stepped down on 6th May 1974. The Guillaume affair was more an excuse for than a cause of his resignation, although he proclaimed that he was taking "political responsibility" for "instances of negligence" in connection with the scandal.

As spectacular as this Stasi triumph might have seemed, Wolf would characterize it in his memoirs as an own goal for Communist East Germany, since Guillaume's discovery had brought down the man who more than any other had tried to normalize relations between East and West Germany. Brandt's *Ostpolitik* (eastern policy) had replaced the Federal Republic's Hallstein Doctrine, according to which West Germany would consider the recognition and assumption of diplomatic relations with East Germany by any Western state to be a hostile act. Brandt was so important to the East German leadership that in 1972, with Wolf's help, it had prevented his political demise. A constructive, secret-ballot vote of no confidence in the German parliament, launched by conservative opposition leader Rainer Barzel, failed after two deputies from the Christian Democratic Union (CDU) Party abstained. Wolf later claimed that he had paid one of those deputies 50,000 deutschmarks to withhold his vote, and evidence later emerged that another had been an "unofficial collaborator" of the Stasi who had also been bribed to do likewise. It was thus all the more regrettable, from Wolf's perspective, that Brandt quit two years later. On 7th May 1974, he wrote in his journal: "Brandt has in fact resigned. The irony of history: For years, we made plans and undertook measures

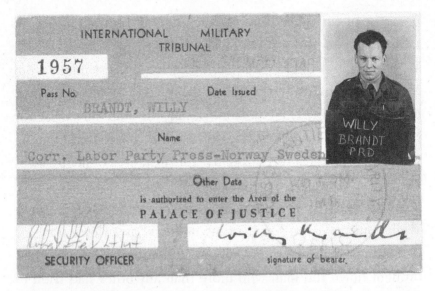

INTERNATIONAL   MILITARY
TRIBUNAL

1957

Pass No.   Date Issued

BRANDT, WILLY

Name

Corr. Labor Party Press-Norway Sweden

Other Date

is authorized to enter the Area of the

PALACE OF JUSTICE

SECURITY OFFICER   signature of bearer.

WILLY
BRANDT
PRD

Willy Brandt's press accreditation card for the International Military Tribunal.

against Brandt. Now, when we really don't want and even fear it, this accident has to happen. We are pulling the trigger and firing the bullet."[2]

Another irony, if not tragedy, of history was that Brandt and Wolf's early political and career biographies were similar in so many respects. The two men knew each other for twenty-nine years and had lived side by side for many months as correspondents in the Nuremberg Trial press camp.

In the autumn of 1945, Brandt was still an unknown. As a left-leaning socialist and member of the Socialist Workers Party (SAP) from the northern German city of Lübeck, Thomas Mann's home town, he had joined the anti-Nazi Resistance and later gone into exile after the party was banned in 1933. Two years before that he had quit the more moderate SPD, whose leader he would become after the war, to protest its lack of courage in dealing with the conservative German government of the time. In Norwegian exile, he led the battle of the SAP against fascism. Born Herbert Frahm, he renamed himself Willy Brandt and launched a journalistic career to supplement his political activism. In 1937 he reported on the Spanish Civil War. When Germany occupied Norway in the Second World War he fled to Sweden and continued his activities.

On 8th November 1945, six months after Germany's surrender in the Second World War, Brandt returned to Germany as a correspondent for Oslo's *Arbeiderbladet* and other labour-union newspapers.[3] Shortly before the beginning of the trial, he travelled via Bremen and Frankfurt to Nuremberg. He was accredited by the British consulate in Oslo. Brandt was deeply depressed when, after nine years of exile, he saw the landscape of rubble to which Germany had been reduced. He compared it to a "ghostly dream" and "one of those terrible visions that come over you sometimes between sleep and waking".[4]

Wolf, who was ten years Brandt's junior, also emigrated, being forced to flee Nazi Germany with his family in 1933. He came from far better circumstances than his future adversary. Brandt was born out of wedlock, never knew his father, was raised by his step-grandfather and grew up in the labour movement. By contrast, Wolf came from the educated upper-middle classes and was introduced to literature as a child. His father, Friedrich Wolf, was a fervent Communist from a Jewish background, but also a doctor, homeopath and playwright, whose 1929 drama *Cyankali (Cyanide)* was a big stage hit. Set among the Berlin working classes, it attacked the injustice of paragraph 218 of the German legal code, which banned abortion and essentially turned 800,000 women a year into criminals. The play was written for political purposes, and critics gave it a mixed reception.

In his review for the *Neue Leipziger Zeitung* Erich Kästner, who would also encounter Markus Wolf in Nuremberg, dismissed it as a "work of artlessness" that owed its power not to aesthetics but to "its genuine social emotion and its subject matter".[5]

Friedrich Wolf's political activism became obvious when he published his programmatic essay "Art is Weapon". For him, art could never be divorced from purpose, and he sought to use it to encourage social and political healing. His *Professor Mamlock*, written in exile in 1933, was a bitter attack on anti-Semitism and earned him a reputation beyond the German-speaking world. Two years previously, the Nazi *Völkischer Beobachter* had called him one of "the most perniciously dangerous representatives of Eastern European Jewish Bolshevism". As of 1934, Friedrich Wolf lived in Moscow with his family.

Markus, who was born in the south-western German town of Hechingen, originally wanted to be an airplane mechanic and studied at university in the Soviet capital with that aim in mind. But as the German Wehrmacht advanced on the city in 1941, he transferred to the distant Party Academy of the Executive Committee of the Comintern. It was charged with training people of various nationalities for both sabotage missions in Germany and assignments after the war. It also polished future Communist functionaries, taught them the history of the Communist International and gave instruction in everything from handling firearms to conducting discussions and winning over allies. But after Wolf had finished his first year at the academy it was dissolved, likely as a concession to the Soviet Union's allies in the fight against the Nazi Germany.[6]

Influenced by his father, Markus Wolf began a career as a radio journalist at the Deutscher Volkssender, a German exile broadcaster run by the German Communist Party (KPD) that could be picked up within the Third Reich. He became an announcer who commented on developments on the front and conducted psychological warfare. By that point he had joined the KPD. After the end of the war, thanks to German Communist leader Walter Ulbricht, he was sent—he claimed against his will—to Berlin to help found an anti-fascist German radio station in the Soviet occupation zone. This was how he became a co-director, with 600 people under him, of the Reichrundfunk, the former central radio broadcaster of Nazi Germany. He commented on foreign political affairs, worked as an announcer under the pseudonym Michael Storm and was responsible for the station's main political programmes.

In the Press Camp

As Wolf later noted, in his working life he was always the youngest. He was a mere twenty-two when he reported from the Nuremberg Trial and only twenty-nine when he became the head of the East German Foreign Intelligence Agency. He was a protégé of his father, who became a politician in cultural affairs and an ambassador to Poland after the war. That is "a key to understanding Markus Wolf", as one biographer has written.[7] In November 1945, Markus Wolf arrived in Nuremberg together with two Russian officers as a correspondent for the Berlin Rundfunk radio broadcaster and the *Berliner Zeitung* newspaper. It was an assignment for which he had put himself forward to his editors. Poor road conditions meant that the journey from Berlin took longer than usual, so he missed the start of the trial, and an unpleasant surprise awaited him when he tried to register at the press camp, where he was turned away as a German. He insisted that he was a Soviet, and in fact he had been in possession of a Soviet passport, albeit lapsed, since the age of sixteen. The US officers responsible for registration overlooked the expiration date and not only allowed him into the camp but issued him a press identification card under the American-sounding name Mark F. Wolf. He stayed in Nuremberg until the end of the trial, which was rare for correspondents.

Wolf would give his time in the press camp literary form in his 1995 work *Secrets of Russian Cuisine*, a curious combination of a cookbook and a portrait of Russia. A rather anecdotal, light-hearted chapter titled "Nuremberg Sakuska" explored the culinary side of the city, the quality of the food and the amazement of the American head of the kitchen in Schloss Faber-Castell at Wolf and his companions—the first Soviets in the press camp. "We were the sensation of the day!" wrote Wolf. "Russians who ate with knives and forks as normal people did and didn't even smack their lips!" The new arrivals were less impressed with the standards of American cooking, with its reliance on bacon and tinned corn. With a healthy pinch of irony, Wolf described accompanying the prominent Soviet writer Vsevolod Vishnevsky to dinner one evening at the Grand Hotel, "where the food was better". Vishnevsky got so drunk, however, that he made an embarrassment of himself and was flown out of Nuremberg the following day on the orders of the Soviet delegation.

Wolf shared a room in the Russian house with three Soviet colleagues, among them Boris Polevoy, who wrote his novel *Story of a Real Man* there. It was a melodrama about a Soviet fighter pilot, the titular "real man", who lost his legs after being shot down, only to return to the skies with prosthetic replacements to battle the Germans. After an initial bout of writer's block the story flowed out of Polevoy, who finished it in nineteen days. *"Real Man* became a bit of evening therapy for the everyday reality of the trial at which the most horrific crimes were discussed in the most unemotional of tones," he later remarked.

Markus Wolf enjoyed the alcohol-fuelled social evenings he spent with Polevoy and the others, writing: "Now and again, my roommates Boris Polevoy, Sergey Krushinski and Yuri Korolkov, who had made names for themselves as writers, would read bits of their new manuscripts. Occasionally they competed with one another like singers on the Wartburg for the attention of our charming interpreter. There was always something around that could be used for *sakuska* [small snacks]: a hard sausage, a glass

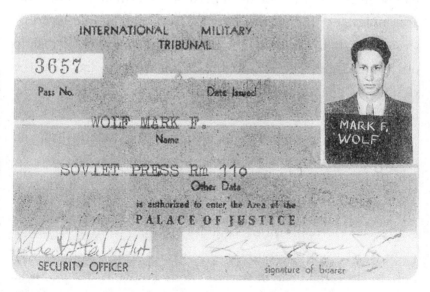

Press card for the International Military Tribunal issued to "Mark F. Wolf".

of pickles or preserved mushroom, if sometimes only a piece of bread and an onion."[8]

Criminals and Other Germans

Like Wolf's roommates, Willy Brandt also worked on a book in Nuremberg, not a novel but a work of non-fiction titled *Forbrytere og andre tyskere* (*Criminals and Other Germans*) for a Scandinavian readership. The book would later come back to haunt him in Germany—rather unfairly. In it, Brandt juxtaposed the sort of criminality on trial in Nuremberg with the *other* Germany, refusing to acknowledge the idea of collective German guilt. Brandt rejected Vansittartism, arguing that reality was far more complex. He described in great detail how infernally systematic the Nazis' implementation of their plans had been and how too many of his fellow Germans had become accomplices to their crimes. But Germans, he insisted, weren't "born criminals". Special circumstances had made them into instruments and victims. Brandt bemoaned the fact that the victors had not allowed German judges at the Nuremberg Trial to hold the accused accountable for their deeds in the name of the German people. In conclusion he demanded social and institutional bulwarks against relapses into nationalism.

The book was published in 1946 in Norway, and a Swedish version also appeared that year. It was never published in its entirety in German during Brandt's lifetime. All that appeared were short excerpts intended by his adversaries to discredit him. In 1961, the head of Bavaria's conservative Christian Social Union Party, Franz Josef Strauss, sneered, "One thing we should be allowed to ask Mr Brandt is what he was doing for twelve years abroad." Brandt's enemies spread rumours that he had written a foreign-language book titled *Germans and Other Criminals*, in which he had shown his "true" face as an advocate of collective German guilt.

The truth was precisely the opposite: Brandt's words were twisted to defame him.[9] *Criminals and Other Germans*, which has been available to Germans in their native language since 2007, was in fact an attempt to combat anti-German sentiment in Norway. In 1946 Norwegians remembered German occupation all too well, and Vansittartism had powerful supporters including the Nobel laureate Sigrid Undset and conservative politician Carl Joachim Hambro. Brandt was writing, among other things, to counter Undset's assertion that Germans were governed by a "herd mentality... namely cruelty".[10]

Brandt was not a German apologist, and his experiences with the locals in Franconia were by no means positive. "In and around Nuremberg, you have to look far and wide to find anyone who will admit to being a true-believing Nazi rather than just possessing a party membership number," he wrote. One day, wearing a Norwegian military uniform and an armband identifying himself as a "war correspondent", he accompanied a Danish colleague to interview the Duchess of Coburg in her home city. Her voice trembled with emotion, Brandt reported, as she related the outrageous injustice visited upon her husband, who had been interned, although he had only been President of the German Red Cross during the Third Reich. He had given his all for Germany and the cause of peace, the aristocratic lady assured Brandt, and had been a victim of his "idealism".[11] In reality, Carl Eduard Herzog von Sachsen-Coburg und Gotha had been an avid supporter of Hitler and a ranking member of the SA.[12] After the war he was accused of crimes against humanity, although he was ultimately classed as "fellow traveller" and only punished with a fine of 5,000 deutschmarks.

Brandt differentiated between guilt and responsibility. For him, even those found innocent of direct complicity in Nazi crimes shared in the responsibility of the collective. Moreover, he utterly rejected the common view that Nazi barbarism was akin to a natural catastrophe beyond human control.

Brandt spent several months in Nuremberg, staying until Christmas 1945, then again in the new year until February, and then again in the spring and late summer of 1946. In a letter to his journalistic colleague Olaf Solumsmoen on 27th November 1945 he wrote, "It is frantically interesting here," although he also complained about feeling very isolated. He didn't know whether his articles were reaching Oslo, nor whether they were being published. Contact was very difficult. There were no direct telephone connections, and Brandt's articles couldn't contain any breaking news because they were delayed for days before appearing. He had to adapt to these circumstances. It's no surprise, then, that *Arbeiderbladet* only published six reports with his byline.[13]

Brandt mostly filed factual news reports and protocols that focused on events without a great deal of reflection. For example, his piece on 24th November 1945 ran under the headline "Yesterday the American prosecutor presented new, unknown documents revealing Hitler's plans"; one the following day read "New important revelations are expected in Nuremberg"; and one in December was titled simply "Review of the Nuremberg Criminals". As the last headline suggests, that article surveyed the defendants one by one: "Göring has lost a lot of weight. He seems in better health than in the past twelve years. The external indications of past power and grandeur have disappeared… There's not much left of Ribbentrop, if indeed there was anything to him other than the external polish of a wine dealer… Sauckel, the former regional leader of Thuringia who had 12 million foreign labourers under him during the war, seems to be in a good mood. Often, he sits there grinning. In terms of his repulsive external appearance, he's not far behind Streicher."[14] Brandt didn't specify what he found so repulsive, and he avoided any form of analysis or intellectual engagement with the trial, strictly confining himself to descriptions.

Like other correspondents, Brandt built up emotional armour to defend himself against the horrors made public in Nuremberg, which would have led even the strongest personalities to the brink of a nervous breakdown. Later he would recall that on more than one occasion he had been close to following the lead of an American colleague who had sent a telegram home reading: "I can't take it. I have no words any more."[15]

Criminals and Other Germans was unlike his articles, which depicted the trial's daily revelations with journalistic distance. Brandt devoted most of his attention as a writer to the book and worked on it obsessively, wanting to publish it as soon as possible. It was in this forum that he strove for intellectual depth.[16] Brandt forewent the extensive external descriptions of the defendants he included in his articles. Instead, he showed himself to be a precise political observer and an exacting researcher. The book was his attempt at "describing clean-up operations between the ruins", both "on the streets and in people's minds". During his time in Nuremberg Brandt undertook several trips through what remained of his former homeland, and he combined his impressions of the trial with accounts of his travels. He explored the question of whether there had been a German Resistance movement and shone a spotlight on the policies of the Western Allies and the Soviets. On the basis of conversations conducted with Germans, he discussed post-war living conditions in the country. He was keenly interested in the situation in the four different occupation zones and the future of Germany in Europe. The book was divided into seven chapters, only two of which dealt with the Nuremberg trials. One of those consisted of a record, akin to the minutes of a meeting, of the four prosecutors enumerating their evidence at the trial. But *Criminals and Other Germans* is not a straightforward account of the trial from beginning to end. In fact, Brandt departed Nuremberg months before the verdicts were announced.

Katyn

Given the fact that, as Chancellor, Brandt advocated aligning Germany with the West, as well as anti-totalitarianism and anti-Communism, it's surprising that his book optimistically predicted that there would be no break between the Soviet Union and the Anglo-Saxon Allies "because it's not in the interest of either side". In 1945 and 1946, he treated the Soviet Union with kid gloves. In February 1945, six years after the Red Army had attacked Finland, Brandt wrote that "experience in the Balkans, in Finland and in Poland" didn't suggest that "any comprehensive and brutal interventions in the forms of social life in these countries are intended by the Russian side".[17] Brandt was also still convinced that the Soviet Union represented no threat to Polish freedom. Indeed, he envisioned peaceful cooperation with the Soviet Union—although he himself had seen how the Soviet secret police had helped the Spanish Communists eliminate their rivals during the Spanish Civil War. In 1944, he wrote from Scandinavian exile: "As socialists we have a vested interest in close, friendly relations with the Soviet Union." Such relations, he added, were "one of the crucial conditions for the future of the German people and the stabilization of peace in Europe".[18]

This stance influenced Brandt's reporting from Nuremberg. In both his articles and his book, he studiously ignored the Stalin-ordered massacre of Katyn, even though it was the subject of one part of the trial. In the spring of 1940, 4,400 Polish POW officers were killed in the forest of Katyn near Smolensk. On several occasions since 1943, also during those weeks in which the disputes surrounding Katyn had attracted international attention, Brandt had met with representatives of the Polish Socialist Party. But he failed to mention Katyn in anything he published during or immediately after the war. He would first broach the topic in his 1989 memoirs.[19]

Between 22,000 and 25,000 Poles were murdered on Soviet territory during the Second World War. The mass executions of Katyn were followed by numerous other killings of Polish military officers, police officials and intellectuals. In the spring of 1943 German troops who were occupying the area exhumed the bodies in Katyn, and the Nazi regime publicly blamed the Soviets for the massacre. The intent was, on the one hand, to celebrate the Nazi "liberation" of the people of the Soviet Union from the yoke of Bolshevism and, on the other, to confront the

Western Allies with Soviet atrocities. Above all, Goebbels and his fellow propagandists wanted to drive a wedge through the anti-Nazi alliance.

Moscow reacted by blaming Germans for the murders. Stalin feared that the Katyn massacre could discredit the Soviet Union internationally and insisted it be added to the list of charges against the major war criminals in Nuremberg. The other prosecutors urged General Rudenko to forgo this accusation since it would give defence lawyers the opportunity to reject the charge and to accuse one of the powers responsible for conducting the trial of a horrific crime. But Rudenko stood his ground and propagated the falsehood that Katyn was another Nazi atrocity. He deliberately overstated the number of dead as 11,000 and blamed the killings on a pioneer battalion code-named "Staff 537" under the leadership of an officer called Arne.

The *Neue Zeitung* passed on this version of events, but a former officer named Reinhardt von Eichborn, who had served in "Staff 537", read it and instantly recognized Rudenko's charge as a lie. In reality, what was actually known as "Unit 537" had been an intelligence group, the officer in charge was a man named Friedrich Ahrens, and the unit had been quartered from December 1941 to January 1943 in barracks some kilometres from Katyn. Eichborn travelled to Nuremberg to testify and refute the accusations levelled against his unit. The court also heard from Friedrich Ahrens, who testified on 1st July 1946. Ahrens and Eichborn were joined by a further exonerating witness, while three Soviet witnesses immediately swore to the contrary.

One evening, a putative representative of the Soviet press approached Ahrens, who was quartered in the building on

Novalisstrasse for witnesses not suspected of war crimes and was allowed to move freely about Nuremberg. As he made his way back to his quarters, he thought he was being watched. The next day, when he reported his suspicions that the Soviet secret service was threatening him to the general secretariat of the court, he was promptly prohibited from leaving the witness house.[20] The matter increasingly became a source of embarrassment and confusion for the court since the Western Allies had a good idea, thanks to Polish evidence among other things, that the Soviets were actually responsible for the massacre. Ultimately, Judge Lawrence ordered the charge dropped. It wasn't until 1990, under Mikhail Gorbachev, that the Soviet Union took responsibility for the massacre, acknowledging it as a Stalinist atrocity and apologizing to the Polish people.

In 1946 Soviet commentators on the Nuremberg Trial not only propagated the idea that German soldiers had carried out the killings. They also made a great show of their outrage at the accused who testified to the contrary, including the former Nazi radio journalist Hans Fritzsche. One of the most vocal critics was Markus Wolf, whose dramatic words surely earned him the approval of his superiors. "Attributing their own crimes to others has always been and remains among the most popular methods of these defamatory muckrakers," Wolf proclaimed in his daily radio commentary for Berliner Rundfunk on 3rd July 1946. "As chance had it, directly after Fritzsche, attention turned to Katyn, the lowest Nazi provocation of this kind. I would advise you, dear listeners, to read through the Nuremberg reports on the Katyn massacre very carefully in order to acquaint yourselves with the entire repulsiveness of the methods with which Fritzsche works. While he bellows in front of the microphone about the alleged crimes of others, Fritzsche knows only too well that the Polish officers in Katyn were murdered by the [German] Security Service, acting on direct orders from above."[21] Sixty years after the start of the Nuremberg Trial, the *Tagesspiegel* newspaper asked him about his reporting on the Katyn massacre. "Back then I thought it was a German crime," he claimed. "I didn't have any information [to the contrary] from the Soviet prosecutors."[22]

Stalinist Media Work

In Nuremberg, the twenty-two-year-old Wolf rigorously adhered to the Stalinist dictum "You're either with us or against us". His reporting was informed by a Marxist insistence on the primacy of social class and served the predetermined propaganda goal of "using the entire trial as a lever to unleashe a wave of hatred in the [German] people and of revulsion [for the defendants]".[23] At the start of the proceedings, the central administration for education in the Soviet occupation zone demanded that special broadcasts about the trial that should end with the statement "The Nuremberg defendants are Germany's worst enemies".[24] An essential component of this campaign was depicting the accused not as people but as embodiments of an abstract idea to be rejected. Individual characteristics and traits were irrelevant. As Wolf made clear to his listeners, it didn't matter which books the defendants borrowed from the prison library and how often they attended religious services, since discussing such things "would be to pay them an honour they truly don't deserve".[25] Over and over, the capitalist system as a whole was blamed for the crimes of National Socialism.

Wolf was well versed in ratcheting up emotions. His commentaries were full of vivid descriptions of the destruction and immeasurable suffering caused by German troops in the Soviet Union. His report in the *Berliner Zeitung* on 28th January 1946 included the testimony of Auschwitz survivor Marie-Claude Vaillant-Couturier, whose inner strength and confidently down-to-earth manner fascinated Wolf and many others. He also called for the death penalty across the board. "All twenty-one of the accused without exception deserve to die," he said in his daily radio report on 31st July, adding that "progressive humanity" demanded this punishment.

Wolf admired Stalin and assiduously pushed the Soviet leader's agenda and put his media policies into practice. He was aware of Stalin's purges, but not even the murders of tens of thousands of people could shake his faith in the dictator. Even many years later, he still insisted that Stalin "remained the embodiment of our cause, a good and noble cause".[26] The court didn't heed Wolf's call for the comprehensive death penalty. While twelve of the defendants were sentenced to die, three received life imprisonment, four were given lengthy prison terms and three were acquitted. In his commentary on the verdicts Wolf supported the position of the Russian judge, who had also demanded the death penalty for all the accused but had been outvoted by the Western judges.

Unlike Brandt, who was sceptical about the fairness of the de-Nazification proceedings, calling them a "bureaucratic witch hunt",[27] Wolf took a hard line. Moreover, he completely rejected Brandt's contention that German judges should have been part of the trial. In his final commentary on the trial, titled "The World Court Has Its Judgment", Wolf wrote that the German people had lacked sufficient wisdom and, later, strength to "free itself from its own evil". For that reason, an international court was needed to render judgment on the war criminals. Wolf ultimately viewed the trial positively and appealed to Germans to learn from their mistakes. This final commentary was broadcast in both Germany and Austria.

Wolf had no way of knowing that one day he would be measured against his own words. In 1993, in an attempt to bring him to trial for "treason and affairs of intelligence espionage", a prosecutor representing reunified Germany cited several sentences from his final commentary on the Nuremberg Trial, including the rhetorical question "After this trial, who would stoop… to robbing others of their freedom?" This was precisely what his detractors accused Wolf and the other main leaders of Communist East Germany of doing.

Brandt and Wolf regularly crossed paths in the press camp but took no notice of each other. "I only became aware later of Willy Brandt, who reported for the Norwegians—no one knew him yet," Wolf remarked in a 2005 interview in the *Tagesspiegel*. "I had an office in the Palace of Justice, where the trial took place, and the first thing I learned was how to operate a teletypewriter. There I sent two fifteen-minute reports to Berlin every day. As of 1946, they were published in print in the *Berliner Zeitung* as being reported 'by the special correspondent of Berliner Rundfunk'. I only spoke directly over the telephone in extraordinary circumstance." Wolf carried one reminder of the press camp with him for the rest of his life—literally. On New Year's Eve 1945/46, intoxicated revellers had loosened a chandelier in the ballroom of Schloss Faber-Castell and a crystal had fallen and hit his head, leaving behind a scar on his forehead.

When he finally departed Nuremberg, Wolf continued to work for Berliner Rundfunk until 1949, before launching his mercurial career via the East German embassy in Moscow as the head of the Communist foreign intelligence service.

Brandt's time in Nuremberg was a major crossroads in his life. In 1945, he was unsure whether he should stay in Norway or return to Germany. He was a Norwegian citizen—his German citizenship had been revoked and wouldn't be restored until 1948. Moreover, his job and social life were in Scandinavia. He had a wife and child in Norway, as well as a lover, Rut Bergaust, whom he would later marry. The press camp was a chance for Brandt to test his chances in the land of his birth, to which he remained emotionally attached. He wrote to Social Democrat Kurt Schumacher, who was working to rebuild the SPD, and re-established contact with various colleagues and relatives on his trips through the country. In May 1946 he gave a lecture titled "Germany and the World" in his home town, Lübeck, and that year he was offered the mayorship of the city.

Brandt, today known as a "pragmatic visionary", did in fact act pragmatically in deciding that Lübeck would be too confining and that he would rather work as a Norwegian citizen in Berlin. He became a press attaché for the Norwegian military mission there and was elected an SPD deputy to the Bundestag in 1949. Although he had remained a member of the "unorthodox Communist" SAP until 1944,[28] the key moment in his relationship to the practical reality of that ideology came in the spring of 1948 when the Communist Party in Czechoslovakia seized power in a coup d'état, ending democracy there. That changed Brandt, in the words of biographer Peter Merseburger, "from a supporter of an anti-fascist alliance with the Communists to a so-called Cold Warrior".[29] He would remain such until the first years after the construction of the Berlin Wall.

As the peaceful revolution in East Germany was coming to a head, Wolf would try to portray himself as the face of reform at the mass demonstration against the Communist regime on East Berlin's Alexanderplatz on 4th November 1989. The former head of the foreign intelligence division of the Stasi wasn't able to win over the majority of his fellow citizens. In the years that followed he did succeed, however, in establishing a reputation as something of a grandee of Eastern European espionage. He often appeared as an intellectual in German media. In 1986 he began writing books. His most highly regarded work was *The Troika*, the story of the divergent biographies of his brother Konrad Wolf, a famous East German director, and two friends. It appeared simultaneously in the West and the East in the spring of 1989 and caused a stir with its critical, autobiographically inflected reminiscences of Stalin's terror in 1930s Moscow.

If Markus Wolf is to be believed, he tried in his later years to engineer a reconciliation with Brandt. In his memoirs he wrote of the Nobel peace laureate: "I personally apologized to Willy Brandt. I myself experienced his greatness as a human being when, shortly before his death in 1992, he publicly came out against me being prosecuted. I never got the chance to see him in person. He felt that a meeting would cause him too much pain."[30]

XI

Rebecca West's Doomed Affair

"Fascism is a headlong flight into fantasy from
the necessity for political thought."

REBECCA WEST, "THE NECESSITY AND GRANDEUR
OF THE INTERNATIONAL IDEAL" (1935)

W hen it became clear that the main Nuremberg Trial would
go on at least until the late summer of 1946, people in the
court were frustrated and bored. After the storm surrounding
Göring's cross-examination, the long-winded sessions with the
other defendants and witnesses became a slog. Levi Shalitan,
editor of the Yiddish newspaper *Undzer Veg*, called it the "chewing
gum trial"—and not only because both the accused and security
personnel constantly chewed the stuff. "Chewing gum itself was
the best metaphor for the trial," Shalitan wrote. "The sweetly
bitter menthol taste has long faded, and all that remains in your
mouth is a tedious stretching and sucking."[1] On 23rd May 1946,
doubting that the mountains of paper and countless words were
serving any purpose at all, British judge Norman Birkett complained that his life was slipping away in a shocking waste of time.

In other German cities, Nazi functionaries had been convicted in smaller trials lasting only a few weeks. But Nuremberg

was different. The monotonous judicial attention to the tiniest details got on everyone's nerves. Moreover, the legal teams of the Allies mistrusted one another. The Anglo-American judges thought that Soviet witnesses lacked credibility and Soviet prosecutorial work was inadequate—Birkett called it "extremely primitive".[2] His frustration knew no bounds, so he sought out diversion, particularly as there was nothing he could do to change his circumstances.

Birkett was a literature enthusiast and traded occasional poems with one of his fellow judges, with whom he enjoyed having dinner parties and playing poker in the evenings. Longing for such casual forms of fun was one of the main topics of their verse. Birkett, for example, once wrote a poem addressed to the main US judge, Francis Biddle (1886–1968), during a court session: "Birkett to Biddle after one long dreary afternoon/At half-past four my spirits sink/My mind a perfect trance is:/But oh! The joy it is to think/Of half-past seven with Francis."[3]

Before the trial, the sixty-year-old Biddle had hoped to be appointed president of the court as a whole, but for diplomatic reasons he had to demur to Britain's Sir Geoffrey Lawrence. That, however, did nothing to undermine his high opinion of himself. "Lawrence depends on me for everything and I'll run the show," he once proclaimed in his journal, after being forced to take a back seat.[4] Jealousy and jockeying for power marked Biddle's relationship with Robert H. Jackson, who, despite being his junior, had been one rung above him on the career ladder for years. In 1940, when Jackson was promoted to head the US Department of Justice, Biddle took his vacated place as Attorney General. But now the tables were turned. Jackson was the one who had to win over others with his arguments, while it was down to Biddle to render judgment on his success.

Jackson's staff in Nuremberg despised Biddle. Thomas J. Dodd, who would succeed Jackson as chief counsel when the latter returned to the USA, didn't mince words in his private correspondence about the man and his judicial abilities. "Biddle is as nasty as he can be—but everyone here knows he is a faker and worse, a man without character," he wrote to his wife. "He will make a farce of this case yet and he is doing the Nazis' handiwork now." He concluded another letter with the words, "What hands in which to place high responsibility"; on another occasion he exclaimed, "What an ass of a man he is."[5] Conversely, Biddle greeted Jackson's unconvincing cross-examination of Göring with schadenfreude, writing to his wife of his rival sitting in the courtroom "unhappy and beaten, full of a sense of failure".[6]

Biddle came from an old, well-respected Philadelphia family. In the eyes of his legal colleagues he was a self-styled gentleman, with an often snobbish manner and a tendency to massage his ego at others' expense. Birkett shared his dissatisfaction with his role in Nuremberg. Whereas Biddle was peeved that he hadn't been made the court president, Birkett, who was originally supposed to chair the court, was only an alternative judge, with no vote of his own on verdicts. But Biddle made no secret of his disgruntlement, and his touchiness alone disqualified him for the task of presiding over the court, at least in the eyes of American prosecutor Telford Taylor, who wrote that he "could never have projected the aura of fairness that Lawrence radiated".[7]

Rebecca West (1892–1983), the *grand dame* of British journalism, viewed Biddle entirely differently. When she arrived in Nuremberg in late July 1946, where she replaced Janet

Flanner for *The New Yorker* and later reported for the *Daily Telegraph*, it caused a stir.[8] Born Cicily Fairfield, she took the pseudonym Rebecca West from a character in Henrik Ibsen's play *Rosmersholm*. She studied acting in London, although she soon quit the stage to join the women's suffrage movement. As Rebecca West she started writing as a literary critic, and by the age of twenty she was already famous for her cuttingly witty articles.

She got pregnant by H.G. Wells, one of the many authors she panned, after curiosity had led the two of them to start a literary friendship, then a romantic affair. But Wells, who had an open marriage and for whom West was only one of numerous liaisons, had no intention of changing his lifestyle habits, and he and West agreed to keep his paternity secret. She gave birth to a son, whom she passed off as her nephew and with whom she would have a difficult relationship for the rest of her life. Later he took his revenge by writing a book in which he revealed the identity of both his parents.

In 1928 West met the banker Henry Maxwell Andrews and the pair married two years later. At first their relationship was a source of stability, and the self-confident and unconventional West built a career as a journalist and author of socially critical novels. But although her work made her materially wealthy, her emotional life was barren. After seven years Andrews left her. Both had affairs, but in the long term West remained unfulfilled. Travelling to Nuremberg in the summer of 1946 was thus a welcome change of scenery. The woman Harry S. Truman would later dub the "best reporter in the world" was in search of adventure.

What she found in Nuremberg, however, was anything but adventurous. The reality was the same as that which left Birkett and Biddle so depressed. The best symbol of Nuremberg was a yawn, she complained. Being isolated in such narrow confines took its toll on everyone involved with the trial. "To live in Nuremberg was, even for the victors, in itself physical captivity," she wrote.[9] West, too, soon realized that the only amusement to be had was at the evening get-togethers, and she was glad when she met Biddle at a dinner party shortly after her arrival. They had encountered one another twice previously, most recently in 1935, when West interviewed him for a series of reports on economic and social reforms in the wake of the Depression. They had got on well, and both had felt a charge of sexual attraction.

When West told him that she was in Nuremberg to report for *The New Yorker*, Biddle replied that the magazine was one of the few things that kept him going in the city. Biddle had followed West's life from afar via her books, and he was a literature enthusiast who had himself published a novel. Gradually their conversation turned to the trial. When West expressed her fear that she knew too little about the background, Biddle invited her to his villa to fill her in on the details. The two grew close, meeting up again and again and taking walks together on the weekends through nearby forests and villages. West was captivated by Biddle's charisma. "Isn't it curious that the only aristocrat on the bench is an American?" she remarked to one of his colleagues.[10]

In no time they became lovers. Despite their attempts to keep their relationship secret, the entire trial community was soon whispering about their affair, and for a while West even moved into Biddle's villa. It was very fitting, West noted, that a "highly erotic" painting of Venus with Amor hung over Biddle's bed. No doubt, what art historian and court interpreter Philipp Fehl later called the "air of boorish and idle sensuality" in Nuremberg encouraged the two to abandon their inhibitions.[11] "There was hardly a man in the town who had not a wife in the United States," West would write, not failing to add a jibe about those women's ages, but "to the desire to embrace was added the desire to be comforted and to comfort." The result was a great number of often short-lived romances which West proudly defended. "These temporary loves were often noble, though there were some who would not let them be so."[12]

One of those West was talking about was her German colleague Gregor von Rezzori, who saw his own promiscuity rather less romantically. "It was a morally destitute time, and I behaved accordingly," the well-known bon vivant wrote in his autobiography. "When our third and youngest son was born [in 1946], a few days later a girl came into the world in the same Hamburg hospital. Both of the mothers asserted in their half-conscious state that I was the father of these new citizens of the earth."[13]

Like Biddle, the fifty-three-year-old West was sexually frustrated. She hadn't had sex with her husband in years and had privately written off any sort of sex life. For his part, the sixty-year-old Biddle told her that his wife, Katherine, had refused to sleep with him for the past eighteen months as punishment for the pain she had suffered giving birth to her second child.[14] Both West and Biddle gave each other the feeling of being desirable despite their relatively advanced ages. In Nuremberg they compensated for what had been denied them in their homeland. Their cosy life as a twosome was briefly interrupted when West returned to England for several weeks on 16th August. It was during this time that she wrote letters full of tenderness and flirtation. West sent some of her reports for *The New Yorker* to Biddle for editing, and he returned them with his comments. In one description of the Nuremberg court building she mentioned an allegorical representation of Eros in a corridor, a marble statue of a dog waiting for its master, which West considered a symbol of the loneliness and emotional stress in the city. Biddle pressed her to return to Germany, telling her he couldn't wait to hear her British-inflected "lovely, Francis, lovely" again.

Their physical relationship, which recommenced after West returned on 26th September, was reflected in her work. As historian Anneke de Rudder has correctly noted, West's reports "thoroughly sexualized the Nuremberg Trial".[15] Whether she was trying to create a scandal or just wanted to come up with an unusual take on the defendants, she described Göring's sexual aura to a much greater extent than any of her fellow correspondents. Hans Habe compared the former Reich Marshal to an unemployed chauffeur, Shirer likened him to a maritime radio operator and Philipp Fehl was reminded of a Renaissance condottiere à la Cesare Borgia. West, on the other hand, wrote: "Göring's appearance made a strong but obscure allusion to sex... Sometimes, particularly when his humour was good, he recalled the madam of a brothel. His like are to be seen in the late morning in doorways along the steep streets of Marseille, the professional mask of geniality still hard on their faces though they stand relaxed in leisure, their fat cats rubbing against their spread skirts." In her 7th September "Letter from Nuremberg" for *The New Yorker*, she likened the trial to a historic peep show in which the defendants were lowering their trousers. Moreover, she intentionally feminized former Hitler Youth leader Baldur von Schirach, writing that he was "like a woman".[16]

Accusations of insufficient manliness, homosexuality, impotence and "womanly" behaviour had been staples of wartime propaganda. A famous British soldiers' song, sung to the melody of the "Colonel Bogey March", featured the lyrics: "Hitler has only got one ball/Goebbels's got two, but very small/those of Goering are very boring/ and poor old Himmler has no balls at all." The reports filed by Rebecca West, the suffragette, partook of the same machismo and sexism. For her the war of words had never ended. On the contrary, she kept on fighting, just as her lover was rendering judgment upon the battle between the prosecution and the defence.

"Greenhouse with Cyclamens"

West often drew inspiration for her articles from her private life. She reacted like a seismograph to external stimuli, which prompted chains of association. During her relationship with Biddle she moved back and forth between Villa Conradi, his residence in Nuremberg, and the press camp. On one golden autumn evening, while walking in the park at Schloss Faber-Castell she saw that the door to the greenhouse was open. She had never taken any note of it before, but it provided the title for her extended essay on the Nuremberg Trial, "Greenhouse with Cyclamens". When she went into the structure she was astonished to see the perfect rows of flowers upon flowers: flax lilies, primulas and above all cyclamens. West found what she saw absurd. Germany had been destroyed. The economy had ceased to function. The people of Nuremberg were unable to buy necessities like shoes, water kettles and blankets. But in the park of the press camp, one business was flourishing. The one-legged gardener, a veteran who had served on the Eastern Front, had got permission from the aristocratic castle owners to sell flowers to Allied customers, and business was booming. When West first spoke with the ambitious florist, he was mostly interested in whether more trials would follow the first one, the verdict of which was about to be rendered. That was necessary for him to profit from the lucrative Christmas season.

West used this conversation to explore the character and mentality of the German people. In her mind, the gardener was prototypical. "There are, of course, countless workmen in other countries who, like this man, are industrious to the point of nobility; but there was something different and peculiarly German and dynamic in his self-dedication," she wrote. "In these other countries a good or a bad workman will enjoy his leisure, take pride in proving his worth in his trade-union branch, and will be prepared to argue that he and every man ought to be many-sided. But this grower of potted plants saw himself simply as a grower of potted plants, and was more than satisfied with that limitation; indeed, it was to him not a limitation at all, it was enfranchisement." The positive result of this mentality, for West, was the quality of the work that was produced. But there was a negative side: "He would have had no sympathy with a British workman's innocent desire to win a football pool and leave his job and escape in the holiday of independent means, or with the French workman's recurrent impulse to break the bars of the rigid industrial system in which he feels himself imprisoned and escape into a strike. He did not want to escape from his greenhouse, he wanted to escape into it. This did not necessarily demonstrate that he had a more agreeable character." West's implication was clear. The gardener was a solipsist lacking in social and moral awareness and responsibility.

A few months previously, in "Germany and the Germans", Thomas Mann had proposed that there was "a secret union of the German spirit with the demonic",[17] a constant push and pull of destructive and creative forces. Mann focused, among other things, on music, which he regarded as the pinnacle of the German soul. "It has felt and feels more strongly than ever today that such musicality of soul is paid for dearly in another sphere—the political, the sphere of human companionship." German soulfulness, in Mann's estimation, all too often resulted in provincialism and fear of the rest of the world. The German character was vulnerable to being seduced, which led to subservience. There was no Faust without Mephisto. Germans' relationship to their world was abstract and mystical, not socially binding as it was for other peoples.

West saw the origin of what Mann criticized as a mystical tendency in the German love of fairy tales. For her, Schloss Faber-Castell was an "architectural fantasy", a fairy tale made of stone and thus a symbolic expression of the collective German mentality. Meanwhile, on the prestige buildings of Nazi period, she wrote: "These were curious results of an excessive preoccupation with fairy tales; for that was the dream behind all this villa-building. It revealed itself clearly in this Schloss. Its turret windows were quite useless unless Rapunzel was to let down her hair from them; its odd upper rooms, sliced into queer shapes by the intemperate steepness of the tiled roof, could be fitly occupied only by a fairy godmother with a spinning wheel; the staircase was for the descent of a prince and princess that should live happily ever after." And West didn't stop there: "It was perhaps the greatest misfortune of the German people that their last genius, Wagner, who flowered at the same time as their political integration, their military conquests, and their industrial hegemony, and who has never had his domination over them so much as threatened by any succeeding artist, should have kept so close to the fairy tale in his greatest works. It is as if Shakespeare had confirmed the hold of Dick Whittington and Jack and the Beanstalk on the English mind; and it means that the German imagination was at once richly fecund and bound to a primitive fantasy dangerous for civilized adults."[18]

Clichés

West clearly knew her Brothers Grimm, but she was on less solid ground with architecture and design. The new Schloss and its tower, which were added between 1903 and 1906 to the Faber-Castell complex, was anything but a second fairy-tale Neuschwanstein Castle. On the contrary, it harked back to the Middle Ages. The architect, Theodor von Kramer, wrote in his memoirs, "In keeping with the express wish of the client, the entire complex of buildings has the character of a fortress."[19] Count Faber-Castell was less inspired by fairy tales than by his own family history, which stretched back to the eleventh century. Schloss Faber-Castell was by no means as archetypically German or Romantic as West would have had her readers believe. It was a unique creation that showed creative openness and strove for international architectural validity. The music gallery in its ballroom, for instance, featured decorative elements from the Italian Renaissance.[20] A Louis XVI room, a Javanese room and a Gobelin hall further evidenced the stylistic variety. The artists who contributed to the new Schloss were also an international lot. The "bosomy and gold-encrusted [dining-room] fresco representing the phases in the life of German womanhood", as West called it, was created by the Milwaukee-born painter Carl von Marr, while the still lifes were the work of Lazar Binenbaum.[21] West presented her readers with a cliché German castle, but in reality Schloss Faber-Castell was something else entirely.

West's view of Germans was not only clichéd but hostile. Like most of the correspondents in the press camp, she harboured major aversions to the Allies' former enemies. That didn't just include the unofficial proscription of any sort of sympathy, which isolated the vanquished from the victors. West also got caught up in one of the most predominant features of discourse in the Anglo-American media, the fear that Germany could one day take up arms again. In March 1946, an article in *Reader's Digest* suggested that excessive sympathy with the Germans would only lead to a defeated, humiliated, vengeful Germany rising from the ashes and launching a third attempt to take over the world.[22]

While West remained relatively moderate towards Germany in her published writings, she let her hostility flow freely in her private comments. She had done so even before the most heinous crimes of Nazism had been committed. When she visited Germany in the 1930s, she asked her sister in a letter why the British had not put every man, woman and child of that "abominable nation" to the sword in 1919. "The insane mercy and charity of the Treaty of Versailles makes me gnash my teeth," she wrote.[23]

Such tirades may be excusable considering the crimes committed by Germany and the Germans, but West's other views cast her in a less than flattering light. Between 1936 and 1938, she travelled to the Balkans and became a fervent supporter of Serbian nationalism. The result was her 1941 epic travelogue *Black Lamb and Grey Falcon: A Journey through Yugoslavia*. In it she extolled the virtues of everything "Slav", while dismissing "the Croat" as an inferior "weakened by Austrian influence as by a profound malady".[24] It's no accident that scholars today characterize West as racist, with some even going even so far as to compare her views with Nazism in terms of crude racial stereotypes and advocation of violence.[25] In this context, we should also take note of passages like the one in which West described Albert Speer as "black like a monkey".[26]

In any case, she mocked Germans as a "great galumphing fool of a people" and German women particularly, lacking in both "intellectual pretentions and domestic skills".[27] Like other female observers, she noted that the trial was an almost exclusively male affair. But the number of women reporters was in stark contrast to that of the main figures in the legal proceedings. Women like West were central to the journalistic depiction of the trial. West couldn't resist making a gender-conscious barb at the builders of Schloss Faber-Castell: "Nothing can have been so offensive to the spirit of the Schloss as these women correspondents. Its halls had been designed for women who lived inside their corsets as inside towers... [and] whose feet were encased in shoes that prevented them from hurrying and advertised their enjoyment of infinite leisure."[28]

Of course, the female correspondents in the press camp had no time to enjoy any such leisure. They were required to churn out reports. And for West their industry made them into models of emancipation belying stereotypes and capable of serving as role models to re-educate people. She highlighted

Francis Biddle in his brother George's fresco *Life of the Law* in the US Department of Justice, 1937.

one Jewish-French colleague: "Madeleine Jacob burned the air in the corridors, she rushed so fast along them... her superbly Jewish face was at once haggard and bright with contentious intellectual gaiety. It would have been very hard for the builders of the Schloss to grasp the situation: to understand that these ink-stained gipsies had earned the right to camp in their stronghold because they had been on the side of order against disorder, stability against incoherence."[29]

"You are a good kid, but of course it is my wife I really love"

Without doubt, West led a more liberated life in Schloss Faber-Castell than the countesses of the past whom she considered prisoners. Nonetheless, her affair with Biddle soon showed how little had changed in the way powerful men viewed women. The judge considered her just another romantic dalliance and had no intention of allowing her to disturb the external image of his intact, monogamous marriage that was so important in the USA. Biddle became palpably nervous when his wife announced that she wanted to visit him in Nuremberg. Katherine Garrison Chapin was a well-regarded poet whose verses had been set to music and performed by prestigious orchestras like the New York Philharmonic. Both Biddle and Katherine were respected public personalities, and after the trial he aimed to further ascend the social ladder in the USA. There was no way he could let a divorce damage the credit he had built up in Nuremberg or endanger his legal career with something that cast him in a bad light. His brother, the painter George Biddle, had immortalized him as a family man of impeccable moral integrity in a fresco that adorned a wall of the US Department of Justice, and he had to live up to that image.

He had told his wife that he had come into contact with the famous writer Rebecca West but implied that he only spent time with her as a replacement for Katherine's literary circle. When Katherine cancelled her visit because of difficulty with travel arrangements, Biddle was clearly relieved. During this period West had gone to Berlin, where she had reported for *The New Yorker*, and the ever-diligent Biddle was swamped with work. After a marathon 218 days of court sessions, he was now preparing verdicts for the defendants. It was thanks to his change of opinion in these days that Albert Speer escaped Nuremberg with his life. Together with the Soviet judge, Biddle had originally called for the death penalty for the former Reich Armaments Minister, but a stalemate arose between their British and French colleagues, who favoured imprisonment, and Biddle ultimately came round and agreed to a twenty-year prison term. In his verdict he wrote: "In mitigation, it must be recognized that... he was one of the few men who had the courage to tell Hitler that the war was lost and to take steps to prevent the senseless destruction of production facilities, both in occupied territories and in Germany. He carried out his opposition to Hitler's scorched earth program in some of the Western countries and in Germany by deliberately sabotaging it at considerable personal risk."[30]

When West returned from Berlin to Nuremberg, she immediately went to Biddle's villa. He found her surprisingly self-conscious and reserved, not at all like in her passionate letters. West said she was feeling fatigued, but she clearly suspected that her affair was nearing its conclusion. Her friend Emanie Arling had told her in a letter that August that, had Biddle's wife joined him in Nuremberg, West would have had no chance with him. But both West and her lover were anticipating the final verdicts. West knew her emotions didn't matter. This was a historic event the entire world had feverishly awaited and would be closely following. Biddle bore direct responsibility for the outcome, while West would have to find the right words to describe it.

West was present in the courtroom on 1st October when the sentences were read out, and she acknowledged the defendants' composure as they heard their fates: "We had learned what they did, beyond all doubt, and that is the great achievement of the Nuremberg trial. No literate person can now pretend that these men were anything but abscesses of cruelty. But we learned nothing about them that we did not know before, except that they were capable of heroism to which they had no moral right, and that there is nothing in the legend that a bully is always a coward."[31] The only verdict she disagreed with was the acquittal of Hans Fritzsche, the head of radio in Goebbels' Propaganda Ministry.

After the verdicts had been rendered Biddle and West visited Prague, which they agreed was the most beautiful city they had ever seen. It was a melancholy trip, overshadowed by their imminent parting. While there, they went to the cinema to see a film whose title was like an omen: David Lean's melodrama *Brief Encounter*. It dealt with a grand, hopeless romance between a married woman and a married man who knew their relationship had no future. The fictional plot no doubt struck West and Biddle close to home.

Before Biddle returned to the USA, he accompanied West back to England. They parted ways in Ibstone. Of the two, West seems to have been hit harder by the end of the affair—after all, her marriage had long since ceased to exist on anything but paper. H.G. Wells, to whom she had remained close, had died in August, and now Biddle was also leaving her forever. "Katherine has got him," she wrote with resignation in her diary. West once even compared her to an alligator. Her sense of loss caused her to suffer "an infection of the gums, toxic neuritis of the left arm and shoulder, and a high fever". West was wont to fall ill in times of emotional duress. Back in 1941, she had written that the body calling for help "makes the appeal as strongly as possible".[32]

A short time later, when West began composing "Greenhouse with Cyclamens", she remarked that, like the defendants, many lovers had no interest in seeing the Nuremberg Trial end: "The illusion was strong that if these delights could go on forever they would always remain perfect. It seemed to many lovers that whatever verdicts were passed on the Nazis at the end of the trial, much happiness that might have been immortal would then be put to death."[33] It was West's sorrowful way of admitting that her own relationship was fated to pass once the judgments had been rendered. She didn't want to let Biddle get away with cancelling the relationship the moment the trial was over. She was angry that, for Biddle, she had been merely someone to pass time with who could offer solace and companionship in bed—ultimately, like so many other women in Nuremberg, she was nothing more than a diversion and object of lust. In August 1946, she had written to her friend Dorothy Thompson that she dreamed of divorcing her husband and emigrating to the United States.[34] But Biddle had assigned her the role of the classic extramarital lover. He didn't feel any genuine strong emotion, to say nothing of love, for her. West was lucky that she didn't know what he truly thought. On 21st July 1946, for example, he had written in his diary: "Tomorrow dinner will meet Rebecca West and will make English love if she hasn't grown too fat."[35]

In "Greenhouse with Cyclamens", in order to describe the situation in Nuremberg, Rebecca West has an anonymous man say to his lover: "You are a good kid, but of course it is my wife I really love."[36] It's easy to imagine these being Francis Biddle's actual words. If so, this oblique, accusatory reference was the only role he ever played in any of her works.

XII

Martha Gellhorn, Hemingway's Shadow and the Shock of Dachau

"You're brave. Nothing ever happens to the brave."

MARTHA GELLHORN

I n June 1946, a few months before she arrived in Nuremberg, Martha Gellhorn (1908–98) celebrated an unexpected theatrical triumph in London. The idea of writing a play was a flight of fancy, and she had to be convinced to do it, since the thirty-eight-year-old had no experience as a playwright nor any ambition to go into drama. Gellhorn had published novels and short stories, but above all she was a journalist, and a passionate one. "I love journalism," she wrote in her book *Travels with Myself and Another*. "It is always a chance to see and learn something new."[1] She was especially keen on covering stories that involved injustice.

In 1941, in the middle of the Second World War, she was "disgusted" with her colleague John Dos Passos for proposing at a PEN conference in London that now was not the time for writers to write. "If a writer has any guts he should write all the time, and the lousier the world the harder a writer should work," she fumed in a letter to publisher Max Perkins on 17th October 1941. "For if he can do nothing positive, to make the world more liveable or less cruel or stupid, he can at least record truly, and that is something no one else will do, and it is a job that must be done. It is the only revenge that all the bastardized people will ever get: that someone writes down clearly what happened to them."[2] Gellhorn was anything but an objective observer. She was an opinionated reporter who always took sides and pushed favoured causes. Her pieces contained both observations of great sensitivity and enraged indictments. For her, journalism was a means of disciplining those who pulled the strings.

Incensed at the suffering of common people and the ruling classes' lust for power, Gellhorn discovered her calling as a war correspondent during a century of armed hostilities. "I never really found my own private disorderly place in the world except in the general chaos of war," she would recall to a friend in 1960.[3] Working as what we today would call an embedded journalist, she covered battles from the Spanish Civil War to Vietnam to the 1989 American invasion of Panama. But the Second World War would always remain central to her life. Gellhorn was one of the greatest chroniclers of the conflict and a pioneer of female front-line reporters in a terrain almost completely dominated by men. In addition to her talent as a writer, the secrets to her success were her insatiable curiosity, her courage and her social skills. Gellhorn was a good listener who enjoyed drinking whisky and talking to soldiers in English, German and French in bombed-out basements and muddy battlefields.

It was curiosity that brought her together with Ernest Hemingway during Christmas 1936. Gellhorn ran across the celebrity writer in a bar in Key West while vacationing there with her mother. He was a "a large, dirty man in untidy some-what soiled white shorts and shirt". Mustering her courage, Gellhorn introduced herself. Neither his grubby appearance nor the fact that he was married to his second wife prevented them from flirting. Soon their relationship intensified, and in 1940, after Hemingway had secured a divorce, they married.

Martha Gellhorn was born in St Louis to parents of very different backgrounds. Her father, a German Jew who had fled to America to escape anti-Semitism, was a gynaecologist, while her Protestant mother was a well-known suffragist, member of high society and friend of US First Lady Eleanor Roosevelt. Gellhorn always insisted that her parents' marriage was a union of equals, something that contributed to the failure of her relationship with Hemingway. Gellhorn's had been a privileged childhood that included trips to Europe and a private education. She later enrolled at Bryn Mawr college near Philadelphia, but she found the atmosphere there just as oppressive as in her home city. There was nothing she feared more in life than boredom. So she quit university and became a cub reporter.

After jobs at various newspapers and a stay in Paris, the vivacious Gellhorn became a literary star, landing a hit with her 1936 short story collection *The Trouble I've Seen*. This narrative cycle consisted of a series of connected fictional portraits of victims of the Depression, for instance a young prostitute and an elderly lady reduced to relying on social benefits. In his review of the book Graham Greene praised her "amazingly unfeminine style". The press compared her style to Hemingway's, and he was flattered when this self-confident, attractive young woman approached him—all the more so because she regarded him as the great literary master. Back in 1931 she had already declared that the code by which she lived her life was a passage from Hemingway's *A Farewell to Arms*: "'You're brave. Nothing ever happens to the brave.' Which is somehow enough—a whole philosophy—a banner—a song—and a love. And something to fill up time—busily, passionately."[4]

Shortly after they met, she and Hemingway decided to go to Spain to write about the Spanish Civil War. Soon Gellhorn's dispatches were appearing in *Collier's Weekly*, where they were widely read. Driven by her sense of personal mission and pugnacious temperament, Gellhorn homed in on vivid details to give readers the sense of witnessing the events live. "Write what you see" was her professional credo, and she claimed to have turned herself into a "walking tape recorder with eyes" that didn't think or judge but merely chronicled in words what she witnessed and heard.[5]

In the years that followed, Gellhorn reported from Hitler's increasingly powerful Germany. In the spring of 1938, a few months prior to the Munich Agreement, she was in Czechoslovakia, a country that would shortly be partly annexed, partly occupied by the Third Reich. After the start of the Second World War she described the events of the conflict in her 1940 novel *A Stricken Field*. She also reported directly about the war for *Collier's* from places as far-flung as Finland, Hong Kong, Burma, Singapore, Java, the Caribbean and England.

Hemingway's Shadow

Gellhorn and Hemingway lived together for four years, including in Cuba, before marrying in December 1940, but he grew increasingly upset by her long absences from his side. In 1943, when she left their estate near Havana to report from the Italian front, he famously sent her a cable asking, "Are you a war correspondent or a wife in my bed?" He had long resented her independence and regarded her as a competitor. Shortly before the Normandy landings, he himself went to the European front while trying to torpedo Gellhorn's similar assignment. In a particularly treacherous move, in the autumn of 1944 Hemingway put himself forward as a correspondent for *Collier's*, the very magazine for which she herself worked. The publisher had decided to hire a permanent reporter to cover the fighting, and because Hemingway was more famous than Gellhorn he got the job. This act of betrayal hurt her, but she reacted in characteristic fashion. Lacking journalistic accreditation, she sneaked on to a hospital ship and passed herself off as a nurse to witness the Allied landings in Normandy. She was the only journalist present on the ground at D-Day and was able to report more authentically on the events of 6th June 1944 than Hemingway could.

Their conflict continued in what they wrote. Whereas Hemingway tended to stress the heroic side of war in his reports, Gellhorn reduced battle to its brutal essence, as though intentionally contradicting her husband. "A battle," she wrote, "is a jigsaw puzzle of fighting men, bewildered terrified civilians, noise, smells, jokes, pain, fear, unfinished conversations and high explosives."[6]

On Christmas Eve Gellhorn and Hemingway met up in Rodenbourg, Luxembourg, for a Christmas dinner organized by an American colonel. The evening was a disaster. Hemingway and Gellhorn got into a row in which he berated her in front of the other guests, saying that she lacked any talent whatsoever as a writer. By that point, their marriage had devolved into an endless stream of insults and cruelties. When Gellhorn arrived back in London after a dangerous sea passage she told him she had had enough. She was simply ill-suited to the role of loyal wife at the great genius's side—for all her life she had refused to be intimidated by male egos. So she filed for divorce.

Hemingway had tried to dominate Gellhorn and rein in her professional ambitions. She claimed that he wanted her to change her name to Martha Hemingway so that he would be associated with her works. Hemingway even attacked her family background, accusing her of "Prussian blood" and "krautism".[7] For her part, after their divorce Gellhorn had nothing good to say about her ex-husband, although she deliberately portrayed herself exclusively as the innocent victim. In truth, she could give as well as she got. Many people considered her dogmatic, ruthless and insensitive, and even those closest to her suffered from her stubborn and sometimes overbearing behaviour. For instance, in 1969 she positively eviscerated her adopted son Sandy in a series of letters. "Motivation comes from within: the world was not invented to amuse and satisfy you; or make your way a bed of roses," Gellhorn wrote. "Motivation comes from guts, imagination and will, within. You have none. You are a poor and stupid little fellow in my eyes. I'd be so damned ashamed to be you, I'd want to jump off a cliff."[8] Gellhorn's empathy and sensitivity were seemingly reserved for the victims of war.

Months before divorcing Hemingway, Gellhorn had an affair with General James Gavin, the commander of the 82nd Airborne Division and, after the war, of the US forces in Berlin. Among other things, Gavin was a major influence on Gellhorn because he gave her direct insights into how front-line soldiers experienced the war. They met under circumstances ripe for a film. During the Battle of the Bulge, soldiers from Gavin's division found Gellhorn wandering around in the snow without accreditation or military uniform and brought her back to headquarters. She and Gavin, the youngest division commander in the US Army and a married man with children, fell in love immediately. Their romance caught fire in liberated Paris, then the ruins of Berlin, until an insanely jealous Marlene Dietrich began spreading nasty rumours about Gellhorn and herself seduced Gavin. He originally wanted to get a divorce and marry Gellhorn, but she couldn't picture herself leading the life of an army wife and used his affair with Dietrich as an excuse to end their relationship.

Love Goes to Press

Although Gellhorn had numerous affairs and married and divorced again, outsiders always considered Hemingway the most important man in her life, and his shadow would dog her for the rest of her days. Much to her dismay, she was often reduced to "Mrs Hemingway" and was continually asked what he was like. Gellhorn's only play, *Love Goes to Press*, was about two women war correspondents with all the problems that job entailed, including competition, long phases of separation and stereotypical gender roles. This indirect final reckoning with her ex-husband premiered in 1946 in London's Embassy Theatre.

The two heroines of the play, Annabelle and Jane, are well-known reporters who are unlucky in love and happy in war. At a press camp on the southern Italian front, where the pair are surrounded by male colleagues, Annabelle considers how to make peace with her husband, a fellow war correspondent who steals her best stories and publishes them as his own, justifying his behaviour with the idea that front-line reporting is too dangerous for a woman anyway. Meanwhile, Jane falls for a public relations officer. But when he extols the virtues of the idyllic post-war life he envisions in the country, which strikes her as incomparably boring, Jane—an adrenaline addict—takes to her heels.

Gellhorn wrote *Love Goes to Press* in the early summer of 1945 in London with her colleague Virginia Cowles. The play was conceived as a comedy, Gellhorn wrote in the programme notes, intended to make audiences smile and earn some money. The plot was based on Gellhorn and Cowles's real-life experiences in the Sessa Aurunca press camp in southern Italy during the Allied invasion. Annabelle and Jane were unmistakable stand-ins for the two authors, and despite Gellhorn's claims that the male characters were entirely fictional and not intended to caricature any real-life figures, Annabelle's husband, Joe Rogers, was obviously based on Hemingway. Rogers—a famous author and notorious "drunk all the time" alcoholic—has a problem with his wife's success and plagiarizes from her. "It turned out he married me to silence the opposition," Annabelle says at one point in the play.[9] That recalled an anecdote involving one of Hemingway's army officer buddies, Buck Lanham: "As Lanham was driving them on dangerous roads that might at any moment be strafed by fighter planes, they caught sight of a V2 vapor trail. Stopping to watch it, Gellhorn noted the time and place and turned to Hemingway, saying, 'Remember this, Ernest… That V2 is my story, not yours.'"[10]

During a stay in London in 1944, Hemingway had written sketches about two female war correspondents in which he had made fun of their loose morals and unethical conduct. It is conceivable that he based the figure of Janet Rolfe, an elegant and ambitious blonde, on Gellhorn, whom Hemingway called, in his parting words, "my beloved phony and pretentious bitch". In fact, although she later refused to discuss her marriage to the writer, she did use his fame to advance her own career, identifying herself on the book jacket of *A Stricken Field* as "Martha Gellhorn (Mrs Ernest Hemingway)".[11] The play *Love Goes to Press* was in a sense Gellhorn's retort to her ex-husband's unflattering sketches.

Today, the comedy is above all interesting from a feminist perspective. American literature at the time was full of stories about men without women. Gellhorn and Cowles turned the tables and created a world of women without men, whose viewpoint they satirize. In so doing they demonstrated the hollowness of male clichés and pre-assigned gender roles.

A Female War Correspondent in a Male World

Love Goes to Press was written before Gellhorn's stay in the press camp in Stein. Nonetheless, the situation of the female correspondents there was in many respects comparable to the one she had depicted in her stage comedy. There were 140 women reporters attached to the US Army during the Second World War, but they constantly had to fight against discrimination, and the importance of their work was long dismissed by men. The Supreme Headquarters Allied Expeditionary Force

(SHAEF) had ordered that during battle female journalists, like nurses, were to be kept behind front lines. Women were forbidden from travelling on their own, but they also weren't given Jeeps and drivers. Aspersions were also cast upon their work ethic.[12] Charles Madary, later the director of the press camp in Stein, was reported to have assured an interview partner in Luxembourg that female correspondents worked hard and wouldn't cause him many trouble. Nonetheless, he also told anecdotes that ridiculed female reporters' commitment to their jobs, for instance by preferring to visit fashion shows in Paris.[13]

This was the sort of prejudice and stereotyping Gellhorn faced not only from Hemingway but also from her *Collier's* editors, who publicly referred to her as their "girl correspondent".

Martha Gellhorn as "girl correspondent", illustration
in *Collier's Weekly*, 20th January 1940.

Her pieces were often accompanied by illustrations that would today be considered sexist. One of them, for an article on 20th January 1940, depicted her as a glamorous starlet with a blonde mane, wearing lipstick and a tight-fitting dress, as though she were a journalistic Rita Hayworth.[14] By contrast, photos from the time invariably show her dressed simply and functionally.

Gellhorn's male colleagues in the press camp in Stein also thought in clichés and reduced female correspondents to their appearance. Ernest Cecil Deane complained that the residents of the women's wing were demanding and that their vanity caused problems. Meanwhile, a male colleague from *Time* magazine wrote a mocking account of Janet Flanner's story of being outnumbered by French and Soviet reporters who occupied the bathroom in the camp's women's house and refused to admit anyone other than their countrywomen.[15]

The Shock of Dachau

Another person shut out, assuming the descriptions of the bathroom situation were accurate, was Rebecca West. Although neither she nor Gellhorn mentioned it in their writings, the two did encounter one another in Nuremberg. Gellhorn arrived in the city in late September 1946; both were present when the verdicts were announced, and they had met previously. It was a touchy reunion for Gellhorn, since H.G. Wells, the father of West's son, had asked her to marry him in 1935.[16] Rumour had it that Gellhorn had had an affair with Wells about which West knew nothing. In any case, Gellhorn admired West's work but kept her at a distance. She couldn't connect emotionally with her older colleague, whom she found "neurotic"—"almost too mild a word for Rebecca". In 1987, three years after West's death, Gellhorn wrote to West's biographer, Victoria Glendinning, expressing her appreciation of West's writing but confessing to having been uncomfortable around her: "I always lacked Rebecca's tendency to be dazzled. Did you like her gossiping? She must have found me sadly lacking; I'm no good at it and I find a great difference between malice and hate; the latter being respectable."

But what Gellhorn shared with West was a capacity for hatred—particularly of the German people, whom Gellhorn compared to a malarial insect: "What a race are these Germans: considering that we have tried to exterminate the anopheles mosquito I think we could most easily devote time to exterminating the German who brings surer and nastier death," she wrote in August 1944 to her friend Hortense Flexner. These words came after she had witnessed the worst thing she had yet seen in her life in Italy: "They are digging out of the catacombs the bodies of 320 hostages the Germans shot in reprisal for a bomb once thrown in Rome which killed 32 Germans. The smell was something utterly unimaginable and that garbage of human bodies, with nothing of human dignity left, was the most ghastly sight I have ever seen."[17] Gellhorn had no way of knowing something even worse was about to come.

On 29th April 1945, Allied troops liberated the Dachau concentration camp. Gellhorn arrived several days later on 7th May, the date of Germany's surrender to the Western Allies, to report on that event. She had never been injured in war. Indeed, despite her dangerous assignments she had never even suffered a scratch. But what she saw in Dachau cut her to the core: "We have all seen a great deal now; we have seen too many wars and too much violent dying; we have seen hospitals, bloody and messy as butcher shops; we have seen the dead like bundles lying on all the roads of half the earth. But nowhere was there anything like this. Nothing about war was ever as insanely wicked as these starved and outraged, naked, nameless dead."[18] The survivors all looked the same in Gellhorn's eyes. It was impossible to tell their age, and they had no distinguishing features because their faces were so sunken. Some of them had been subjected to inhuman experiments. Some had been deprived of oxygen to ascertain how long German pilots could survive at extreme altitudes, some had been dunked in icy water to determine the effects of extreme temperatures, and some had been injected with malaria in the interests of developing a vaccine for German soldiers. Others had been castrated or sterilized.

Gellhorn described these atrocities in detail in her report for *Collier's*, quoting a Polish physician who had been an inmate in the camp. He was incensed but also ashamed that human beings had been capable of such monstrous deeds. During her tour of Dachau, Gellhorn found no respite from the horror. When she could no longer take the stories told by the doctor she moved on to other parts of the camp: torture spaces no bigger than telephone booths and gas chambers, where she was told to cover her nose with a handkerchief because of the piles of rotting corpses the SS men hadn't had time to burn. She also met a survivor of the "death train" that had transported prisoners from Buchenwald to Dachau during the final days of the Third Reich. "Perhaps his body will live and take strength," she wrote, "but one cannot believe his eyes will ever be like other people's eyes." Some prisoners in Dachau had died of sheer relief when

246 THE WRITERS' CASTLE

they were liberated. Others had succumbed after gorging themselves when they were finally given food, which their bodies
could no longer handle. Others still had perished at the electric
fence where they had raced in joy to greet their rescuers. News
of Germany's surrender and Allied victory reached Gellhorn
while she was in Dachau, and the place would always remain a
symbol for her. Ultimately, she found that such nightmare locations were what war was always about, and she believed that the
Allied triumph would permanently relegate places like Dachau
to the past.

Gellhorn welcomed the execution of at least thirty-nine
German concentration camp guards shot to death by American
GIs despite surrendering: "Behind one pile of dead lay the
clothed healthy bodies of the German soldiers who had been
found in this camp. They were shot at once when the American
Army entered. And for the first time anywhere one could look
at a dead man with gladness." Gellhorn didn't mention that the
dead men were part of a recent replacement troop recruited
after the SS Death's Heads units responsible for the atrocities
in Dachau had fled. Perhaps she was unaware of that fact. But
she was no stranger to the desire for revenge, which recurred as
a leitmotif throughout her writing.

Her 1948 novel *Point of No Return*, for example, was a
revenge fantasy of the highest order, based on her experiences in
Dachau. It centred on an infantry battalion fighting in the Battle
of the Bulge and liberating the concentration camp in the final
months of the Second World War. The hero, Jacob Levy, a young
soldier from St Louis, was uninterested in politics, global events
or his Jewish heritage before finding himself confronted with
the unimaginable horrors of Dachau. (His experiences mirror

Gellhorn's own.) Heinrich, an inmate who has been imprisoned at the camp for twelve years, enlightens him matter-of-factly about the torture and genocide that have taken place there. For Heinrich such monstrosities are part of everyday reality, but Levy recognizes them as a fate that could have been his own in different circumstances. Although Levy was vaguely aware of the murder of Jews, he didn't realize the extent of the geno- cide. His whole life has thus far been based on the belief that, if he behaved like everyone else, he would not only survive but achieve success. Now he's confronted with the question: what happened to all the German Jews who also just wanted to lead normal lives?

The shock transforms Levy in a way he could never previ- ously have imagined. Back in his Jeep, he sees a group of laugh- ing German women who refuse to get out of the way when he honks his horn. Overcome with hatred, he loses control and aims his vehicle at the women, punches the gas pedal, runs them over and then crashes into a tree. In the hospital he admits that he has committed murder, but sees it as a symbolic act. He has finally accepted his Jewish heritage and believes that he needs to sacrifice his own happiness to confront the world with its cul- pability in the Holocaust. The novel concludes with Levy being convicted of involuntary manslaughter and avoiding a prison sentence.

Gellhorn admitted in her postscript that she had written the novel to exorcize the unbearable images of Dachau. Like Levy, she had paid insufficient attention to the concentration camps during the war and hadn't protested against the outrages unfolding there. In this sense, she, like her fictional hero, had failed. She hadn't reckoned with anything like the horrors she

found in Dachau. Gellhorn tried to justify the fictional murder
of the German women in her novel, but it remained an account
of an imaginary act of vengeance. The dark side of Gellhorn's
righteous rage was that it partially blinded her to the moral
implications of some of what she wrote. In contrast to most of
Gellhorn's works, *Point of No Return* was never translated into
German.

In Nuremberg

It was more than a year after the liberation of Dachau that
Gellhorn came to Nuremberg, attending the court session
on 30th September 1946, the second-to-last day of the trial.
"Göring has the ugliest thumbs I have ever seen," she wrote in
her notebook, "possibly also the ugliest mouth." She also noted
that the air conditioning was kept on high, which seemed to
fit the atmosphere of the proceedings: "It is a cold court—no
pity is possible." She didn't mean these words as a criticism.
As historian Lara Feigel writes, "The pitilessness of the Nazis
themselves could only be answered by coldness."[19]

   In the first paragraphs of her subsequent article for *Collier's*,
"The Paths of Glory: Highlights of the grim comedy and dire
tragedy of Nuremberg", Gellhorn focused on the defendants'
appearances, the "strange faces" that "told nothing". "Göring's
terrible mouth wore a smile that was not a smile, but only a
habit his lips had taken," she wrote. "Next to him Hess, with
dark dents for eyes, jerked his foreshortened head on his long
neck, weird, inquisitive and birdlike. Ribbentrop held his mouth
pursed and sat rigid as the blind. Keitel was nothing, a granite

bust badly made of inferior stone." She added: "They were just faces, some cruder than others and all more insignificant than you would believe possible. They were just men after all, with the usual number of legs, arms and eyes, born like other men; they were not ten feet tall and with the revolting masks of lepers. You sat there and watched them and felt inside yourself such outrage that it choked you. These twenty-one men, these nothings, these industrious and once-confident monsters were the last left alive of that small gang which had ruled Germany."

Gellhorn wanted her readers to see the defendants as a pathetically "unimposing gang" rather than regarding the horrors of Nazism as an abstraction. By contrast, she was impressed with the dignity of the judges, particularly Lawrence, who was for her a symbol of justice. In her depiction, he was the voice of history itself—a voice for the principle that individuals could be held accountable for crimes against humanity.

During the two-hour lunch break, Gellhorn wandered through the ruins of Nuremberg. Again she was shocked by the extent of the destruction. In *Point of No Return* she called the bombed-out old town as a "vast rubbish heap". She also described an anonymous, battle-hardened GI remarking: "There was nothing small and clinchy about the bombs we were using. The air force was running a regular bus service over Nürnberg; the noise of the planes was so constant you stopped hearing it."

In the evening, together with others from the press camp, Gellhorn travelled to the nearby town of Ansbach for dinner. There they spoke with an unrepentant, patriotic young German soldier who claimed that Germany had only gone to war because England was preparing to attack. Why did the Germans invade

Poland instead of going after English cities, he was asked. The soldier couldn't answer the question but was certain the Nazi government had good reasons. He also asserted that the numbers of victims in the concentration camps were exaggerated, and that Jews had been brought there for their own safety. It had been a mistake to kill Jews, he admitted, but they hadn't performed any real work, and he had experienced for himself how cunning they were with money. He had great memories of the Hitler Youth and was bewildered that his words didn't convince the correspondents.

The next day, 1st October 1946, the verdicts in the Nuremberg Trial were announced. It took forty-seven minutes for them to be read out. Gellhorn was left feeling empty. To her mind, no punishments were sufficient for the crimes in question. The trial was the least that could be done to strengthen the notion of fundamental human rights. It offered no guarantees that things would be different in future, but it did demonstrate something that Gellhorn found particularly essential: "The hope is that this body of law will serve as a barrier against the collective wickedness, greed and folly of any nation. In these dark times it is only a hope. But without hope we cannot live."[20]

Gellhorn's report on the Nuremberg Trial was quite conventional. Compared to her other pieces, it was a rote exercise containing few surprising insights, judgments or revelations. "She is at her best when angry or moved to pity," Hemingway would write to publisher Charles Scribner in October 1947.[21] But anger and pity were not the emotions Gellhorn felt at the main Nuremberg Trial.

Gellhorn only spent a few days in the Stein press camp, and she never mentioned it in her writings. Maybe she didn't consider it worth discussing. After all, as a war correspondent she was used to far worse accommodation. She had lived during the Spanish Civil War with Hemingway and other colleagues in Madrid's Hotel Florida, a constant target for artillery, which suffered significant damage, whose elevator rarely worked and where hot water was the exception rather than the rule. In contrast to Shirer, for example, who had never reported from the front, she didn't object at all to the relative comfort of Schloss Faber-Castell. Gellhorn, who always wrote about topics in which she was personally invested, preferred to concentrate on the atrocities in Dachau and the trial of the century. Still, Nuremberg was just another station. While there she was already preparing to go to Paris, where that December she covered a conference of foreign ministers.

"Why I Shall Never Return"

Gellhorn came away from Germany with a lifelong aversion to its people. In 1962, sixteen years after Nuremberg and six months after she had covered the Eichmann trial in Jerusalem, she undertook a "short trip to hell" to report on the new generation of Germans for *Atlantic Monthly*. She stayed for three weeks, travelling to universities from Hamburg to Munich where she interviewed students. But, like Rebecca West, she considered Germans irredeemable because of the "egocentricity of German thinking". Back in 1943 she had written to Hemingway: "I'm reading Vansittart's book; everyone criticises him like mad, saying he's a brutal extremist but I do not find this so, and have not found anything yet that seemed to me inaccurate and much that is about as sound as one can hope to see, and all he proposes is the occupation and supervised re-education of Germany, based on the assumption that the Germans will never voluntarily reform themselves."[22] Two decades had done nothing to change Gellhorn's mind. "They're incurable people, in my opinion," she wrote to her close friend, former US presidential candidate Adlai Stevenson. "At present they are in the phase of being quiescent sheep and tigers; but only because they are overweight with butter and cream. Remove those and they will become insane blood-loving sheep and man-eating tigers."[23] Gellhorn was particularly shocked by female German students, whom she characterized as conformist, humourless, boring and, in their servility, "the Arab women of the West".[24] She would conclude her article, titled "Is There a New Germany?", with a resounding no: "In my opinion there is no New Germany, only another Germany. Germany needs a revolution which it has not had and shows no signs of having; not a bloody, old-fashioned revolution, with firing squads and prisons, ending in one more dictatorship, but an interior revolution of the mind, the conscience."[25]

Gellhorn waited another twenty-eight years before she reprised her university tour to mark Germany's reunification. Again, she wanted to discover whether the latest generation of German students was any different than the previous one. As she described in her article, published in *Granta*, "Ohne Mich: Why I Shall Never Return to Germany", she found her hopes for change confirmed.[26] "Their education had completely changed, and now they were cajoled to think for themselves and speak their own ideas." But then came the racist violence in Hoyerswerda, the neo-Nazi attacks on foreigners in Rostock and neo-Nazi marches in many places in East Germany. Gellhorn thought the German government was doing far too little to rein in the latest far-right unrest—and not just the government. What about the students, she asked: "Where were those good kids?" Why wasn't there a rebellion at German universities against the government and this pernicious new neo-Nazi activity? Gellhorn was deeply disappointed and went so far as to hazard a biological explanation: "I think they have a gene loose, though I don't know what the gene is." She herself would remain true to the title of her *Granta* article and never returned to Germany. She died in 1998 in London.

XIII

Painting to Escape the Horror: Wolfgang Hildesheimer and the *Einsatzgruppen* Trial

"If for no other reason than that it distinguishes
between 'human being' (Mensch) and 'man'
(Mann), German is a good language."

WOLFGANF HILDESHEIMER

With the announcement of the verdicts, the Nuremberg Trial became a part of history. The print media and radio treated it as an event of global political significance, and the trial was the subject of documentary films for mass audiences in both the East and the West. By the end of 1946, Stuart Schulberg from the US Office of Military Government for Germany had already been commissioned to make a film, *Nuremberg: Its Lesson for Today*, whose title didn't hide its didactic intention.

Well versed in the dramatic form of fictional films, Schulberg humanized the trial, making US prosecutor Robert H. Jackson into the hero. The film begins with several minutes from his opening speech, and he appears repeatedly throughout. The US War Department hired popular writer and playwright Carl

Zuckmayer, a German refugee from Nazism in the USA, as a civilian cultural consultant to work on the script. After a historical introduction, *Nuremberg: Its Lesson for Today* followed the structure of the trial and used the prosecution's four main charges as an organizing format. Most of the film consisted of official footage from the courtroom, but it also used visual material introduced as evidence against the defendants. The calm, unemotional narration starkly contrasted with the upsetting images, serving as an American-inflected voice of reason. The film was shown in 1948 in southern Germany and in 1949 in West Berlin.

Its Soviet equivalent was *The People's Court*. It was produced by the former front-line reporter Roman Karmen, who resided in Schloss Faber-Castell and shot his own footage in the courtroom.[1] Karmen was a favourite of Stalin and was very famous in the Soviet Union, having captured on film both the capitulation of the German Sixth Army in Stalingrad and the Soviet conquest of Berlin. His 1937 film about the Spanish Civil War, *Madrid in Flames*, had won international acclaim. Karmen's documentary about the trial combined his footage from the proceedings with segments from Nazi weekly film newsreels and images of the advancing Red Army and the liberation of the concentration camps. It was not without didactic pathos. Today we might call Karmen an early exponent of visual framing, since he not only tried to stir up emotion but also repeated key images to drive home select messages. The film attracted lots of viewers to cinemas in the Soviet occupation zone.

The conclusion of the Nuremberg Trial and the cinematic attempts to depict it for posterity, however, were by no means the end of the prosecution of Nazi crimes in the city. In December

1945, the Allies had already agreed on a unified legal basis, Control Council Law Number 10, for holding war criminals accountable for their actions. It also became the foundation for all of what became known as the subsequent Nuremberg trials. In contrast to the Major War Criminals Trial, which was conducted by an international military tribunal, these trials were the exclusive responsibility of US military courts. Jackson resigned his office after the conclusion of the main trial and appointed as his successor Telford Taylor, who had performed well in the proceedings. Twelve subsequent trials were held in Nuremberg between 1946 and 1949 against groups including doctors, military officers, civil servants and diplomats. They demonstrated the extent to which the leaders of German society had supported the Nazi dictatorship.

There were no internationally famous names among the new crop of defendants. Without exception, these were all "second-level" war criminals. As a result, international media interest withered. What was true for the accused also held true for the correspondents. No celebrity authors or journalists attended any of the subsequent trials. The VIPs had long departed Nuremberg, making way for a new guard of correspondents, from which a number of excellent writers also emerged.[2] The press camp, seriously overcrowded when the verdicts in the main trial were announced, gradually emptied. According to a telephone list of the entire personnel at the trial, drawn up at the behest of the Chief of Counsel for War Crimes, only around seventy guests resided in Schloss Faber-Castell by 1948.[3]

As of January 1947, one of them was a young man, completely unknown on the literary scene, who would become the moral conscience of, and an independent spirit within, post-war

West German literature. Wolfgang Hildesheimer (1916–1991) would not have suspected that he would one day win the Georg Büchner Prize (1966) and write a bestseller, *Mozart* (1977), which would be translated around the world and forever change the genre of biography. During his time in Nuremberg he had no ambitions whatsoever to become an author, and neither before nor during this period did he write anything of note. He had published a few journalistic articles, poems and reviews in English, which he regarded as "garbage", expressing his amazement in 1946 at "how poor" they were. It wasn't until 1950 that he began composing literary works in German.[4] A combination of personal interest and chance brought Hildesheimer to Nuremberg, but his time there would set his life on a new path.

Hildesheimer came from a rabbinical family on his grandfather's side. Born in Hamburg, he moved at the age of seventeen with his family to the British Mandate for Palestine in 1933. There, he did a carpenter's apprenticeship and soon discovered a passion for the visual arts. He studied painting and set design in London, returning after stays in France and Switzerland to Palestine, where he served as an information officer for the British government's Public Information Office during the Second World War. Back in London after the war, he tried to earn his keep as a painter, graphic artist and set designer, but it was a hand-to-mouth existence for a fellow who was also something of a dandy.

"Because I was interested in the system of simultaneous interpretation, with which I was completely unfamiliar at the time, I took an interpretation test at the American embassy [in London] and was hired as an interpreter for the Nuremberg court system," Hildesheimer wrote in 1953 to German novelist

Heinrich Böll.[5] The test involved translating a speech by Hitler into English, and once he passed it he was offered the lucrative salary of £850 a year. "I took up the offer because I wanted to convince myself of the truth of the much-cited thesis at the time of German collective guilt, not because I wanted to return permanently to Germany," he added. Whether Hildesheimer really interrupted his career as a visual artist because he was curious as to whether Germans were indeed collectively guilty or whether the money was his primary motivation doesn't matter. Curiosity was in any case one of his main character traits.

The Post-war Collective Guilt Debate

Although the Allies rarely levelled direct accusations of collective German guilt, the issue dominated the public debate of the immediate post-war period, and the German populace was confronted with Allied posters featuring images of the liberated concentration camps and the caption "These atrocities: your fault". This was an unambiguous reference to the culpability of Germans in general, and many were also sensitive about the idea of collective blame because of the total social collapse they had just endured. Tempers ran high. Adolf Grimme, Minister for Education in the state of Lower Saxony, wrote in *Die Welt* on 21st May 1946: "Political life is Germany has hardly awakened. Most Germans still stand on the sidelines. They've had enough of what people call politics. The only two ideas that occupy even the dullest of them are collective guilt and democratization. These two concepts are a focal point encompassing both past and future."

According to a survey carried out in the winter of 1946, 92 per cent of respondents rejected the idea of collective guilt.[6] Cultural and political magazines like *Der Ruf* and *Die Wandlung* published in-depth debates about the issue, often initiated by German émigré intellectuals like Thomas Mann, Hannah Arendt and Franz Werfel. Philosopher Karl Jaspers commented on the Allied posters. In a series of lectures at the University of Heidelberg, published in 1946 as *Schuldfrage* (*The Guilt Question*), he distanced himself from what he considered the banality of the public discourse surrounding guilt and called for greater differentiation than an explanation "that reduces everything to a single level without nuance in order to pass judgment in the style of a bad judge".[7] Jaspers distinguished between four gradations of guilt: criminal guilt, political guilt, moral guilt and metaphysical guilt. They could only be measured by corresponding authorities: the courts, the power and will of the victors, Germans' individual consciences and God.

Not all philosophers accepted Jaspers' ideas. For instance, his student Hannah Arendt, with whom he corresponded about her essay "Organisierte Schuld" (Organized Guilt), was sceptical. In August 1946 she complained that his definition of Nazi policies as a crime (criminal guilt) didn't go far enough. Nazi crimes, in her eyes, defied legal definition, which was precisely what made them so monstrous. There was no punishment harsh enough to fit them. In line with such thinking, Arendt criticized the intention and verdicts of the Nuremberg court. It would be completely insufficient for the Allies to hang Göring, she wrote to Jaspers. The guilt of the Nazi leaders exceeded the scope of all legal systems, nullifying them, so no punishment within those systems could ever be adequate. Jaspers thought Arendt was in danger of inflating the Nazi leaders' status and losing sight of the banality of the accused by raising their guilt beyond the level of the merely criminal. "Bacteria can cause plagues that wipe out whole peoples, but they still remain bacteria," Jaspers argued on 23rd October 1946.[8]

Hildesheimer didn't differentiate in this fashion during his time in Nuremberg. He never questioned the effectiveness of the trials. Like his parents in Palestine, he cast a critical eye on Germans as a whole: "I don't have much in common with the Germans and can't understand how anyone could," he wrote to his parents from the press camp on 10th April 1947. "Beside the fact that they're dirty, I find Germans physically unsympathetic," he proclaimed in another letter. Worse still, he added, the only emotion the masses were still capable of feeling was self-pity, "and that comes completely at the cost of them feeling any guilt".[9]

But Hildesheimer would change his mind over the course of his years in Nuremberg. Personal acquaintance with Germans, especially with artists and museum workers, became friendships, and he openly spoke of them as "family". Hildesheimer's parents were pressuring him to return to Palestine after his engagement as interpreter, but he cautiously prepared them in his letters for his decision to stay in the country of his birth and establish himself as an artist. Doing that required a more positive view of the people around him. By 15th September 1949 he was writing that Germans were "if not for the most part, then to a large part innocent".[10]

The change in Hildesheimer's attitudes towards Germans mirrored that in Anglo-American policies, which increasingly turned away from stigmatization. The two Western powers needed their former enemies as friends. On 18th May 1947, the British deputy military governor in Germany, Brian Robertson, instructed the control commission in his occupation zone to treat Germans "as people of one Christian and civilised race towards another whose interests in many ways converge with our own and for whom we no longer have any ill will". His staff called this the "be kind to the Germans order". Meanwhile the Americans issued a new directive to replace Joint Chief of Staff Directive 1067, which prohibited fraternization with Germans. JCS 1779, which took effect in July 1947, declared: "An orderly and prosperous Europe requires the economic contributions of a stable and productive Germany."[11] The posters with photo collages of concentration-camp victims and the admonition "Remember this! Don't fraternize!" disappeared. The priority was now to help the Federal Republic of Germany achieve international recognition and reinforce the national identity of West Germans.

Ultimately, Hildesheimer's personal answer to the post-war German debate about collective guilt was his decision to stay in Germany after his interpreter's job was over. But the past would revisit him decades later. In 1979, German essayist Fritz J. Raddatz published a critical article in the weekly newspaper *Die Zeit* about the beginning of post-war West German literature. In it, Raddatz posed several provocative questions about respected German authors: "Was Günter Eich a member of the Nazi Party? Did Peter Huckel remain a member of the Reich Writers Chamber? Did Erich Kästner write scripts for Nazi films? Did Wolfgang Koeppen publish in the Third Reich? Did Peter Suhrkamp print odes to Nazism?" The article, which disputed the idea of a completely new beginning in German literature after the war, unleashed a debate in the arts sections of German periodicals about whether well-known writers had been "fellow travellers" of the Nazis. Literary critic Marcel Reich-Ranicki chimed in for the *Frankfurt Allgemeine Zeitung*, asking numerous writers, including Hildesheimer, for statements on the issue.

Starting in 1951, Hildesheimer had been a member of Group 47, an informal platform for the renewal of German literature founded by author Hans Werner Richter in 1947, and he personally knew several of the writers Raddatz had attacked, among them Eich. Hildesheimer's opinion carried weight within Group 47 because he was considered an "un-German"—in the positive sense—outsider. In his obituary, Germany's renowned *Spiegel* magazine called him a "Sunday's child", free from the "very German depressiveness, contrition and provincialism" of the Group 47 circle, as well as a cosmopolitan who straddled genres and possessed his own individual imagination and political views.

Hildesheimer's answer appeared on 9th November 1979 in *Die Zeit* and was titled "Were my friends Nazis?" While he acknowledged that his colleagues had made mistakes, he refused to either excuse or morally condemn them. "Crimes make the criminal, but mistakes don't make the mistaken," he wrote. "We are no longer the people we were twenty, thirty or forty years ago, and when I examine my own mistakes, I can only say: thank God. The past of those close to me before they became close to me is irrelevant to me, which doesn't mean that it is not allowed to be talked about in a relevant context. The question implies a pluperfect that doesn't admit of my or indeed any evaluation. The question should be: was I friends with Nazis? The answer is categorically and unambiguously: no."[12]

Hildesheimer wasn't an outsider in post-war German literature because he had returned to German from a POW camp, foreign exile or—least of all—a period of "inner emigration". He owed his special role and status as "elder statesman" to the fact that he was Jewish, and he was eminently aware of this. Hildesheimer was ambivalent about his Jewishness. In one of his essays he wrote that although he felt Jewish, he wasn't rooted in Jewishness and considered it a destiny that had been thrust upon him without any action of his own.[13] His membership in this category was only significant for him insofar as others recognized it and it was greeted with anti-Semitism. The Nuremberg trials were a life crossroads in this respect. "I was first confronted with Jewishness in the most horrific sense—racial categorization, exclusion and all the other terms in this discourse—when I became a simultaneous interpreter at the Nuremberg trials, which rolled out, systematically and schematically, a story I had only known from reports and rumours while it was going on."[14]

The Hildesheimers hadn't resettled in Palestine in 1933 because they fled the Nazis, although the family, like all Jews in Germany, had faced anti-Semitic hostility. They were Zionists, and Hildesheimer's parents had planned for quite some time to emigrate. The first time Hildesheimer had to face the horrors of Nazism directly, with their full emotional force, was during the subsequent Nuremberg trials, especially the *Einsatzgruppen* Trial, the ninth of the twelve supplementary proceedings. During the "biggest murder trial in history", as it was billed by the Associated Press, Hildesheimer served as an interpreter for Otto Ohlendorf, a man who today is considered the epitome of an intelligent, technocratic mass murderer.

The *Einsatzgruppen* Trial

Ohlendorf was an SS *Brigadeführer* and commander of the mobile terror and killing unit *Einsatzgruppe* D during Germany's military campaign against the Soviet Union, and he freely admitted his deeds in Nuremberg, much to the amazement of the court.[15] After completing his studies, the handsome forty-year-old spent most of the war as a foreign-trade expert in the Economics Ministry. He had only commanded *Einsatzgruppe* D for a single year, between 1941 and 1942. The neutral-sounding term *Einsatzgruppe* (deployment group) was a Nazi euphemism. Ohlendorf's men didn't killed armed enemies on a battlefield. They executed defenceless victims—Jews, Roma, Communists, suspected partisans and so-called anti-socials (the mentally and physically ill)—in the name of genocidal Nazi ideology. *Einsatzgruppen* were originally put together by Heinrich Himmler for deployment in Poland, where, starting in 1939, with the full knowledge of the German Wehrmacht, they murdered more than 60,000 people, mostly Polish elites. Following behind advances made by the German Army, the *Einsatzgruppen* subsequently expanded their murderous actions to the Soviet Union.

Ohlendorf had already been called as a witness in the Nuremberg Trial on 3rd January 1946, and his testimony had deeply shaken the court. When asked by US Colonel John Amen how many people had been killed by *Einsatzgruppe* D under his command, Ohlendorf answered without hesitation: "In the year between June 1941 to June 1942 the *Einsatzkommandos* reported ninety thousand people liquidated." When Amen followed up by asking whether that number included men, women and children, Ohlendorf simply responded, "Yes." When Amen inquired what the "official duties" of the *Einsatzgruppen* had been, he said: "The instructions were that in the Russian operational areas of the *Einsatzgruppen* the Jews, as well as the Soviet political commissars, were to be liquidated." Amen then wanted to know, "And when you say 'liquidated,' do you mean 'killed?'" Ohlendorf replied, "Yes, I mean 'killed'." Göring was incensed. "What does that swine think he'll gain," the former Reich Marshal was said to have asked during a break in the proceedings. "He'll hang one way or the other."

Otto Ohlendorf at the 1947 *Einsatzgruppen* Trial

Ohlendorf was a difficult customer insofar as he recanted some of his earlier testimony on the advice of his attorney at his own trial. He also tried to win over his fellow accused to his would-be exonerating line of argument, in which he claimed he had acted in "putative self-preservation". That claim was based on the idea that he had assumed the conditions required for self-defence had been fulfilled. The liquidation order, Ohlendorf said, had been issued by the SS head of personnel, Bruno Streckenbach, who had in turn been passing on instructions from Hitler. Ohlendorf was trying to deflect responsibility on to Streckenbach, who found himself in Soviet captivity, also claiming that his own life and that of his men would have been in danger had he defied the Führer's command. The idea was to portray himself as a commander who had only followed orders in a situation of enormous pressure.

Moreover, he sought to justify the mass murders as a matter of military security. In October 1948, he testified that "the goal was to liberate the army's rear areas by killing Jews, Gypsies and Communist activists" and anyone who potentially might have threatened security. This line of defence was an abject failure. In June 1951 Ohlendorf was executed in the prison for war criminals in the town of Landsberg am Lech, after a plea for clemency by German politicians and religious figures was rejected.

Hildesheimer was one of a team of interpreters who translated Ohlendorf's words into English, and he found it very trying. "The material you're given and the witness testimony you hear during the Doctors Trial often goes beyond the imagination," he wrote to his parents on 5th February 1947. Eight months later, on 8th October 1947, he added: "This morning I interpreted for the cross-examination of the main defendant Ohlendorf. It was terribly difficult, and I'm still exhausted. But now I've got five days off again."[16] Nearly without exception, the interpreters, including Julia Kerr, the wife of noted theatre critic Alfred Kerr, were Jewish refugees from Europe. During the subsequent trials they were instructed to translate the defendants' whitewashing, evasions and lies with precision and professionalism, not to contradict them. Emotions were not to play any role at all. But it wasn't always possible to keep down such feelings. A man named Armand Jacoubovich, for example, who had lost almost his entire family in the Holocaust, passed out in the interpreters' booth. He subsequently asked to be transferred to the ranks of the translators. One of his colleagues said in a 2005 interview that she had been twenty-one when she began working in Nuremberg and ten years older when she left the city four months later.[17]

Hildesheimer painted. The visual arts were a form of compensation, a therapy and a shield against the horrors that he experienced during the trials. In summer 1947, he finished an abstract oil picture and a portrait. He painted in oil and water-colours, using feathers, matches and whatever else he could get his hands on. He even planned an exhibition of his works in Munich for the spring of 1948. Some thirty years later, he remarked that he set up an art studio in Nuremberg "in order to distract myself with drawing and painting from the horror of the detailed recapitulations of these events, and I succeeded".[18]

In his later years, Hildesheimer sometimes had a strongly pessimistic, even apocalyptic view of the world. The planned Afterword to his fictional biography *Marbot* (1981), which he ultimately left out of the book, began with the words: "The earth is heading toward the end. The tempo of this process accelerates from hour to hour."[19] Concerns about the environment, the arms race and problems in the Third World darkened Hildesheimer's already fundamentally depressive mood. For quite some time he had suffered from psychological distress, with symptoms includ-ing insomnia. It would go too far to blame his experiences as an interpreter alone for his later depression. But Hildesheimer's reaction to his inner despair was the same as it had been during the trials. He turned to the visual arts.

In 1984, he announced that he was giving up writing in the face of the imminent environmental catastrophes he expected. He had already used many of his personal experiences—for instance his sleeping difficulties and his fear that he could still be persecuted by adherents of the Nazi dictatorship—in works like his bestseller *Tynset*. But now he let his pen rest. In an interview with *Stern* magazine he said he found it incomprehen-sible that "anyone could still sit down today and write a fictional story".[20] Publicly stigmatized as a prophet of impending doom and shunned by his fellow writers, he returned to his artistic roots. He mainly painted collages, and once again the visual arts became an alternative universe that saved him.

Painting was one reason Hildesheimer moved in December 1947 from Schloss Faber-Castell to the Grand Hotel in Nuremberg city centre. His studio was in the heart of town and could be reached on foot from the hotel. Before that, he had spent almost a year pleasantly in the press camp. While many of the correspondents complained about the cramped conditions in Schloss Faber-Castell, Hildesheimer, an employee of the occupying authority, enjoyed comparatively princely accommodation in a room of his own. His monthly alcohol rations included three bottles of champagne. "Last month I had Veuve Cliquot [*sic*]... there's also gin," he wrote enthusiastically to his parents. Hildesheimer had his own drinking glasses and towels. "I'm also getting curtains this week and have wallpapered my room with pictures and maps," he told his parents. "I was able to go to the dentist a while ago here. I have a new pair of spectacles, too. All for free by the way. The arrangements are truly fantastic." The only disappointment in Schloss Faber-Castell was aesthetic. "[The castle is an] awful old box, terribly tasteless, a mixture of art nouveau and rococo. But it's very comfortable. There are huge rooms with baths, fantastic food, drink, social spaces and cars constantly at your disposal."[21]

In the Interpreters' Booth

Hildesheimer spent his first weeks in Nuremberg practising for his new job. Before he could be deployed as an interpreter he had to be trained, and he found simultaneous interpretation a challenge. Hitler's interpreter, Paul Schmidt, who was quartered in the witnesses' house, remarked: "The difficulty… resides in the special syntax that distinguishes German from all other languages commonly used at international conferences. Because in German the verb very often comes at the end of sometimes extremely long and labyrinthine sentences, whereas it's required directly after the subject in French or English translation… nearly insurmountable obstacles arise purely in terms of time."[22]

Simultaneous interpretation was an entirely new discipline born during the Nuremberg Trial. It required a novel technology, with everyone wired up with everyone else, which allowed for immediate translation. Separated from the rest of the courtroom by a glass wall, the interpreters could switch between languages with the twist of a knob. A yellow light signalled to the speakers that they should talk more slowly; a red light meant an interruption, for instance, because of technical problems. Previously, interpreters had translated consecutively, with the translation following the original words. A special note-taking technique was used for this. But there was no time for conventional interpreting in Nuremberg since it would have unreasonably delayed the trial.

The interpreters were under enormous pressure—and not just in terms of tempo. They were also required to translate perfectly at the highest of speeds in a war crimes trial of global historical significance. As Siegfried Ramler, Hildesheimer's fellow interpreter, boss and friend, acknowledged in his autobiography, it was an impossible task. The most important talent of a simultaneous interpreter, he said, was a lack of perfectionism.

The second- or third-best choice of an equivalent word was also legitimate. The defendants, whose necks were literally on the line, saw the situation differently. One of the accused in the Major War Criminals Trial, Fritz Sauckel, whose strong Franconian accent proved a major headache for the interpreters, believed until his final breath that he had been sentenced to death because of a mistranslation.

Nor were prosecutors exempt from being misconstrued. Jackson, whose cross-examination of Göring was highly criticized, also owed his perceived failure to a translation. Initially, he sought to connect the former Reich Marshal with German planning for the Second World War. He introduced as evidence a document concerning the "preparation for the liberation of the Rhine". But Göring spotted a mistake and pointed out that the passage in question had nothing to do with Germany's 1936 remilitarization of the Rhineland, but rather the freeing of the River Rhine of obstacles. The German word *Freimachung* had been incorrectly rendered into English.

Every word was a battle in Nuremberg, and the correct choice of terms could be a matter of life and death, so great attention was paid during the selection of interpreters as to whether the candidates would in fact be up to the job. Along with excellent language skills, they also had to possess broad cultural background knowledge and be familiar with specialist legal, political and medical terminology. Although their work demanded extreme concentration, they were forced to perform it amid a constant din since the interpreters' booth wasn't sound-proofed. Hildesheimer repeatedly complained in his letters about the strain this put him under. "You can imagine that this is a somewhat nerve-wracking job," he wrote to his sister. And he added to his parents in July 1947: "I'm extremely worn down and very stressed despite the relatively short working hours."[23]

Three teams of twelve interpreters took turns according to a rota. Working hours were in fact not a source of stress. Hildesheimer was only on the job for one and a half hours each in the morning and afternoon. The next day he had off, aside from having to check the transcriptions. But the work was psychologically challenging because the interpreters had no time to comprehend the content of what they translated—that's how hard they had to concentrate on the sheer act of rendering words from one language in another. It was only later, when they read the transcripts or compared the minutes from the testimony with the audio recordings, that they realized the gravity of what had been said. Those deferred emotions took their toll over time. One symptom was a strange psychological identification with the accused. "Things are in full swing with the *Einsatzgruppen*, and although it's very trying, interpreting is very interesting because you involuntarily imitate them," Hildesheimer remarked. "I'm capable of the entire spectrum from irony to rage to tears. You involuntarily act things out."[24]

Hildesheimer didn't just work in the courtroom. Once in a while, he also had to interpret during interrogations outside the Palace of Justice. In 1948, one assignment of this kind took him to Copenhagen. His short working hours left him with considerable free time, which he used to travel within Germany and also to make trips to Austria and Italy. Via the Red Cross, he worked for a while for an educational programme for children, teaching them to draw. He went to concerts, opera performances and exhibitions, but more than anything he created visual art.

Hildesheimer kept interpreting until the end of his job in Nuremberg in 1949, but his work increasingly shifted to preparing a textual record of the trials, and he was made an editor. In the interest of transparency and general understanding, American authorities had decided to document the subsequent trials in writing. The result was not an unabridged, popularly inaccessible, dry-as-dust collection of transcripts. The fifteen volumes of the *Trials of War Criminals before the Nuernberg Military Tribunals under Control Council Law No. 10*, published by the US government, served as the official documentation of the individual charges and verdicts as well as the relevant administrative materials.

As a member of the editorial team, Hildesheimer was responsible for the selection, compiling, editing and indexing of Volumes Three (the Judges Trial) and Five (the *Einsatzgruppen* Trial). Later in life he would notice the usefulness of his intense engagement with language as an interpreter and editor for his incipient literary work. He had actually only got to know the German language, he said, when he came back to Germany and compared it with other languages. It was this comparison that had shown him the richness and superb qualities of the German tongue.

Hildesheimer heard from Otto Ohlendorf once, indirectly, after the latter was sentenced to death on 10th April 1948. As interpreter Peter Uiberall reported, the interpreters received a letter specifically addressed to them in which Ohlendorf expressed his gratitude that, thanks to their work, he had been given a fair say.[25]

In October 1949, when his work as an editor was over, Hildesheimer moved to the town of Ambach on the Starnberger

See. In 1957 he turned his back for good on Germany, moving to Switzerland, where he lived reclusively until his death in 1991. His motivation for emigration was indirectly related to his experiences in Nuremberg—at least in the estimation of his fellow interpreter Henry A. Lea. Lea, who later taught German Literature in the USA and published on Hildesheimer's works, saw the post-war German desire for a return to the good old days and Hildesheimer's own abiding fear of anti-Semitism as motivations for his relocation. Lea had worked with Hildesheimer on numerous court sessions during the *Einsatzgruppen* Trial and had observed his reactions up close. "When he was asked in 1964 why he didn't live in Germany, [Hildesheimer] replied 'Ich bin Jud' [I'm a Jew]," Lea told German author Hermann Kesten for his anthology *Ich lebe nicht in der Bundesrepublik* (*I Don't Live in the Federal Republic*). "Two-thirds of all Germans are anti-Semites. They always were and always will be." In an unrelated interview, Hildesheimer reaffirmed his accusation of general anti-Semitism, commenting that it was "inherent in Germans and will never be expunged".[26]

Ironically, it was the son of one of the Nuremberg defendants who injected a bit of hope into Hildesheimer's political outlook the year before the latter's death. In 1990, a few months after the fall of the Berlin Wall, German President Richard von Weizsäcker—whom Hildesheimer most likely had met in Nuremberg when as a lawyer he defended his father, Ernst von Weizsäcker, in the Ministries Trial—invited the interpreter-turned-author to give a reading at his official residence in Berlin. The event came at a very symbolic point in Germany's history, with a host of leading cultural and political personalities in attendance. Hildesheimer read from his fictional biography

Marbot. It was a great source of satisfaction for him as a Jewish author, who had left Germany for reasons including anti-Semitism, to be invited to a celebration of German reunification. This was a gesture for the future.

Richard von Weizsäcker and his wife found it very important to offer Hildesheimer a public forum and had worked hard to find an appropriate date. The two men's admiration was mutual. Wolfgang Hildesheimer called Weizsäcker "the best president since Heuss"—the groundbreaking journalist, democrat and the first man to hold that largely symbolic but influential office in West Germany. Hildesheimer singled out Weizsäcker's historic speech on the fortieth anniversary of the end of the Second World War as his crowning achievement. In that address, Weizsäcker had become the first German leader to portray 8th May 1945 as a day of liberation for everyone, including Germans.[27]

XIV

A Kind of Afterword:
Golo Mann's Plea for Rudolf Hess

"It had always been my view that the whole Third Reich was
a scandalously stupid episode in German history, woven from
a series of accidents, mistakes and avoidable idiocies, and by
no means the inevitable result of what happened before."

GOLO MANN

O n 24th November 1945, a few days after the start of the
Nuremberg Trial, Thomas Mann was asked by Associated
Press for a statement of his position on the event. The result-
ing article, abridged and framed as an interview, appeared in
the *New York Daily News* five days later. Taking up the heated
discussions at the time about the legality of the International
Military Tribunal, Mann explained why he thought the Allies'
general approach was correct. Mann took seriously the criticism
aimed at the four Allies that the trial was a legal farce in which
the victors were merely flexing their muscles. In his opinion,
though, such objections were outweighed by the trial's purpose
as a moral crucible. He confided to his diary: "In this trial, the
issue is what should come next and what the primary intellectual

and moral state of reality was at the point when fascism impiously rose up against it. It is taking place on the threshold of the future."[1] In other words, the trial was an event with a broad pedagogical intent, driving home a political and moral point.

Erika Mann supported the tribunal more unreservedly than her father. As she wrote in the synopsis for her planned book "Alien Homeland", "Germans cannot be trusted to take proper care of their own war criminals."[2] To her mind, incorrigible Nazis, such as were still be found in German courts, could hardly be expected to render judgments about their former peers. Erika also spoke out against US Senator Robert A. Taft, who had been an opponent of America's entry into the Second World War, when he criticized the Nuremberg Trial in October 1946.[3]

Her brother Golo Mann (1909–94) was far more critical. The third of the Mann children and a prize-winning historian and journalist, by his own admission he suffered all his life under the burden of being Thomas's son and the sibling of Erika and Klaus, who achieved fame at an early age. He knew he wasn't his father's favourite. In his old age, while editing Thomas's diaries for publication, he could read his father's opinion of him in passages like this one of 24th January 1920: "Golo, more and more a problematic personality, dishonesty, uncleanly and hysterical."[4] Even if their relationship had improved over the years, with Thomas developing respect for his son's historical writings, Golo's adolescence had been a struggle to emancipate himself from the family patriarch. From an early age he became a loner, both within the family and intellectually. Many conventional German historians shunned him because of his narrative style—his biography of Albrecht Wenzel Eusebius von

Wallenstein, the Bohemian military leader and statesman during the Thirty Years' War, included a fictional interior monologue. That earned him an unjust reputation for being a popular historian without academic credibility. Swinging back and forth between the political Left and Right, he remained an individualist who defied all labels throughout his life. He also cultivated this image. Significantly, in his final years he agreed to be buried in Kilchberg cemetery with the other Manns, but not in the family mausoleum where Thomas, Katia and his siblings Erika, Monika, Elisabeth and Michael were laid to rest.

In the autumn of 1945, Golo began working as a programme director and censor at Radio Frankfurt in Bad Nauheim. Before that, while serving as a US soldier in London, he was an announcer for the German division of the American Broadcasting Station. After a short stay in Luxembourg, where he took part in the so-called "war of the airwaves", he wanted to help establish a free German radio broadcaster, which he envisioned being open to journalists of all political stripes except former Nazis. True to this aim, Communists like Hans Mayer and Stephan Hermlin were also welcome. Mann was tasked with monitoring their contributions and those of their colleagues. As all three men later admitted, they often had to grit their teeth to work together, but they treated one another fairly.

Mann frequently travelled to Nuremberg, and one foggy day in December 1945 he was involved in a car accident that left him with an injured leg and put him in hospital for weeks. It is impossible to say whether he ever stayed overnight at or even visited Schloss Faber-Castell. Most of his correspondence from 1944 to 1946 was lost. In a letter to Katia on 6th December 1945, he wrote that he hoped to see Erika in Nuremberg, which might indicate that he went out to the press camp, especially as he knew others who resided there. As a US citizen, Golo would in any case have been admitted to the building, and he did in fact meet with his sister. On 9th December he conducted a fourteen-minute radio interview with her in which she discussed her impressions of Mondorf-les-Bains and the legal particularities and global historical importance of the Nuremberg Trial.[5]

Thirty-six years old at the time, Golo was sceptical about what he saw and heard from the press section of the courtroom, although, as a censoring authority taking direct orders from US occupiers, it wouldn't be until later that he could freely state his views. In an interview he confessed that after eight months he had tired of his identity as one of the victors and his hatred for Germany had "melted away like snow in the May sun".[6] Whereas Erika regarded Germans as a people culpable for the crimes of Nazism and Thomas Mann didn't believe Germany would be able to reform itself, Golo rejected the collective guilt thesis as oversimplifying the many facets of Germany's historic downfall. He preferred the term "collective liability", suggested by his teacher Karl Jaspers. "Liability and guilt—guilt in the criminal sense—are two fundamentally different concepts," Golo wrote in 1987, "and after their victory as well as during the war, the Allies were no angels themselves."[7] War crimes committed by the victors were never mentioned in Nuremberg, he complained. Golo Mann's biographer, Urs Bitterli, cited another passage from his private correspondence in which he attacked "the deeds of this mob of victors", while cautioning, however, that the crimes of the Nazis should not be relativized in any way.[8]

Golo Mann criticized the Nuremberg court not for its punishment of the Nazi perpetrators but for the arbitrary nature of those punishments. In an interview on the fortieth anniversary of the end of the Second World War, he proposed that the accused should simply have been interrogated and then "executed by victors' decree" rather than being sentenced by a legal tribunal.[9] Privately, he expressed far more understanding for some of the defendants, writing to the widow of executed military commander Alfred Jodl that it had been utterly capricious and random as to which of the accused had been sentenced to death: "One was executed while another was allowed to help build up the Bundeswehr [the post-war German military]. I'm only slightly exaggerating here… The best thing would have been to exempt military men altogether from the proceedings."[10]

The Last Prisoner of Spandau

It wasn't until the late 1960s, when he called for the release of Hitler's former secretary and deputy, Rudolf Hess, one of the defendants at the Nuremberg Trial, that Golo Mann expressed such views in public, and not simply in the relative safety of his private correspondence. Hess had been incarcerated since 1941. That year, without Hitler's knowledge, he had commandeered an airplane and flown to Scotland in a wild attempt to negotiate a peace settlement with the British government via the Duke of Hamilton. His mission was hardly very promising. Hess's peace proposal would have had Britain returning all the colonies it had lost in the First World War and creating two separate spheres of influence, giving Germany a free hand on the European continent while London could do what it wanted in the British Empire. The foremost exponent of the cult of personality surrounding the Führer, Hess threatened Britain with Germany's putative military superiority and demanded that the Churchill government step down for peace to be concluded. In a German-language book he authored, Karl Anders, a correspondent for the BBC in Nuremberg, wrote, "Either Hess was in fact already insane… or the Führer's deputy was simply dumb."[11] Anders wasn't alone in this opinion among the press corps.

Whatever the case may have been, Hess was mistakenly convinced that the mood in Britain had turned in favour of a peace settlement with the Third Reich, and he feared the consequences for Germany of a two-front war at a time when Hitler was setting a date for the Wehrmacht to attack the Soviet Union. His secret mission was also likely a desperate attempt to compensate for a loss of his own power, with which he sought to impress Hitler. But whatever his motivation, Hess completely failed. The British immediately took him into custody when he landed and after the war he was sent to Nuremberg.

Back in 1941, in the middle of the war, both Thomas and Erika Mann had drawn hope from Hess's spectacular flight to Britain, seeing it as a setback for Hitler, a shock for the German public and a sign that the circles around Hitler were by no means as stable as they were portrayed to the outside world. The fact that such a major figure would seek "shelter from the English" would open Germans' eyes, wrote Thomas Mann in his diary.[12] Erika even planned to write a book about Hess, but, as with "Alien Homeland", her plans never came to fruition—although in this case the refusal by the British authorities to provide her with the necessary documents was probably also a factor.[13]

By the time of the Nuremberg Trial Hess seemed disoriented, strangely out of place and yet defiant. During testimony concerning the most horrendous atrocities he demonstratively read trashy novels with titles like *Loisl, The Story of a Girl*. His own attorney cast doubt on his mental competence. Göring, visibly embarrassed by the state of the former party comrade sitting next to him, continually interrupted his testimony, instructing him not to talk for so long. Initially, when questioned by the prosecution, Hess said he couldn't remember much, but on 1st December he declared that he was faking such lapses for tactical reasons and that from now on he would have full command of his memory and would take responsibility for everything he had done, signed or co-signed. Over the entire trial, he never acknowledged any wrongdoing. In his final statement he stressed that he regretted nothing, calling Hitler the "greatest son my people has ever produced in its thousand-year history". Hess was convicted of having conspired to destroy peace and planned a war of aggression. He was sentenced to life in the military prison in Spandau, on the outskirts of Berlin.

The life sentence was taken literally, and as the decades passed some Germans began to lobby for his release. In 1966, when his fellow prisoners Baldur von Schirach and Albert Speer were allowed to leave, a movement started to have Hess treated likewise. One year later, his son Wolf Rüdiger founded what he called the "Assistance Group for Rudolf Hess's Freedom" to collect signatures for a petition on his behalf. Among the signatories were the British lead prosecutor in Nuremberg, Sir Hartley Shawcross, as well as anti-Nazi clergyman pastor Martin Niemöller, writer Carl Zuckmayer, future German President Richard von Weizsäcker and Golo Mann. At the centre of the petition were humanitarian concerns, with the group arguing

that "this prisoner has undergone more than the amount of personal suffering to which he was sentenced".

By that point, Hess was seventy-two years old. He had been
behind bars since 1941, and it was apparent that he had been
a victim of the power politics of the Cold War. The Soviets
had repeatedly vetoed requests for his release, and Spandau
Prison was a curiosity. The prison, originally constructed to
hold 600 inmates, was the only place in the world in which the
former Allies of the Second World War still cooperated with one
another. It housed a single prisoner, watched over by alternating
guards from the four victors. The annual costs for food, administration and cleaning ran in the millions.

The Aftermath of a Foreword

Golo Mann, who greatly respected Wolf Rüdiger Hess's efforts
and was in personal contact with him, didn't mince his words.
For him, Rudolf Hess was by far the most innocent of all the
Nazi leaders, "a most deeply harmless human being" with "nothing at all evil about him", a romantic and a lover of nature, not
a "man of war". Life imprisonment should always contain the
possibility of parole, Mann argued, for Hess as for anyone else;
otherwise it was a harsher form of punishment than death. Hess's
continuing incarceration was thus "a judicial act of murder hor-
rifically stretched out over time".[14]

Golo Mann made these statements in 1985 and allowed Wolf
Rüdiger to use them in the Foreword to the 1994 edition of his
book *Rudolf Heß: "Ich bereue nichts"* (*Rudolf Hess: "I Regret
Nothing"*). Although Mann explicitly distanced himself from the

historical views expressed in that book, his position regarding Rudolf Hess sparked a political controversy. After earning fame as a Georg Büchner Prize winner, historian and pundit, Mann went from being an acolyte of Willy Brandt to a spokesperson of the Right. The student unrest, and particular the Red Army Fraction terrorism in 1970s West Germany, drove him into the arms of the ultra-conservative Bavarian leader Franz Josef Strauss, whose 1979 campaign for chancellor he supported.

For many people, that made Golo Mann a persona non grata. Intellectuals at the time were expected to be on the Left. Friendships disintegrated or turned into outright enmity. For example, since 1963 Mann had had regular contact with the playwright Rolf Hochhuth, whose drama *Der Stellvertreter* (*The Representative*) he had reviewed positively. Hochhuth, an admirer of Mann's Wallenstein biography, felt very grateful to and flattered by his older literary colleague and often consulted him on historical questions. But in the end, the two men's friendship disintegrated in a quarrel over the state premier of Baden-Württemberg, Hans Filbinger. In a 1978 article for *Die Zeit*, Hochhuth had called Filbinger "a nightmare of a jurist" because he had handed down death sentences as a navy judge during the Third Reich. In August of that year, Filbinger was forced to step down. Golo Mann was displeased and vented his anger at Hochhuth for unleashing the affair. "I was always for the underdog, and Filbinger has been the underdog during the past weeks," Mann wrote to Hochhuth a month after the state premier's resignation. "By the way, I don't know him personally. I've only ever seen him once or twice, and I didn't like him... Nonetheless I feel sorry for him. I remain convinced that he has been the victim of an injustice you started, willingly or unwillingly. Everything afterwards was a chain reaction."[15]

Golo Mann tended to extremes of affinity and antipathy and had a very black-and-white idea of justice. It was intransigence that led him to take up the cause of the still-imprisoned Rudolf Hess again in the 1980s. But he completely underestimated how much the extreme Right in West Germany had come to identify with the former Deputy Führer. It's hard to say whether this miscalculation was the result of naivety or unwillingness to acknowledge the facts. In 1985, Mann allowed himself to be used for a podium discussion about Hess by the ultra-nationalist group Conservative Action. Unaware of the political thrust of the event, he agreed to record an introductory video message. It was these words that were used later as the Foreword to Wolf Rüdiger Hess's book about his father. After Rudolf Hess's 1987 suicide, the far-right group German Conservatives, which wanted to re-establish Germany's borders not just of 1937 but of 1914, cited Mann, without his knowledge, in their obituary notice. His angry protest and insistence that he would never support an association with such aims fell on deaf ears.[16] His political apostasy was all too apparent. Mann was pigeonholed in the media as a militant reactionary. Frustrated, he wrote to the diplomat and author Baron Burkhard von Müllenheim-Rechberg: "I assume Hochhuth has also seen the [obituary] notice and will publicly characterize me as a proven neo-Nazi. That's just the way the world is."

What distinguished Golo Mann from most other supporters of Rudolf Hess was a sense of gratitude he felt because the latter had protected his maternal grandfather, Alfred

Pringsheim, despite his Jewish background, during the Third Reich. Pringsheim, a Munich mathematician, was good friends with Professor of Geopolitics Karl Haushofer, who was in turn close to Hess. The future Deputy Führer had been a student and for a time an assistant of Haushofer. "Again and again, thanks to Haushofer's mediation, Rudolf Hess held a protecting hand over Alfred Pringsheim, sparing him the humiliations already visited upon German Jews in the 1930s long before the first true pogrom," Mann stated in the Foreword to the book by Hess's son. "As his grandson I cannot forget this fact."

Golo Mann was the only one in his family to credit Hess for the help he had offered. Erika Mann never mentioned it, characterizing Hess instead as a fanatic and foolish Hitler henchman. Her estate contained a fictionalized manuscript, titled "Memory of Rudolf Hess and his Prize Essay of November 1921", about Hess winning an anonymously sponsored essay contest at Munich University. The prescribed question entrants had to answer was: "What will the man be like who raises Germany back up to its former heights?" In his essay Hess had described a passionate, ruthless and selfless dictator clearly modelled upon his idol Adolf Hitler, and though its high-flying praise of the future Führer might have been veiled, it could not have been any more hagiographic. Erika scornfully cited from this "revolting portrayal", written by a "semi-lunatic" with an "idiotic gaze" and "ice-cold eyes"—a portrait of Hess utterly unlike her brother Golo's harmless romantic.

During the Nuremberg Trial, Erika encountered Hess's wife, Ilse, whom she described as completely simple-minded, and she had no affection either for Karl Haushofer, whom she interviewed a year after the Second World War ended. Haushofer's son Albrecht had been involved in the 20th July 1944 assassination attempt on Hitler and had been arrested. He was executed by an SS unit as the Red Army was marching into Berlin. Karl Haushofer, who had already come in for SS scrutiny after Hess's flight to Scotland, was also arrested after the failed assassination attempt and confined for a month at Dachau concentration camp. Psychologically broken, he lived out of the public eye until the end of the war. In March 1946 he and his wife committed suicide.

Erika Mann interviewed him in September 1945. The result was a bitter, nigh on hateful essay, "Besuch beim Karl Haushofer" (A Visit with Karl Haushofer), in which she stressed the conflicts between father and son. The geopolitics professor and former Wehrmacht officer Karl Haushofer had been a pioneer of the Nazi aim of conquering "living space" in Eastern Europe. People had even called him "Hitler's brain", and Haushofer was personally acquainted with the Nazi leader from visiting Rudolf Hess in Landsberg Prison after the failed 1923 "Beer Hall Putsch". Haushofer believed that the German people would have to enlarge its "living space", an idea that provided pseudo-scientific support for Hitler's expansionist aggression and aim of creating a massive German-dominated empire in Europe and northern Africa. Small peoples, Haushofer believed, would inevitably have to give way. Erika was particularly keen to attack these geopolitical convictions. For her, Haushofer was a paradigm, a symptomatic representative of the German elite that had done nothing to stop Hitler. Was he not put to shame by his son's martyrdom, she asked. For her it didn't matter that, at the latest after Hess's flight to Scotland, Haushofer distanced himself from the Nazis, that he had himself been persecuted by them or that he had lost his son as part of the German Resistance to Hitler. And she completely ignored Haushofer's role in protecting her grandparents.

Erika's "intransigent hatred", as Mann family biographer Tilmann Lahme calls it,[17] was the opposite of Golo's support for Rudolf Hess to be granted parole, and these two positions would be emblematic for segments of post-war West German society. Erika sympathized without reservation with the student movements of the 1960s and their opposition to earlier genera-tions' suppression of the German past. Her biographer, Irmela von der Lühe, surmised that, had she not died in 1969, Erika would have "approved of and supported" the radicalism with which many younger Germans held their parents accountable for what had gone before.[18] Golo, as we have seen, sympathized in the 1970s with conservatives like Strauss, who referred to the ascension of the Willy Brandt government as a leftist coup d'état. However, his support was based on what he saw as the continual attacks and "massive hatemongering" against the Bavarian leader.[19] One of Strauss's major political allies was Alfred Seidl, who was named Bavarian Interior Minister in 1977. He was none other than Rudolf Hess's attorney during the Nuremberg Trial.

If we read the views on the Nuremberg Trial against the backdrop of the later debate about Hess, it's conspicuous that there was no room at the time of the proceedings for the sort of mildness later advocated by Golo Mann. Although he later joined Mann and Seidl in arguing for Hess's release, in his final arguments at the trial Hartley Shawcross, out of a sense of professional duty, asked for the death penalty for all of the defendants.[20] Without exception, the Soviet correspondents found that Hess deserved the death penalty.

For observers in the courtroom, Hess was a riddle. Many considered him mentally incompetent, even after his admission, genuine or otherwise, that his memory lapses were fake. "Mad as a hatter and very ill" was how the artist Laura Knight described him in a letter to her husband from Nuremberg. "He looks thin as a rake and dark green in colour." In her painting *The Nuremberg Trial* she depicted him as collapsed inwards upon himself and emphasized his thinning hair. "Hess looks crazy now," she wrote in her letter. "The sickest man one ever saw. He has a round, bald patch like a monk's on the top of his head."[21] The tonsure was a monastic mark of devotion to God—Knight interpreted Hess's lack of hair of the top of his head as a sign of his cultish worship of the Führer.

Probably the most honest position taken during the trial came from Gregor von Rezzori, who freely admitted that he couldn't understand the man Rudolf Hess or his deeds. Like all the defendants, the inaccessible Hess couldn't be put in any sort of proper perspective. In contrast to many of his colleagues who confidently rendered judgments about the accused, Rezzori wrote, "Evil doesn't want to be comprehended."[22] The subsequent debates about Hess were full of commentators who did in fact try to comprehend "evil" in line with their own feelings, as much as they varied from individual to individual. Indifference was not an option, at least as far as anyone was willing to admit. Otherwise, the emotional spectrum ran from hatred to mercy to support to reverence for a purported martyr. We should recall that right-wing extremist memorial marches to Rudolf Hess took place annually between 1988 and 2004. The West German government eventually adopted a position of mildness, asking the former Allies, who remained legally in control of Berlin, to release the then ninety-year-old Hess for humanitarian reasons. They had no success.

NOTES

Foreword

1 X. Qian in S. Radlmaier (ed.), *Der Nürnberger Lernprozess*.

2 Today Schloss Faber-Castell is used by the Faber-Castell company for high-profile events. It also contains a museum devoted to the history of the firm. On the seventy-fifth anniversary of the Nuremberg Trials Faber-Castell commissioned a multi-media permanent exhibit on the press camp.

3 See R. Boyes, "Der Fetteste überlebt".

4 W. Wagner, *Lebens-Akte*, p. 75.

5 See Hildesheimer to his parents on 26th April 1947 in W. Hildesheimer, *Die sichtbare Wirklichkeit bedeutet mir nichts*, p. 296.

6 S. Kinnebrock, "Frauen und Männer im Journalismus", p. 122.

7 V. Ocampo, *Mein Leben ist mein Werk*, p. 252.

8 The present book also benefited from the discovery of rich new source material, for instance the unpublished letters of Ernest Cecil Deane, the liaison officer between the press camp and the court. Other material has also emerged in the estates of Erika Mann, Peter de Mendelssohn and William Stricker. See also S. Radlmaier, *Das Bleistiftschloss als Press Camp*, and S. Radlmaier (ed.), *Der Nürnberger Lernprozess*. Together with filmmaker Reiner Holzemer, Radlmaier produced a documentary film titled *IMT Press Camp*, featuring Markus Wolf, Ray D'Addario and the translator Simone Herbulot speaking in original historic locations. The film is part of the permanent exhibition in the castle museum and can be viewed by visitors taking a tour of the building.

1. A Castle Made of Pencils

1 A. Diller and W. Mühl-Benninghaus (eds), *Berichterstattung über den Nürnberger Prozess gegen die Hauptkriegsverbrecher 1945/46*, p. 11. See also B. Mettler, *Demokratisierung und Kalter Krieg*.

2 M. Gemählich, *Frankreich und der Nürnberger Prozess gegen die Hauptkriegsverbrecher 1945/46*, p. 170.

3 Speer, *Inside the Third Reich*, p. 608, https://archive.org/details/insidethirdreich00spee/page/n3/mode/2up?q=bets

4 T. Taylor, *Anatomy of the Nuremberg Trials*, p. 279.

5 P. de Mendelssohn, *Zeitungsstadt Berlin*, p. 607.

6 H.-U. Wagner, https://zeitgeschichte-online.de/geschichtskultur/der-nuernberger-hauptkriegsverbrecherprozess-als-medienereignis#_ftn21

7 W. Schaber, "Der Fall Ullmann", p. 116.

8 E.W. Michel, *Promises Kept*, pp. 113–14.

9 A. Weinke, *Die Nürnberger Prozesse*, p. 49.

10 L. Jockusch, "Justice at Nuremberg?", pp. 122, 126 f.

11 J. Wilke, B. Schenk, A.A. Cohen and T. Zemach, *Holocaust und NS-Prozesse*, p. 64.

12 H. Krösche, *Zwischen Vergangenheitsdiskurs und Wiederaufbau*, p. 60 f.

13 Ibid., p. 66.

14 R. Tüngel and H.R. Berndorff, *Auf dem Bauche sollst du kriechen*, p. 131 ff.

15 Deane to his wife, 16th January 1946.

16 See R. Weber, *Dateline*.

17 Mendelssohn to Spiel, 18th November 1945.

18 Ibid.

19 F. Prinz zu Sayn-Wittgenstein, *Schlösser in Franken*, p. 24 f.

20 W. Brandt, *Verbrecher und andere Deutsche*, p. 13.

21 Hildesheimer to Teltsch, January 1947 in Hildesheimer, *Die sichtbare Wirklichkeit bedeutet mir nichts*, p. 285.

22 Most of the surviving photographs were taken by Ray D'Addario, who lived in the castle and worked as a US Army photographer.

23 E. Triolet in S. Radlmaier (ed.), *Der Nürnberger Lernprozess*, p. 263.

24 https://www.tuttartpitturasculturapoesiamusica.com/2016/06/Laura-Knight.html

25 William Stricker's estate, which includes several photos of the press camp, can be found in digitized form in the Internet archive of the Leo Baeck Institute in New York (William Stricker Collection). It also contains a

digitized copy of the *Nürnberger Extra Blatt*, privately printed in an
edition of 300 in 1946.

26 Deane to his wife, 20th October 1945.
27 T. Taylor, *Anatomy of the Nuremberg Trials*, p. 263 f.
28 Deane to his wife, 22nd December 1945.
29 Mann to her parents, 24th March 1946.
30 H. Krösche, *Zwischen Vergangenheitsdiskurs und Wiederaufbau*, p. 65.
31 Deane to his wife, 14th May 1946.
32 S. Radlmaier, *Das Bleistiftschloss als Press Camp*, p. 21.
33 B. Polewoi, *Nürnberger Tagebuch*, p. 126.
34 H. Gaskin (ed.), *Eyewitnesses at Nuremberg*, p. 26.
35 B. Polewoi, *Nürnberger Tagebuch*, p. 128.
36 B. Gribben, *Weighted Scales*, p. 53.
37 J. Flanner, *Paris, Germany…*, p. 126.
38 B. Polewoi, *Nürnberger Tagebuch*, p. 127.
39 Deane to his wife, 6th December 1945.
40 Ibid.
41 E. Kästner, *Streiflichter aus Nürnberg*, p. 495.
42 S. Simon, *La Galerie des monstres*, p. 18.
43 P. Fehl, "Die Geister von Nürnberg", p. 280.
44 H. Gaskin (ed.), *Eyewitnesses at Nuremberg*, p. 104.
45 A. Döblin, *Wie das Land 1946 aussieht*, p. 320.
46 See W. von Koppenfels, "Orwell und die Deutschen" and L. Feigel, *The Bitter Taste of Victory*, p. 39 ff.
47 A. Rückerl, *NS-Verbrechen vor Gericht*, p. 92. On historians' and legal experts' opinions about the trial see I. Gutmann, E. Jäckel, P. Longerich and J.H. Schoeps (eds), *Enzyklopädie des Holocaust*, Vol. 2, p. 1019–47.
48 W. Brandt, *Links und frei*, p. 404.
49 See M. Voslensky, "Stalin war mit Nürnberg unzufrieden" and G. Ueberschär (ed.), *Der Nationalsozialismus vor Gericht*, p. 52 ff.
50 H. Habe, *Die Irrtümer von Nürnberg*, p. 238.
51 O. White, *Conquerors' Road: An Eyewitness Report of Germany 1945*, p. 179.
52 A. Mitscherlich cited in K. Scherpe, *In Deutschland unterwegs*, p. 325.
53 S. Radlmaier (ed.), *Der Nürnberger Lernprozess*, p. 296 f.
54 T. Fitzel, "Eine Zeugin im Nürnberger Prozess", p. 64 f.
55 C. Maier, "Die Reportage in der ersten Hälfte des 20. Jahrhunderts", p. 106.
56 See Polevoy and Rezzori's reports on the trial in S. Radlmaier (ed.), *Der Nürnberger Lernprozess*, pp. 105, 289.
57 See M. Lerner's Preface in V.H. Bernstein, *Final Judgement*, p. 2.

2. American Defeats, or The Melancholy of John Dos Passos

1 J. Dos Passos, *The Fourteenth Chronicle*, p. 556.
2 Emphasis added.
3 K. McLoughlin, *Martha Gellhorn*, p. 25.
4 N. Kadritzke, Afterword to J. Dos Passos, *Das Land des Fragebogens*, p. 134.
5 J. Dos Passos, *The Fourteenth Chronicle*, pp. 600–1.
6 Deane to his wife, 30th October 1945.
7 E. Hemingway, *Selected Letters*, p. 670.
8 J. Dos Passos, *Tour of Duty*, pp. 251–2.
9 Ibid., p. 309.
10 T. Ludington, *John Dos Passos*, p. 427.
11 That, for instance, was the opinion of Erich Kästner and Peter de Mendelssohn. See C. Maier, "Die Reportage in der ersten Hälfte des 20. Jahrhunderts", p. 104 f.
12 J. Dos Passos, *The Fourteenth Chronicle*, pp. 558–60.
13 J. Dos Passos, *Tour of Duty*, pp. 304–6.
14 A. Weinke, *Die Nürnberger Prozesse*, p. 41.
15 Ibid.
16 Dos Passos to Upton Sinclair, 30th December 1945, in J. Dos Passos, *The Fourteenth Chronicle*, p. 563.

3. Countess Katharina and Gestapo Head Rudolf Diels

1 A. Weinke, *Die Nürnberger Prozesse*, p. 31.
2 K. Wallbaum, *Der Überläufer*, p. 261.
3 Ibid., p. 349.
4 https://www.faber-castell.de /111-jahre-castell-9000
5 R. Kölbel, "Roland Graf von Faber-Castell", p. 350.
6 In 1998, Asta Scheib published a novelistic biography of Countess Ottilie von Faber-Castell titled *Eine Zierde in ihrem Hause* (*An Embellishment in her House*). One of the topics it covered was her scandalous divorce from Count Alex, which ended with her being found to blame and forced to endure being separated from her children and ostracized by society. She followed her heart and later married the man she loved. German broadcaster ARD made a television movie from this source, stylizing Ottilie as an early fighter for women's rights. On the divorce see R. Kölbel, "Roland Graf von Faber-Castell", p. 352.

7   On the life of Count Roland von Faber-Castell see the interview with his son Wolfgang in J. Franzke (ed.), *Das Bleistiftschloss*, p. 17.
8   E. Randol Schoenberg, "Austria Hangs on to Hitler's Vermeer", *La Opus*, 22nd March 2011, https://www.laopus.com/2011/03/austria-hangs-onto-hitlers-vermeer.html
9   C. Kohl, *Das Zeugenhaus*, p. 133.
10 Ibid.
11 R. West, "Greenhouse of Cyclamens I" in *A Train of Powder*, p. 25.
12 J. Franzke and P. Schafhauser, "Faber-Castell", p. 351.
13 My gratitude goes to Peter Schafhauser for his in-depth information on the history of the Faber-Castell family and castle.
14 J. Franzke (ed.), *Das Bleistiftschloss*, p. 108.
15 D. Sprecher, "Abenteurerin zwischen den Welten", p. 334.
16 C. Kohl, *Das Zeugenhaus*, p. 167 ff. Later in life, Countess Katharina had an extramarital affair with Swiss billionaire and music patron Paul Sacher. The relationship produced two children. In 1969 she and Count Roland divorced.
17 K. Wallbaum, *Der Überläufer*, p. 263.
18 Ibid. There was an entry to that effect in a file maintained by the Counter Intelligence Corps.
19 J. Franzke (ed.), *Das Bleistiftschloss*, p. 19.
20 K. Wallbaum, *Der Überläufer*, p. 279.
21 B. Carter Hett, "This Story Is about Something Fundamental", p. 207.

4. Erich Kästner's Broken Promise

1   Mendelssohn to Spiel, 26th November 1945.
2   E. Kästner, *Werke*, Vol. 6: *Splitter und Balken*, p. 461.
3   S. Hanuschek, *Keiner blickt dir hinter das Gesicht*, p. 323.
4   E. Kästner, *Gesammelte Schriften für Erwachsene*, Vol. 7, p. 76.
5   Mendelssohn to Kästner, 28th March 1961.
6   P. de Mendelssohn, *Unterwegs mit Reiseschatten*, p. 149.
7   Ibid., p. 148.
8   M. Payk, *Der Geist der Demokratie*, p. 86.
9   See the facsimile of the front page of issue one: https://www.stefan-heym-gesellschaft.de/wp-content/uploads/2015/10/451018-Die-Neue-Zeitung-Titel-klein-sw.jpg
10 P. de Mendelssohn, *Unterwegs mit Reiseschatten*, p. 149.
11 F.J. Görtz and H. Sarkowicz, *Erich Kästner*, p. 180.

12 P. de Mendelssohn, *Der Geist in der Despotie*, p. 13.

13 H. Ould (ed.), *Writers in Freedom: A Symposium of the XVII. International Congress of the P.E.N. Club, held in London*, p. 94.

14 E. Kästner, *Streiflichter aus Nürnberg*, p. 499.

15 M. Payk, *Der Geist der Demokratie*, p. 108.

16 It is unclear where Kästner resided in Nuremberg. His biographer, Sven Hanuschek, speculates that he lodged privately since he often stayed with friends during his travels at the time. (Email from Sven Hanuschek to the author, 19th November 2020.) It is unlikely and unproven that Kästner stayed in the press camp, as S. Radlmaier asserts in *Das Bleistiftschloss als Press Camp*, pp. 32, 41.

17 Mendelssohn to Spiel, 26th November 1945.

18 E. Kästner, *Streiflichter aus Nürnberg*, p. 493 ff.

19 B. Wagener, "Inländische Perspektivierungen", p. 204.

20 See G. Reus, "Was Journalisten von Erich Kästner lernen können".

21 On 25th November 1945 Mendelssohn published an article for *The Observer* titled "Overwhelmed by Documents at Nuremberg".

22 P. de Mendelssohn, "Eine schreckliche Stadt", p. 155.

23 M. Payk, *Der Geist der Demokratie*, p. 121 f.

24 E. and K. Mann, *Escape to Life*, p. 108.

25 K. Beutler, *Erich Kästner*, p. 132.

26 S. Hanuschek, *Keiner blickt dir hinter das Gesicht*, pp. 335, 346.

27 Ibid., p. 354.

28 M. Payk, *Der Geist der Demokratie*, p. 117.

29 Ibid., p. 122.

30 L. Feigel, *The Bitter Taste of Victory*, p. 228.

31 B. Wagener, "Inländische Perspektivierungen", p. 195.

32 S. Hanuschek, *Keiner blickt dir hinter das Gesicht*, p. 318.

5. Erika Mann, Her "Beloved Lunatic" and an Unpleasant Reunion

1 Klaus Mann was present at the press conference and asked Göring a question. See the German version of Mann's autobiography, *Der Wendepunkt*, p. 680.

2 J. Flanner, "Letter from Nuremberg, December 17, 1945", *The New Yorker*, 2nd January 1946, p. 48.

3 W.L. Shirer, *End of a Berlin Diary*, p. 315.

4 E. Mann, article for the *Evening Standard*, 29th November 1945, https://www.monacensia-digital.de/mann/content/titleinfo/33254

5 H. Habe, *Brief nach Kilchberg*, p. 14.

6 E. Mann, *Briefe und Antworten*, Vol. 1, p. 30.

7 I. von der Lühe, *Erika Mann*, p. 88.

8 I. von der Lühe, "The Big 52", p. 27 f.

9 A. Weiss, *In the Shadow of the Magic Mountain*, p. 202.

10 I. von der Lühe, *Erika Mann*, p. 252.

11 Ibid., p. 77.

12 E. Mann, *Briefe und Antworten*, Vol. 1, p. 66.

13 I. von der Lühe, *Erika Mann*, p. 260.

14 Erika Mann's letters and manuscripts can be accessed at https://www.monacensia-digital.de/nav/classification /41691

15 Deane to his wife, 18th March 1946.

16 See E. Mann, https://www.monacensia-digital.de/mann/content/titleinfo/33269 and R. West, *A Train of Powder*, p. 26.

17 I. von der Lühe, *Erika Mann*, p. 407 f.

18 In December 1945 she told a radio interviewer: "The trial is less about creating a stir and entertaining people in the present than educating them for the future. And the enormously diligent, sometimes even pedantic way the monstrously copious body of evidence is presented, calmly and undramatically… is very advantageous in view of history." E. Mann, *Blitze überm Ozean*, p. 362.

19 W. Brandt, *Links und frei*, p. 403.

20 I. von der Lühe, "The Big 52", p. 34.

21 E. Mann, "Überraschender Besuch" in S. Radlmaier (ed.), *Der Nürnberger Lernprozess*, p. 143.

22 T. Lahme, *Golo Mann*, p. 182.

23 I. von der Lühe, *Erika Mann*, p. 278.

24 On the suppression of the Nazi past during the early years of the *Süddeutsche Zeitung* see K. von Harbou, *Als Deutschland seine Seele retten wollte*.

25 Ibid., p. 82.

26 S. Radlmaier (ed.), *Der Nürnberger Lernprozess*, p. 183.

27 *Süddeutsche Zeitung*, 27th August 1946, reprinted in W.E. Süskind, *Die Mächtigen vor Gericht*, p. 161. See also R. André, "W.E. Süskind beim Nürnberger Prozess".

28 Mann to Neumann, 3rd June 1946.

29 H. Kurzke, *Thomas Mann*, p. 530.

30 K. von Harbou, *Als Deutschland seine Seele retten wollte*, p. 67.

31 https://www.monacensia-digital.de/mann/content/titleinfo/33348

32 During his activity as a correspondent at the Nuremberg trials Süskind resided in a "badly heated room in the home of a locksmith couple" on Fürther Strasse. At the court he was usually kept separate from his uniformed colleagues from the Allied countries, who, as he himself noticed, sought to avoid him anyway because of the prohibition on fraternization with the former enemy. See W.E. Süskind, *Die Mächtigen vor Gericht*, p. 18.

33 K. von Harbou, *Als Deutschland seine Seele retten wollte*, p. 85 f.

34 W.E. Süskind, *Gekannt, verehrt, geliebt*, p. 51.

35 W.E. Süskind, "Die tänzerische Generation", p. 593.

36 T. Taylor, *Anatomy of the Nuremberg Trials*, pp. 496–7.

37 W.E. Süskind, *Die Mächtigen vor Gericht*, p. 153.

38 F. Utley, *The High Cost of Vengeance*, p. 188 f. On Betty Knox's biography see also A. Stafford, *Wilson, Keppel and Betty*.

6. William Shirer and the Good Wehrmacht General

1 T. Taylor, *Anatomy of the Nuremberg Trials*, p. 220.

2 X. Qian in S. Radlmaier (ed.), *Der Nürnberger Lernprozess*, p. 20.

3 B. Polewoi, *Nürnberger Tagebuch*, p. 76. When the US Executive Trial Counsellor was invited to dinner at the castle in September 1945 he found the food "wonderful". T.J. Dodd, *Letters from Nuremberg*, p. 132.

4 Deane to his wife, 6th December 1945.

5 K. Cuthbertson, *A Complex Fate*, p. 127.

6 W.L. Shirer, *End of a Berlin Diary*, p. 269.

7 M. Strobl, "Hitler will Frieden", *Die Zeit*, 2nd August 2012.

8 K. Cuthbertson, *A Complex Fate*, p. 312.

9 Ibid., p. 294 ff., 313.

10 See Jürgen Schebera's Afterword in W.L. Shirer, *End of a Berlin Diary*, p. 456.

11 R.G. Vansittart, *Lessons of My Life*.

12 W. Brandt, *Links und frei*, p. 353.

13 In 1950 Erika Mann asked her friend Bill, as she called Shirer, to write an essay on her by then deceased brother Klaus. Shirer obliged, composing among other things the Afterword for Klaus Mann's autobiography.

14 W.L. Shirer, *End of a Berlin Diary*, p. 329.

15 Ibid., p. 267.

16 https://babel.hathitrust.org/cgi/pt?id=uc1.b4153667&seq=23

17 W.L. Shirer, *Rise and Fall*, p. 99.

18 C. Kohl, *Das Zeugenhaus*, p. 59.

19 W.L. Shirer, *End of a Berlin Diary*, pp. 322–23.

20 W.L. Shirer, *Twentieth Century Journey: The Start*, p. 176.
21 W.L. Shirer, *Twentieth Century Journey: A Native's Return*, p. 26.
22 Ibid., p. 203.
23 See W.E. Süskind, "Die tänzerische Generation", p. 591. He added: "No one should see dancing girls as artists, and it is equally unjust to jazz if someone tries to make an art form of it."
24 For critical discussions of Shirer's analysis of the origins of Nazism see Golo Mann's Introduction in W.L. Shirer, *The Rise and Fall of the Third Reich*, and K. Epstein, "Shirer's History of Nazi Germany".
25 M. Fisher, "William Shirer at 'Journey's End'," *The Washington Post*, 10th August 1989.
26 W.L. Shirer, *Twentieth Century Journey: A Native's Return*, p. 260.
27 G.D. Rosenfeld, "The Reception of William L. Shirer's The Rise and Fall of the Third Reich in the United States and West Germany, 1960–62", p. 118.
28 W.L. Shirer, *Twentieth Century Journey: A Native's Return*, p. 450.
29 Ibid., p. 453 ff.

7. Alfred Döblin's Didactic Deception: The Phantom Resident of Schloss Faber-Castell

1 All quotations from "Der Nürnberger Lehrprozess" refer to A. Döblin, *Kleine Schriften*, Vol. 4, pp. 170–216.
2 A. Döblin, *Autobiographische Schriften und letzte Aufzeichnungen*, p. 491. On "The Educational Nuremberg Trial" see W. Schoeller, *Döblin*, p. 655 ff.
3 See the Afterword by Christina Althen in A. Döblin, *Kleine Schriften*, Vol. 4, p. 670.
4 In an email to Christina Althen on 29th April 1992, Döblin's son Claude confirmed that his father had not followed the Nuremberg Trial in the city. Thanks to Althen for sharing this information.
5 A. Döblin, *Autobiographische Schriften und letzte Aufzeichnungen*, p. 491.
6 See https://www.faber-castell.de/corporate/historie/press-camp; L. Heid, "German Schrecklichkeit", *Die Zeit*, 19th November 2015; "Nürnberger Prozesse. Pressecamp im Schloss des Bleistiftkönigs", *Der Spiegel*, 17th November 2005.
7 The documentary was still accesible on YouTube as of August 2023 at https://www.youtube.com/watch?v=fCJNkhPGdyk. The purported

press identification appears at 15:47 and an illustration depicting Döblin wearing headphones in the courtroom at 16:00.

8 Email from Peter Hartl to the author, 23rd February 2021.

8. Janet Flanner and the Cross-Examination of Hermann Göring

1 Z.P. Lesinska, *Perspectives of Four Women Writers on the Second World War*, p. 55.

2 B. Wineapple, *Genêt*, p. 77.

3 Ibid., p. 127.

4 J. Flanner, "Uber alles", *The New Yorker*, 9th January 1932, p. 48.

5 J. Flanner, "Fuhrer II", *The New Yorker*, 7th March 1936, p. 27.

6 A. Weiss, *Paris war eine Frau*, p. 200.

7 J. Flanner, "Letter from Cologne", *The New Yorker*, 31st March 1945, p. 58.

8 J. Flanner, "Letter from Nuremberg", *The New Yorker*, 5th January 1946, p. 46.

9 J. Flanner, *Darlinghissima: Letters to a Friend*, pp. 50, 64.

10 Ibid., p. 73.

11 B. Wineapple, *Genêt*, p. 197 f.

12 D.M. Kelley, *22 Cells in Nuremberg*.

13 G.M. Gilbert, *Nuremberg Diary*.

14 A. Speer, *Inside the Third Reich*, pp. 604–5.

15 J. Flanner, "Letter from Nuremberg", *The New Yorker*, 23rd March 1946, p. 81.

16 J. Flanner, "Letter from Nuremberg, March 22", *The New Yorker*, 30th March 1946, p. 76.

17 Ibid, p. 77.

18 J. Flanner, *Darlinghissima*, p. 17 (fn), p. 106.

19 See C. Rollyson, "Reporting Nuremberg".

20 R. West, "Extraordinary Exile", *The New Yorker*, 7th September 1946.

21 https://www.newyorker.com/magazine/1946/09/07/extraordinary-exile. West's *New Yorker* articles were later published in a slightly modified form in her 1955 book *A Train Full of Powder*.

22 B. Wineapple, *Genêt*, p. 200.

23 J. Flanner, "Letter from Königstein", *The New Yorker*, 18th September 1948, p. 96.

24 "Letter from Berlin, July 12", *The New Yorker*, 2nd August 1947, p. 42.

25 B. Wolbring, "Nationales Stigma und persönliche Schuld", p. 346.

26 J. Flanner, *Darlinghissima*, p. 54. After the main Nuremberg Trial Flanner lived primarily in her adopted home, Paris, continuing to write for *The New Yorker* until the ripe old age of eighty-three. In 1975, three years before her death, she returned to New York a much-revered and multiple-award-winning writer.

9. The French Stalinism of Elsa Triolet

1 U. Hörner, *Elsa Triolet und Louis Aragon*, p. 171.

2 See interview with Louis Aragon in Agnès Varda's documentary film *Elsa la rose* (1965).

3 S. Nadolny, *Elsa Triolet*, p. 54.

4 D. Shostakovich, *Testimony*, p. 247–8.

5 See T. Balachova, "Le Double Destin d'Elsa Triolet en Russie". This has been confirmed by recent research in Soviet archives.

6 A. Vaksberg and R. Gerra, *Sem' dnej v marte. Besedy ob emigracii*, p. 176.

7 R. Nestmeyer, *Französische Dichter und ihre Häuser*, p. 122. At the centre of the discord was Salvador Dalí, whose eccentric depiction of sexual subjects offended the party but delighted surrealists.

8 U. Hörner, *Die realen Frauen der Surrealisten*, p. 184.

9 M. Stemberger, "Zwischen Surrealismus und Sozrealismus", p. 84.

10 See M. Delranc-Gaudric, "La Valse des juges".

11 E. Triolet, *Elsa Triolet choisie par Aragon*, p. 258.

12 P. Daix, *Avec Elsa Triolet*, p. 35.

13 See M. Delranc-Gaudric, "La Valse des juges".

14 It's not entirely clear when precisely Triolet was in Nuremberg. Many years later, she claimed in a Foreword to a novel that she arrived in the city in 1945. See M. Delranc-Gaudric, "La Valse des juges". Triolet described in detail the interrogation of Baldur von Schirach, which took place on 23rd, 24th and 27th May. So it's assumed she attended the proceedings on those days.

15 F. Raddatz, "Traum und Vernunft", p. 114 f.

16 I. Ehrenburg, "In Nürnberg", p. 169 f.

17 S. Radlmaier (ed.), *Der Nürnberger Lernprozess*, p. 200.

18 U. Hörner, *Die realen Frauen der Surrealisten*, p. 202.

19 U. Hörner, *Louis Aragon und Elsa Triolet*, p. 129.

20 S. Nadolny, *Elsa Triolet*, p. 130.

21 Ibid., p. 204.
22 See M.-T. Eychart, "L'Allemagne entre mythe et réalité".
23 M. Delranc-Gaudric (ed.), *Elsa Triolet*, p. 210.

10. Willy Brandt, Markus Wolf and the Katyn Massacre

1 A. Reichenbach, *Chef der Spione*, p. 112 f.
2 M. Wolf, *Spionagechef im geheimen Krieg*, p. 496.
3 W. Brandt, *Verbrecher und andere Deutsche*, p. 12.
4 P. Merseburger, *Willy Brandt*, p. 227.
5 A. Reichenbach, *Chef der Spione*, p. 29.
6 Ibid., p. 49.
7 Ibid., p. 31.
8 M. Wolf, "Nürnberger Sakuska", p. 89.
9 See J. Siegerist, *Verbrecher und andere Deutsche. Das Skandal-Buch Willy Brandts*, Bremen, 1989.
10 See E. Lorenz's Introduction in W. Brandt, *Verbrecher und andere Deutsche*, p. 11.
11 W. Brandt, *Links und frei*, p. 405
12 See J. Oltmann, "Seine Königliche Hoheit der Obergruppenführer", *Die Zeit*, 18th January 2001, https://www.zeit.de/2001/04/Seine_Koenigliche_Hoheit_der_Obergruppenfuehrer/komplettansicht?utm_referrer=https%3A%2F%2Fde.wikipedia.org%2F
13 W. Brandt, *Verbrecher und andere Deutsche*, p. 13.
14 W. Brandt, "Nürnberger Verbrecher-Revue", p. 129 ff.
15 W. Brandt, *Erinnerungen*, p. 145.
16 In 1946, Brandt also worked on two pamphlets: *Norden i Nürnberg* (*The North in Nuremberg*) and *Nürnberg—Norge—dommen* (*Nuremberg—Norway—the Judgement*), which appeared that year in Stockholm and Oslo. See A. Bourguignon, "Willy Brandt et le procès de Nuremberg".
17 R. Behring, "Normalisierung auf Umwegen", p. 48.
18 Ibid., p. 47.
19 Ibid., p. 49.
20 C. Kohl, *Das Zeugenhaus*, p. 164.
21 A. Diller and W. Mühl-Benninghaus (eds), *Berichterstattung über den Nürnberger Prozess gegen die Hauptkriegsverbrecher*, p. 185.
22 M. Wolf, "Göring versuchte noch, den Chef zu spielen", *Der Tagesspiegel*, 1st November 2005, https://www.tagesspiegel.de/kultur/goering-versuchte-nochden-chef-zu-spielen/655412.html

23 C. Bartlitz, "Von 'gewöhnlichen Ganoven' und 'erbärmlichen Kreaturen'",
    p. 87.
24 H. Krösche, *Zwischen Vergangenheitsdiskurs und Wiederaufbau*, p. 62.
25 C. Bartlitz, "Von 'gewöhnlichen Ganoven' und 'erbärmlichen Kreaturen'",
    p. 69.
26 A. Reichenbach, *Chef der Spione*, p. 41.
27 P. Merseburger, *Willy Brandt*, p. 227.
28 R. Behring, "Normalisierung auf Umwegen", p. 40.
29 P. Merseburger, *Willy Brandt*, p. 282.
30 M. Wolf, *Spionagechef im geheimen Krieg*, p. 294.

11. Rebecca West's Doomed Affair

1   L. Jockusch, "Justice at Nuremberg?", p. 131.
2   H. Montgomery Hyde, *Norman Birkett*, p. 507.
3   L. Feigel, *The Bitter Taste of Victory*, p. 187 f.
4   Ibid., p. 157.
5   T.J. Dodd, *Letters from Nuremberg*, pp. 202, 215, 310.
6   L. Feigel, *The Bitter Taste of Victory*, p. 171.
7   T. Taylor, *Anatomy of the Nuremberg Trials*, p. 226.
8   Lawrence's wife wrote of West, "I don't see why all this fuss is being
    made over her." See C. Rollyson, *Rebecca West*, p. 248.
9   R. West, *A Train of Powder*, pp. 9, 8.
10 C. Rollyson, *Rebecca West*, p. 248.
11 P. Fehl, "The Ghosts of Nuremberg", *The Atlantic*, March 1972, p. 70.
12 R. West, *A Train of Powder*, pp. 13–14.
13 G. von Rezzori, *Mir auf der Spur*, p. 287.
14 West to Arling, 13th August 1946 in R. West, *Selected Letters*, p. 214.
15 A. de Rudder, *Ein Prozess der Männer*, p. 53.
16 R. West, *A Train of Powder*, pp. 5–6.
17 T. Mann, "Germany and the Germans", pp. 5–6.
18 R. West, *A Train of Powder*, pp. 24–5.
19 *Faber-Castell. Zum Jubiläum 1761–2011*, Stein, 2011, p. 107.
20 Ibid., p. 104.
21 See K. Kuehl, "Das Schloss Faber-Castell in Stein".
22 See the Afterword by N. Kadritzke in J. Dos Passos, *Das Land des
    Fragebogens*, p. 139.
23 L. Feigel, *The Bitter Taste of Victory*, p. 190.
24 A. Hastings, "Special Peoples", p. 382.

25 Ibid., pp. 383, 385; A. Knezevic, "Inhabitants of the Proud Bosnia", p. 134.
26 R. West, *A Train of Powder*, p. 4.
27 L. Feigel, *The Bitter Taste of Victory*, p. 190. West's German protagonist Gerda in *Black Lamb and Grey Falcon* is also depicted negatively.
28 R. West, *A Train of Powder*, p. 26.
29 Ibid.
30 T. Taylor, *Anatomy of the Nuremberg Trials*, p. 596.
31 R. West, *A Train of Powder*, p. 60.
32 L. Feigel, *The Bitter Taste of Victory*, pp. 207–8.
33 R. West, *A Train of Powder*, p. 14.
34 R. West, *Selected Letters*, p. 216.
35 T. Taylor, *Anatomy of the Nuremberg Trials*, p. 547.
36 R. West, *A Train of Powder*, p. 14.

12. Martha Gellhorn, Hemingway's Shadow and the Shock of Dachau

1 M. Gellhorn, *Travels with Myself and Another*, p. 60.
2 Gellhorn to Perkins, 17th October 1941 in M. Gellhorn, *Selected Letters*, p. 118.
3 Ibid., p. 278.
4 Ibid., p. 11.
5 Gellhorn had a problematic relationship with objectivity and preferred not to admit that she added subjective value judgments to her empiric reporting. K. McLoughlin, *Martha Gellhorn*, p. 59.
6 M. Gellhorn, *The Face of War*, p. 135.
7 C. Rollyson, *Beautiful Exile*, p. 176.
8 Martha Gellhorn to Sandy Gellhorn, 5th September 1969 in M. Gellhorn, *Selected Letters*, p. 350. Sandy grew up in boarding schools and later had problems with drug addiction and ran foul of the law.
9 M. Gellhorn and V. Cowles, *Love Goes to Press*, p. 19.
10 C. Rollyson, *Nothing Ever Happens to the Brave*, p. 208.
11 Hemingway is said to have remarked that Gellhorn was more ambitious than Napoleon. See C. Moorehead, *Martha Gellhorn*, p. 305.
12 See C.M. Edy, *The Woman War Correspondent, the U. S. Military, and the Press*.
13 G. Mellinger and J. Ferré (eds), *Journalism's Ethical Progressions*, p. 123.

14 K. McLoughlin, *Martha Gellhorn*, p. 149.

15 S. Radlmaier, *Das Bleistiftschloss als Press Camp*, p. 17.

16 Gellhorn to Glendenning, 22nd September 1987 in M. Gellhorn, *Selected Letters*, p. 467.

17 Ibid., pp. 170, 169.

18 M. Gellhorn, *The Face of War*, p. 184.

19 L. Feigel, *The Bitter Taste of Victory*, p. 203.

20 M. Gellhorn, *The Face of War*, p. 212.

21 C. Rollyson, *Nothing Ever Happens to the Brave*, p. 223.

22 Gellhorn to Hemingway, 1st December 1943 in M. Gellhorn, *Selected Letters*, p. 155.

23 Gellhorn to Stevenson, 26th December 1962 in M. Gellhorn, *Selected Letters*, p. 297.

24 M. Gellhorn, "Is There a New Germany?", *Atlantic Monthly*, February 1964, p. 74.

25 Ibid., p. 69.

26 M. Gellhorn, "Ohne Mich".

13. Painting to Escape the Horror:
Wolfgang Hildesheimer and the *Einsatzgruppen* Trial

1 On Roman Karmen's stay in the press camp see F. Hirsch, *Soviet Judgment at Nuremberg*, p. 136.

2 For example, Richard Tüngel, co-founder of the respected German weekly *Die Zeit*, Harold Kurtz, who would become a renowned biographer, and the historian and professor Paul G. Fried.

3 http://www.rijo.homepage.t-online.de/pdf/EN_NU_45_occwc.pdf

4 S. Braese, *Jenseits der Pässe*, p. 152.

5 Hildesheimer to Böll, 7th September 1953 in W. Hildesheimer, *Briefe*, p. 39.

6 A. Merritt and R.L. Merritt (eds), *Public Opinion in Occupied Germany*, p. 160 ff.

7 K. Jaspers, *Die Schuldfrage*, p. 19.

8 See H. Arendt and K. Jaspers, *Briefwechsel, 1926–1969*.

9 W. Hildesheimer, *Die sichtbare Wirklichkeit bedeutet mir nichts*, pp. 292, 332 f.

10 Ibid., p. 486.

11 L. Feigel, *The Bitter Taste of Victory*, p. 237.

12 S. Bräse, *Jenseits der Pässe*, p. 463 f.

13 Hildesheimer sketched out his Jewish idenity in a 1978 radio piece "My Jewishness" and a 1984 lecture "The Jewishness of Mr Bloom" at the Ninth International Joyce Symposium in Frankfurt. See W. Hirsch, *Zwischen Wirklichkeit und erfundener Biographie*, p. 107 f.

14 W. Hildesheimer, *Gesammelte Werke in sieben Bänden*, Vol. 7: *Vermischte Schriften*, p. 163.

15 R. Ogorreck and V. Ries, "Fall 9: Der Einsatzgruppenprozess (gegen Otto Ohlendorf und andere)".

16 W. Hildesheimer, *Die sichtbare Wirklichkeit bedeutet mir nichts*, pp. 278, 341.

17 https://he.bdue.de/fileadmin/verbaende/he/Dateien/PDF-Dateien/fotoausstellung/BDUE_Fotoausstellung_Frankfurt_Begleitheft_Web.pdf

18 S. Bräse, *Jenseits der Pässe*, p. 145.

19 W. Hirsch, *Zwischen Wirklichkeit und erfundener Biographie*, p. 261.

20 S. Bräse, *Jenseits der Pässe*, p. 518.

21 W. Hildesheimer, *Die sichtbare Wirklichkeit bedeutet mir nichts*, pp. 285, 288, 295.

22 P. Schmidt, *Der Statist auf der Galerie*, p. 45.

23 S. Bräse, *Jenseits der Pässe*, p. 138.

24 W. Hildesheimer, *Die sichtbare Wirklichkeit bedeutet mir nichts*, p. 344.

25 Ibid., p. 342.

26 W. Hirsch, *Zwischen Wirklichkeit und erfundener Biographie*, p. 112. See also H.A. Lea, *Wolfgang Hildesheimers Weg als Jude und Deutscher*.

27 S. Bräse, *Jenseits der Pässe*, p. 546 ff.

14. A Kind of Afterword: Golo Mann's Plea for Rudolf Hess

1 T. Mann, *Zu den Nürnberger Prozessen*, p. 832 f.

2 https://www.monacensia-digital.de/mann/content/titleinfo/33269

3 T. Mann, *Tagebücher 1946–1948*, p. 49.

4 T. Mann, *Tagebücher 1918–1921*, p. 372.

5 Golo Mann was in Nuremberg on 6th and 9th December 1945 and on 16th January 1946. For the wording of his letter to Katia see ibid., p. 771.

6 U. Bitterli, *Golo Mann*, p. 111.

7 G. Mann, *Briefe 1932–1992*, p. 306.

8 U. Bitterli, *Golo Mann*, p. 137.

9 "Professor Golo Mann erinnert sich. Mehr Scham als Freude, Interview mit Klaus Lieber", *Brückenbauer*, No. 18, 1st May 1985, p. 14.

10 U. Bitterli, *Golo Mann*, p. 222.
11 K. Anders, *Im Nürnberger Irrgarten*, p. 23.
12 T. Mann, *Tagebücher 1940–1943*, p. 1051.
13 I. von der Lühe, *Erika Mann*, p. 412
14 See the Foreword by Golo Mann in W.R. Hess, *Rudolf Heß: "Ich bereue nichts"*, pp. 9–13.
15 U. Bitterli, *Golo Mann*, p. 213.
16 G. Mann, *Briefe 1932–1992*, p. 470.
17 T. Lahme, *Golo Mann*, p. ii.
18 I. von der Lühe, *Erika Mann*, p. 364.
19 J. Koch, *Golo Mann*, p. 346.
20 See T. Taylor, *Anatomy of the Nuremberg Trials*, p. 500.
21 D. Zwar, *Talking to Rudolf Hess*, p. 36.
22 S. Radlmaier (ed.), *Der Nürnberger Lernprozess*, p. 289.

BIBLIOGRAPHY

Primary Sources

Anders, K., *Im Nürnberger Irrgarten*, Nuremberg, 1948.

Arendt, H. and Jaspers, K., *Briefwechsel, 1926–1969*, ed. L. Köhler and H. Saner, Munich, 1985.

Bernstein, V.H., *Final Judgement: The Story of Nuremberg*, New York, 1947.

Brandt, W., *Erinnerungen*, Berlin, 1989.

Brandt, W., *Links und frei. Mein Weg 1930–1950*, Hamburg, 1982.

Brandt, W., "Nürnberger Verbrecher-Revue" in S. Radlmaier (ed.), *Der Nürnberger Lernprozess*, pp. 129–33.

Brandt, W., *Verbrecher und andere Deutsche. Ein Bericht aus Deutschland 1946*, Bonn, 2007.

D'Addario, R., *Der Nürnberger Prozeß. Das Verfahren gegen die Hauptkriegsverbrecher 1945–1946*, text: Klaus Kastner, Nuremberg, 1994.

Daix, P., *Avec Elsa Triolet*, Paris, 2010.

Deane, E.C., *Letters*, Reel 1, Hoover Institution Library and Archives.

Der Nürnberger Prozeß. Das Protokoll des Prozesses gegen die Hauptkriegsverbrecher vor dem Internationalen Militärgerichtshof 14. November 1945–1. Oktober 1946, 42 vols, Nuremberg, 1947–49 (CD-ROM: Digitale Bibliothek, Vol. 20, Berlin, 1999).

Diller, A. and Mühl-Benninghaus, W. (eds), *Berichterstattung über den Nürnberger Prozess gegen die Hauptkriegsverbrecher 1945/46. Edition und Dokumentation ausgewählter Rundfunkquellen*, Potsdam, 1998.

Döblin, A., *Autobiographische Schriften und letzte Aufzeichnungen*, Olten and Freiburg, 1977.

Döblin, A. (published under the pseudonym Hans Fiedeler), *Der Nürnberger Lehrprozess*, Baden-Baden, 1946; also printed in A. Döblin, *Kleine Schriften IV*, ed. A.W. Riley and C. Althen, Düsseldorf, 2005, pp. 170–216.

Döblin, A., *Wie das Land 1946 aussieht* in *idem, Schicksalsreise. Bericht und Bekenntnis*, Solothurn and Düsseldorf, 1993, pp. 312–22.

Dodd, T.J., *Letters from Nuremberg: My Father's Narrative of a Quest for Justice*, ed. C.J. Dodd, New York, 2007.

Dos Passos, J., (German edition), *Das Land des Fragebogens. 1945: Reportagen aus dem besiegten Deutschland*, Hamburg, 1999.

Dos Passos, J., *The Fourteenth Chronicle: Letters and Diaries of John Dos Passos*, ed. T. Ludington, Boston, 1973.

Dos Passos, J., *Tour of Duty*, Boston, 1946.

Ehrenburg, I., "In Nürnberg" in S. Radlmaier (ed.), *Der Nürnberger Lernprozess*, pp. 160–72.

Fehl, P., "Die Geister von Nürnberg", *Sinn und Form*, 51 (2), 1999, pp. 275–98.

Flanner, J., *Darlinghissima: Letters to a Friend*, ed. N. Danesi Murray, New York, 1985.

Flanner, J., *Janet Flanner's World: Uncollected Writings 1932–1975*, ed. I. Drutman, New York, 1979.

Gaskin, H. (ed.), *Eyewitnesses at Nuremberg*, London, 1990.

Gellhorn, M. and Cowles, V., *Love Goes to Press*, ed. S. Spanier, Lincoln and London, 1995.

Gellhorn, M., "Ohne mich. Why I Shall Never Return to Germany", *Granta*, December 1992, pp. 201–8.

Gellhorn, M., *Selected Letters*, ed. C. Moorehead, New York, 2006.

Gellhorn, M., *The Face of War*, New York, 1988.

Gellhorn, M., *Travels with Myself and Another*, New York, 1979.

Gilbert, G.M., *Nuremberg Diary*, New York, 1947.

Habe, H., *Brief nach Kilchberg. Zum 60. Geburtstag von Erika Mann* in *Aufbau*, New York, 5th November 1965.

Habe, H., "Die Irrtümer von Nürnberg" in S. Radlmaier (ed.), *Der Nürnberger Lernprozess*, pp. 236–40.

Hemingway, E., *Selected Letters (1917–1961)*, ed. C. Baker, New York, 1981.

Hildesheimer, W., *Briefe*, ed. S. Braese and D. Pleyer, Frankfurt, 1999.

Hildesheimer, W., *Die sichtbare Wirklichkeit bedeutet mir nichts. Die Briefe an die Eltern 1937–1962*, Vol. 1, ed. V. Jehle, Berlin, 2016.

Hildesheimer, W., *Gesammelte Werke in sieben Bänden*, Vol. 7: *Vermischte Schriften*, ed. V. Jehle and C.L. Hart Nibbrig, Frankfurt, 1991.

Jaspers, K., *Die Schuldfrage. Von der politischen Haftung Deutschlands*, Munich, 1987.

Kästner, E., *Gesammelte Schriften für Erwachsene*, Vol. 7, Cologne, 1959.

Kästner, E., "Streiflichter aus Nürnberg" in *idem, Werke*, Vol. 6: *Splitter und Balken. Publizistik*, ed. H. Sarkowicz and F.J. Görtz, Munich, 1998.

Kempner, R.M.W., *Ankläger einer Epoche. Lebenserinnerungen*, in cooperation with J. Friedrich, Frankfurt and Berlin, 1983.

Mann, E., "Alien Homeland", Stadtbibliothek München/Monacensia, estate of Erika Mann, https://www.monacensia-digital.de/mann/content/titleinfo /3326 9

Mann, E., *Blitze überm Ozean. Aufsätze, Reden, Reportagen*, ed. I. von der Lühe and U. Neumann, Hamburg, 2000.

Mann, E., *Briefe und Antworten*, ed. A. Zanco Prestel, 2 vols, Munich, 1984.

Mann, E., Letters, Stadtbibliothek München/Monacensia, estate of Erika Mann, https://www.monacensia-digital.de/nav/classification/41691

Mann, E. and Mann, K., *Escape to Life*, Boston, 1939.

Mann, G., *Briefe 1932–1992*, ed. T. Lahme and K. Lüssi, Göttingen, 2007.

Mann, K., *Der Wendepunkt. Ein Lebensbericht*, Hamburg, 2005.

Mann, T., *Essays*, Vol. 5: *Deutschland und die Deutschen. 1938–1945*, ed. H. Kurzke and S. Stachorski, Frankfurt, 1996.

Mann, T., *Tagebücher 1940–1943*, ed. P. de Mendelssohn, Frankfurt, 2003.

Mann, T., *Tagebücher 1946–1948*, ed. I. Jens, Frankfurt, 2003.

Mann, T., *Zu den Nürnberger Prozessen* in *idem, Tagebücher 1944–1946*, ed. I. Jens, Frankfurt, 2003, p. 832 f.

Mendelssohn, P. de, Letters, Stadtbibliothek München/Monacensia, estate of Peter de Mendelssohn, B 134 and B 59.

Mendelssohn, P. de, "Eine schreckliche Stadt" in S. Radlmaier (ed.), *Der Nürnberger Lernprozess*, pp. 153–60.

Mendelssohn, P. de, *Unterwegs mit Reiseschatten*, Frankfurt, 1977.

Michel, E.W., *Promises Kept: One Man's Journey Against Incredible Odds*, Fort Lee, 2008.

Ocampo, V., *Mein Leben ist mein Werk. Eine Biographie in Selbstzeugnissen*, ed. R. Kroll, Berlin, 2010.

Orwell, G., "As I Please", *Tribune*, 12th January 1945.

Polewoi, B., *Nürnberger Tagebuch*, Berlin, 1971.

Radlmaier, S. (ed.), *Der Nürnberger Lernprozess. Von Kriegsverbrechern und Starreportern*, Frankfurt, 2001.

Rezzori, G. von, "Das Schlusswort von Rudolf Heß" in S. Radlmaier (ed.), *Der Nürnberger Lernprozess*, pp. 287–300.

Rezzori, G. von, *Mir auf der Spur*, Munich, 1999.

Scherpe, K. (ed.), *In Deutschland unterwegs. Reportagen, Skizzen, Berichte 1945–1948*, Stuttgart, 1982.

Schmidt, P., *Der Statist auf der Galerie 1945–50. Erlebnisse, Kommentare, Vergleiche*, Bonn, 1951.

Shirer, W.L., *End of a Berlin Diary*, New York, 1947.

Shirer, W.L., *Twentieth Century Journey: The Start, 1904–1930; The Nightmare Years, 1930–1940; A Native's Return, 1945–1988*, 3 vols, New York, 2020.

Shostakovich, D., *Testimony: The Memoirs of Dimitri Shostakovich as Related to and Edited by Solomon Volkov*, translated by Antonina W. Bouis, New York, 1979.

Simon, S., *La Galerie des monstres. À Nuremberg dans les coulisses du plus grand procès de l'histoire*, Nancy, 1946.

Speer, A., *Erinnerungen*, Berlin, 1969.

Speer, A., *Inside the Third Reich*, New York, 1970.

Süskind, W.E., *Die Mächtigen vor Gericht. Nürnberg 1945/46 an Ort und Stelle erlebt*, Munich, 1963.

Süskind, W.E., "Die tänzerische Generation", *Der deutsche Merkur*, 8, 1924/25, pp. 586–97.

Süskind, W.E., *Gekannt, verehrt, geliebt. 50 Nekrologe aus unserer Zeit*, Munich, 1969.

Triolet, E., *Elsa Triolet choisie par Aragon*, Paris, 1960.

Voslensky, M., "Stalin war mit Nürnberg unzufrieden", *Der Spiegel*, 41, 1986, https://www.spiegel.de/politik/stalin-war-mit-nuernberg-unzufrieden-a-6defab2d-0002–0001–0000–000013519365

Wagner, W., *Lebens-Akte*, Munich, 1994.

West, R., *Selected Letters*, ed. B. Kime Scott, New Haven, 2000.

West, R., *A Train of Powder*, New York, 1954.

White, O., *Die Straße des Siegers. Eine Reportage aus Deutschland 1945*, Munich, 2006.

Wolf, M., "Nürnberger Sakuska" in S. Radlmaier (ed.), *Der Nürnberger Lernprozess*, pp. 87–9.

Wolf, M., *Spionagechef im geheimen Krieg. Erinnerungen*, Berlin, 1997.

Zuckmayer, C., *Als wär's ein Stück von mir. Horen der Freundschaft*, Vienna, 1966.

Secondary Sources

André, R., "W.E. Süskind beim Nürnberger Prozess" in S. Braese (ed.), *Rechenschaften. Juristischer und literarischer Diskurs in der*

Auseinandersetzung mit den NSMassenverbrechen, Göttingen, 2004, pp. 25–46.

Balachova, T., "Le Double Destin d'Elsa Triolet en Russie (Documents des Archives moscovites)" in M. Delranc-Gaudric (ed.), *Elsa Triolet*, pp. 93–101.

Bartlitz, C., "Von 'gewöhnlichen Ganoven' und 'erbärmlichen Kreaturen'. Täterbilder in der Berichterstattung des Berliner Rundfunks über den Nürnberger Prozess 1945/46" in U. Weckel and E. Wolfrum (eds), *Bestien und Befehlsempfänger*, pp. 66–91.

Behr, M. and Corpataux, M., *Die Nürnberger Prozesse. Zur Bedeutung der Dolmetscher für die Prozesse und der Prozesse für die Dolmetscher*, Munich, 2006.

Behring, R., "Normalisierung auf Umwegen. Polen in den politischen Konzeptionen Willy Brandts, 1939–1966", *Vierteljahreshefte für Zeitgeschichte*, 58 (1), 2010, pp. 35–68.

Benda, E., "Der Nürnberger Prozeß. Grundlage eines neuen Völkerrechts?" in U. Schultz (ed.), *Große Prozesse. Recht und Gerechtigkeit in der Geschichte*, Munich, 1996, pp. 340–50.

Beutler, K., *Erich Kästner. Eine literaturpädagogische Untersuchung*, Weinheim, 1967.

Bitterli, U., *Golo Mann. Instanz und Außenseiter*, Zurich, 2004.

Bourguignon, A., "Willy Brandt et le procès de Nuremberg", *Guerres mondiales et conflits contemporains*, 4 (252), 2013, pp. 95–112.

Boyes, R., "Der Fetteste überlebt", *Der Tagesspiegel*, 17th April 2010, www.tagesspiegel.de/meinung/my-berlin-der-fetteste-ueberlebt /1803114.html

Braese, S., *Jenseits der Pässe: Wolfgang Hildesheimer. Eine Biographie*, Göttingen, 2016.

Carter Hett, B., "'This Story Is about Something Fundamental'. Nazi Criminals, History, Memory, and the Reichstag Fire", *Central European History*, 48 (2), 2015, pp. 199–224.

Cuthbertson, K., *A Complex Fate: William L. Shirer and the American Century*, Montreal, 2015.

Delranc-Gaudric, M. (ed.), *Elsa Triolet. Un écrivain dans le siècle*, Paris 2000.

Delranc-Gaudric, M., "'La Valse des juges'. Elsa Triolet au procès de Nuremberg", *Recherches croisées Aragon—Elsa Triolet*, No. 12, Strasbourg, 2009, https://books.openedition.org/pus/7674?lang=de

Edy, C.M., *The Woman War Correspondent, the U.S. Military and the Press: 1846–1947*, Lanham, 2017.

Elsa la rose (1965), directed by Agnès Varda. Paris: Pathé.

Epstein, K., "Shirer's History of Nazi Germany", *The Review of Politics*, 23 (2), April 1961, pp. 230–45.

Eychart, M.-T., "L'Allemagne entre mythe et réalité" in M. Delranc-Gaudric (ed.), *Elsa Triolet*, pp. 65–82.

Feigel, L., *The Bitter Taste of Victory: Life, Love and Art in the Ruins of the Reich*, London, 2016.

Fitzel, T., "Eine Zeugin im Nürnberger Prozess" in G. Ueberschär (ed.), *Der Nationalsozialismus vor Gericht*, pp. 60–72.

Franzke, J. (ed.), *Das Bleistiftschloss. Familie und Unternehmen Faber-Castell in Stein*, exhibition catalogue, Munich, 1986.

Franzke, J. and Schafhauser, P., "Faber-Castell—Die Bleistiftdynastie" in H. Petroski, *Der Bleistift. Die Geschichte eines Gebrauchsgegenstands*, Basel, 1995, p. 331 ff.

Frei, N., "'Wir waren blind, ungläubig und langsam'. Buchenwald, Dachau und die amerikanischen Medien im Frühjahr 1945", *Vierteljahreshefte für Zeitgeschichte*, 3, 1987, pp. 385–401.

Gemählich, M., *Frankreich und der Nürnberger Prozess gegen die Hauptkriegsverbrecher 1945/46*, Berlin, 2018.

Görtz, F.J. and Sarkowicz, H., *Erich Kästner. Eine Biographie*, Munich, 1998.

Gribben, B., *Weighted Scales: American Newspaper Coverage of the Trial of the Major War Criminals at Nuremberg*, 2010, https://scholars.fhsu. edu/cgi/viewcontent.cgi?article=1169&context=theses

Gutmann, I., Jäckel, E., Longerich, P. and Schoeps, J.H. (eds), *Enzyklopädie des Holocaust. Die Verfolgung und Ermordung der europäischen Juden*, 3 vols, Berlin, 1993.

Hanuschek, S., *Keiner blickt dir hinter das Gesicht. Das Leben Erich Kästners*, Munich, 1999.

Harbou, K. von, *Als Deutschland seine Seele retten wollte. Die Süddeutsche Zeitung in den Gründerjahren nach 1945*, Munich, 2015.

Hastings, A., "Special Peoples", *Nations and Nationalism*, 5 (3), July 1999, pp. 381–96.

Hess, W.R., *Rudolf Heß: "Ich bereue nichts"*, Graz and Stuttgart, 1994.

Hirsch, F., *Soviet Judgment at Nuremberg: A New History of the International Military Tribunal after World War II*, Oxford, 2020.

Hirsch, W., *Zwischen Wirklichkeit und erfundener Biographie. Zum Künstlerbild bei Wolfgang Hildesheimer*, Hamburg, 1997.

Hörner, U., *Die realen Frauen der Surrealisten*, Mannheim, 1996.

Hörner, U., *Elsa Triolet und Louis Aragon. Die Liebenden des Jahrhunderts*, Berlin, 1998.

Jockusch, L., "Justice at Nuremberg? Jewish Responses to Nazi War-Crime Trials in Allied-Occupied Germany", *Jewish Social Studies*, 19, 2012, pp. 107–47.

Kastner, K., *Von den Siegern zur Rechenschaft gezogen. Die Nürnberger Prozesse*, Nuremberg, 2001.

Kelley, D.M., *22 Cells in Nuremberg. A Psychiatrist Examines the Nazi Criminals*, London, 1947.

Kinnebrock, S., "Frauen und Männer im Journalismus. Eine historische Betrachtung" in M. Thiele (ed.), *Konkurrenz der Wirklichkeiten. Wilfried Scharf zum 60. Geburtstag*, Göttingen, 2005, pp. 101–32.

Knezevic, A., "Inhabitants of the Proud Bosnia: The Identity of the European Native Muslims", *Islamic Studies*, 40 (1), 2001, pp. 133–77.

Koch, J., *Golo Mann und die deutsche Geschichte. Eine intellektuelle Biographie*, Paderborn, 1998.

Kölbel, R., "Roland Graf von Faber-Castell" in *Fränkische Lebensbilder*, Vol. 21, *Im Auftrag der Gesellschaft für fränkische Geschichte*, Würzburg, 2006, pp. 349–72.

Kohl, C., *Das Zeugenhaus. Nürnberg 1945: Als Täter und Opfer unter einem Dach zusammenlebten*, Munich, 2005.

Koppenfels, W. von, "Orwell und die Deutschen", *Deutsche Vierteljahrsschrift für Literaturwissenschaft und Geistesgeschichte*, 58 (4), 1984, pp. 658–78.

Krösche, H., "Nürnberg und kein Interesse? Der Prozess gegen die Hauptkriegsverbrecher 1945/46 und die Nürnberger Nachkriegsöffentlichkeit", *Mitteilungen des Vereins für Geschichte der Stadt Nürnberg*, 93, 2006, pp. 299–318.

Krösche, H., *Zwischen Vergangenheitsdiskurs und Wiederaufbau. Die Reaktion der deutschen Öffentlichkeit auf den Nürnberger Prozess gegen die Hauptkriegsverbrecher 1945/46, den Ulmer Einsatzgruppenprozess und den Sommer-Prozess 1958*, Oldenburg, 2009.

Kuehl, K., "Das Schloss Faber-Castell in Stein. Zur Bau- und Kulturgeschichte eines Unternehmer-Wohnsitzes" in J. Franzke (ed.), *Das Bleistiftschloss*, pp. 32–65.

Kurzke, H., *Thomas Mann. Das Leben als Kunstwerk*, Munich, 1999.

Lahme, T., *Golo Mann. Biographie*, Frankfurt, 2009.

Lea, H.A., *Wolfgang Hildesheimers Weg als Jude und Deutscher*, Stuttgart, 1997.

Lentner, B., *Propaganda für die Alliierten oder Aufarbeitung des Faschismus? Die Berichterstattung über den Nürnberger Prozeß gegen die Hauptkriegsverbrecher in den deutschen Nachkriegszeitungen*, Eichstätt, 1997.

Lesinska, Z.P., *Perspectives of Four Women Writers on the Second World War: Gertrude Stein, Janet Flanner, Kay Boyle and Rebecca West*, New York, 2002.

Ludington, T., *John Dos Passos: A Twentieth Century Odyssey*, New York, 1980.

Lühe, I. von der, *Erika Mann, Eine Biographie*, Frankfurt, 1996.

Lühe, I. von der, "The Big 52. Erika Manns Nürnberger Reportagen" in U. Weckel and E. Wolfrum (eds), *Bestien und Befehlsempfänger*, pp. 25–37.

Maier, C., "Die Reportage in der ersten Hälfte des 20. Jahrhunderts" in G. Gerber, R. Leucht and K. Wagner (eds), *Transatlantische Verwerfungen. Transatlantische Verdichtungen. Kulturtransfer in Literatur und Wissenschaft 1945–1989*, Göttingen, 2012, pp. 87–109.

McLoughlin, K., *Martha Gellhorn: The War Writer in the Field and in the Text*, Manchester, 2007.

Mellinger, G. and Ferré, J. (eds), *Journalism's Ethical Progressions: A Twentieth-Century Journey*, Lanham, 2020.

Mendelssohn, P. de, *Der Geist in der Despotie*, Frankfurt, 1987.

Mendelssohn, P. de, *Zeitungsstadt Berlin. Menschen und Mächte in der Geschichte der deutschen Presse*, Berlin, 2017.

Merritt, A. and Merritt, R.L. (eds), *Public Opinion in Occupied Germany: The OMGUS Surveys, 1945–1949*, Urbana, Chicago and London, 1970.

Merseburger, P., *Willy Brandt, 1913–1992. Visionär und Realist*, Munich, 2013.

Mettler, B., *Demokratisierung und Kalter Krieg. Zur amerikanischen Informations-und Rundfunkpolitik in Westdeutschland 1945–1949*, Berlin, 1975.

Mitscherlich, A., "Geschichtsschreibung und Psychoanalyse. Bemerkungen zum Nürnberger Prozess (1945)", *Psyche*, 36 (12), 1982, pp. 1082–93.

Montgomery Hyde, H., *Norman Birkett: The Life of Lord Birkett of Ulverston*, London, 1964.

Moorehead, C., *Martha Gellhorn: A Life*, London, 2003.

Nadolny, S., *Elsa Triolet*, Dortmund, 2000.

Nestmeyer, R., *Französische Dichter und ihre Häuser*, Berlin, 2005.

Ogorreck, R. and Ries, V., "Fall 9: Der Einsatzgruppenprozess (gegen Otto Ohlendorf und andere)" in G. Ueberschär (ed.), *Der Nationalsozialismus vor Gericht*, pp. 164–75.

Payk, M., *Der Geist der Demokratie. Intellektuelle Orientierungsversuche im Feuilleton der frühen Bundesrepublik: Karl Korn und Peter de Mendelssohn*, Munich, 2008.

Raddatz, F., "Traum und Vernunft. Louis Aragon" in *idem, Essays 2: Eros und Tod. Literarische Portraits*, Hamburg, 1990.

Radlmaier, S., *Das Bleistiftschloss als Press Camp*, Stein, 2015.

Reichenbach, A., *Chef der Spione. Die Markus-Wolf-Story*, Stuttgart, 1992.

Reus, G., "Was Journalisten von Erich Kästner lernen können", *Journalistik*, 1, 2018, pp. 26–46.

Rollyson, C., *Beautiful Exile: The Life of Martha Gellhorn*, London, 2002.

Rollyson, C., *Nothing Ever Happens to the Brave: The Story of Martha Gellhorn*, New York, 1990.

Rollyson, C., *Rebecca West: A Life*, New York, 1996.

Rollyson, C., "Reporting Nuremberg: Martha Gellhorn, Janet Flanner, Rebecca West and the Nuremberg Trials", *The New Criterion*, September 1998, https://newcriterion.com/issues/1998/9/reporting-nuremberg

Rosenfeld, G.D., "The Reception of William L. Shirer's The Rise and Fall of the Third Reich in the United States and West Germany, 1960–62", *Journal of Contemporary History*, 29 (1), 1994, pp. 95–128.

Ross, A., *The Rest is Noise*, Munich, 2007.

Rückerl, A., *NS-Verbrechen vor Gericht. Versuch einer Vergangenheitsbewältigung*, Heidelberg, 1984.

Rudder, A. de, "Ein Prozess der Männer. Geschlechterbilder in der Berichterstattung zum Nürnberger Hauptkriegsverbrecherprozess 1945/46" in U. Weckel and E. Wolfrum (eds), *Bestien und Befehlsempfänger*, pp. 38–65.

Sayn-Wittgenstein, F. Prinz zu, *Schlösser in Franken. Residenzen, Burgen und Landsitze im Fränkischen*, Munich, 1984.

Schaber, W., "Der Fall Ullmann—Lherman—Oulmàn", *Exilforschung*, 7, 1989, pp. 107–18.

Schoeller, W., *Döblin. Eine Biographie*, Munich, 2011.

Shirer, W., *The Rise and Fall of the Third Reich*, New York, 1961.

Sprecher, D., "Abenteurerin zwischen den Welten. Das aufregende Leben der Katharina 'Nina' Sprecher von Bernegg (1917–1993)", *Bündner Monatsblatt*, 3, 2016, pp. 333–42.

Stafford, A., *Wilson, Keppel and Betty: Too Naked for the Nazis*, London, 2015.

Stemberger, M., "Zwischen Surrealismus und Sozrealismus. Ambivalenzen der Avantgarde am Beispiel Elsa Triolet" in S. Bung and S. Zepp (eds), *Migration und Avantgarde. Paris 1917–1962*, Berlin and Boston, 2020, pp. 71–117, https://www.degruyter.com/document/doi/10.1515/9783110679366-005 /html

Strickhausen, W., "Im Zwiespalt zwischen Literatur und Publizistik. Deutungsversuch zum Gattungswechsel im Werk der Exilautorin Hilde

Spiel" in T. Koebner, W. Koepke, C.-D. Krohn and S. Schneider (eds), *Exilforschung*, Vol. 7, 1989, pp. 166–83.

Taylor, T., *The Anatomy of the Nuremberg Trials: A Personal Memoir*, Boston, 1992.

Tüngel, R. and Berndorff, H.R., *Auf dem Bauche sollst du kriechen. Deutschland unter den Besatzungsmächten*, Hamburg, 1958.

Ueberschär, G. (ed.), *Der Nationalsozialismus vor Gericht. Die alliierten Prozesse gegen Kriegsverbrecher und Soldaten 1943–1952*, Frankfurt, 1999.

Utley, F., *The High Cost of Vengeance*, Chicago, 1949.

Vaksberg, A. and Gerra, R., *Sem' dnej v marte. Besedy ob emigracii*, St Petersburg, 2010.

Vansittart, R.G., *Lessons of My Life*, New York, 1943.

Wagener, B., "Inländische Perspektivierungen. Erich Kästner als Feuilletonist der Neuen Zeitung" in B. Blöbaum and S. Neuhaus (eds), *Literatur und Journalismus. Theorie, Kontexte, Fallstudien*, Wiesbaden, 2003, pp. 195–226.

Wagner, H.-U., *Der Nürnberger Hauptkriegsverbrecherprozess als Medienereignis. Die Berichterstattung durch die Rundfunksender in den westalliierten Besatzungszonen 1945/46*, https://zeitgeschichte-online. de/geschichtskultur/der-nuernberger-hauptkriegsverbrecherprozess-als-medienereignis

Wallbaum, K., *Der Überläufer. Rudolf Diels (1900–1957)—der erste Gestapo-Chef des Hitler-Regimes*, Frankfurt, 2010.

Weber, R., *Dateline—Liberated Paris: The Hotel Scribe and the Invasion of the Press*, Lanham, 2019.

Weckel, U. and Wolfrum, E. (eds), *Bestien und Befehlsempfänger. Frauen und Männer in NS-Prozessen nach 1945*, Göttingen, 2003.

Weinke, A., *Die Nürnberger Prozesse*, Munich, 2019.

Weiss, A., *In the Shadow of the Magic Mountain: The Erika and Klaus Mann Story*, Chicago, 2008.

Weiss, A., *Paris war eine Frau. Die Frauen von der Left Bank*, Reinbek, 1998.

Wilke, J., Schenk, B., Cohen, A.A. and Zemach, T., *Holocaust und NS-Prozesse. Die Presseberichterstattung in Israel und Deutschland zwischen Aneignung und Abwehr*, Cologne, 1995.

Wineapple, B., *Genêt: A Biography of Janet Flanner*, New York, 1989.

Wolbring, B., "Nationales Stigma und persönliche Schuld. Die Debatte über die Kollektivschuld in der Nachkriegszeit", *Historische Zeitschrift*, 289, 2009, pp. 325–64.

Zwar, D., *Talking to Rudolf Hess*, Cheltenham, 2010.

IMAGE CREDITS

p. 6   The press section in the Nuremberg courtroom, with future German Chancellor Willy Brandt in the middle of the third row © dpa picture alliance/Alamy Stock Photo.

p. 20   Laura Knight, *The Nuremberg Trial* (1946), oil on canvas. Reprinted by permission of Imperial War Museums.

p. 22   Günter Peis, caricature of Hermann Göring in the courtroom, October 1946. Estate of Günter Peis.

p. 32   One of the castle's two dining rooms during the days of the press camp. Reprinted in S. Radlmaier, S. (Ed.), *Der Nürnberger Lernprozess*, Frankfurt a. M. 2001.

p. 59   Robert H. Jackson delivering his opening remarks on 20th November 1945 © dpa picture alliance/Alamy Stock Photo.

p. 103 Female war correspondents attached to the US Army in the autumn of 1944. Third from right Betty Knox, first from right Erika Mann. Courtesy National Archives, photo no. 111-SC-192100.

p. 183 Illustration for Elsa Triolet's "La Valse des juges", *Les Lettres françaises*, 14th June 1946, Bibliothèque nationale de France.

p. 194   Willy Brandt's press accreditation card for the International Military Tribunal. Reprinted by permission of Willy Brandt Archive (WBA) at the Archives of Social Democracy (Archiv der sozialen Demokratie) in the Friedrich Ebert Foundation, Bonn.

p. 199   Press card for the International Military Tribunal issued to "Mark F. Wolf". Reprinted in *Spionagechef im geheimen Krieg. Erinnerungen*, Munich, 1997 (private/family photo).

p. 226   Francis Biddle in his brother George's fresco *Life of the Law* in the US Department of Justice, 1937. Carol M. Highsmith Archive, Library of Congress, Prints and Photographs Division (digital ID highsm.02847), © Erben George Biddle.

p. 242   Martha Gellhorn as "girl correspondent", illustration in *Collier's Weekly*, 20th January 1940. Reprinted in K. McLoughlin, *Martha Gellhorn: The War Writer in the Field and the Text*, New York, 2007.

INDEX

AVAILABLE AND COMING SOON
FROM PUSHKIN PRESS

Pushkin Press was founded in 1997, and publishes novels, essays, memoirs, children's books—everything from timeless classics to the urgent and contemporary.

Our books represent exciting, high-quality writing from around the world: we publish some of the twentieth century's most widely acclaimed, brilliant authors such as Stefan Zweig, Yasushi Inoue, Teffi, Antal Szerb, Gerard Reve and Elsa Morante, as well as compelling and award-winning contemporary writers, including Dorthe Nors, Edith Pearlman, Perumal Murugan, Ayelet Gundar-Goshen and Chigozie Obioma.

Pushkin Press publishes the world's best stories, to be read and read again. To discover more, visit www.pushkinpress.com.

THE PASSENGER
ULRICH ALEXANDER BOSCHWITZ

TENDER IS THE FLESH
NINETEEN CLAWS AND A BLACK BIRD
AGUSTINA BAZTERRICA

AT NIGHT ALL BLOOD IS BLACK
BEYOND THE DOOR OF NO RETURN
DAVID DIOP

WHEN WE CEASE TO UNDERSTAND THE WORLD
THE MANIAC
BENJAMÍN LABATUT

NO PLACE TO LAY ONE'S HEAD
FRANÇOISE FRENKEL

FORBIDDEN NOTEBOOK
ALBA DE CÉSPEDES

COLLECTED WORKS: A NOVEL
LYDIA SANDGREN

MY MEN
VICTORIA KIELLAND

AS RICH AS THE KING
ABIGAIL ASSOR

LAND OF SNOW AND ASHES
PETRA RAUTIAINEN

LUCKY BREAKS
YEVGENIA BELORUSETS

THE WOLF HUNT
AYELET GUNDAR-GOSHEN

MISS ICELAND
AUDUR AVA ÓLAFSDÓTTIR

MIRROR, SHOULDER, SIGNAL
DORTHE NORS

THE WONDERS
ELENA MEDEL

MS ICE SANDWICH
MIEKO KAWAKAMI

GROWN UPS
MARIE AUBERT

LEARNING TO TALK TO PLANTS
MARTA ORRIOLS

THE RABBIT BACK LITERATURE SOCIETY
PASI ILMARI JÄÄSKELÄINEN

BINOCULAR VISION
EDITH PEARLMAN

MY BROTHER
KARIN SMIRNOFF

ISLAND
SIRI RANVA HJELM JACOBSEN

ARTURO'S ISLAND
ELSA MORANTE

PYRE
PERUMAL MURUGAN

RED DOG
WILLEM ANKER

THE COLLECTED STORIES OF STEFAN ZWEIG
STEFAN ZWEIG

AN UNTOUCHED HOUSE
WILLEM FREDERIK HERMANS

WILL
JEROEN OLYSLAEGERS

MY CAT YUGOSLAVIA
PAJTIM STATOVCI

BEAUTY IS A WOUND
EKA KURNIAWAN

BONITA AVENUE
PETER BUWALDA

IN THE BEGINNING WAS THE SEA
TOMÁS GONZÁLEZ

TRAVELLER OF THE CENTURY
ANDRÉS NEUMAN